AF478207

LAW AND WAR

The Amherst Series in Law, Jurisprudence, and Social Thought

EDITED BY

Austin Sarat, Lawrence Douglas, and Martha Merrill Umphrey

Law and War

Edited by

AUSTIN SARAT

LAWRENCE DOUGLAS

MARTHA MERRILL UMPHREY

STANFORD LAW BOOKS

An imprint of Stanford University Press · Stanford, California

Stanford University Press
Stanford, California
© 2014 by the Board of Trustees of the
Leland Stanford Junior University

Library of Congress Cataloging-in-Publication Data

Law and war / edited by Austin Sarat, Lawrence Douglas, and
Martha Merrill Umphrey.
        pages   cm. — (The Amherst series in law, jurisprudence,
and social thought)
    Includes bibliographical references and index.
    ISBN 978-0-8047-8742-0 (cloth : alk. paper)
    1. Law and war. 2. Jurisprudence. I. Sarat, Austin, editor
of compilation. II. Douglas, Lawrence, editor of compilation.
III. Umphrey, Martha Merrill, editor of compilation. IV. Series:
Amherst series in law, jurisprudence, and social thought.
K487.W37L49   2014
341.6—dc23
                                                    2013034123
    ISBN 978-0-8047-8886-1 (electronic)

Printed in the United States of America on acid-free, archival-
quality paper

Typeset at Stanford University Press in 10/14.5 Minion

For my son Ben,
with love and the hope that he will grow up in
a world in which war is less of a problem for law (AS)

For Jacob and Milo,
with hopes for a more peaceful world (LD)

Acknowledgments

The editors wish to extend their sincere thanks for the support of Amherst College, which provides the rich intellectual environment on which this series relies. We are grateful to our Amherst College colleagues David Delaney, Nasser Hussain, and Adam Sitze for their intellectual companionship. We thank our students in Amherst College's Department of Law, Jurisprudence & Social Thought for their interest in the issues addressed in this book. Finally, we would like to express our appreciation for the generous financial support provided by Amherst College's Corliss Lamont Fund.

Contents

CONTRIBUTORS   *xi*

Law and War: An Introduction   *1*
LAWRENCE DOUGLAS, AUSTIN SARAT, AND
MARTHA MERRILL UMPHREY

Limits of Law: Promoting Humanity in Armed Conflict   *23*
SARAH SEWALL

The Individualization of War: From War to Policing in the
Regulation of Armed Conflicts   *48*
GABRIELLA BLUM

Pandemic Disease, Biological Weapons, and War   *84*
LAURA K. DONOHUE

From Antiwar Politics to Antitorture Politics   *154*
SAMUEL MOYN

War Crimes Trials during and after War   *198*
LARRY MAY

INDEX   *223*

Contributors

GABRIELLA BLUM is Professor at Harvard Law School

LAURA DONOHUE is Associate Professor of Law, Georgetown Law

LARRY MAY is W. Alton Jones Professor of Philosophy, Professor of Law, and Professor of Political Science at Vanderbilt University

LAWRENCE DOUGLAS is James J. Grosfeld Professor of Law, Jurisprudence & Social Thought at Amherst College

SAMUEL MOYN is James Bryce Professor of European Legal History at Columbia University

AUSTIN SARAT is Associate Dean of the Faculty and the William Nelson Cromwell Professor of Jurisprudence & Political Science and Professor of Law, Jurisprudence & Social Thought at Amherst College

SARAH SEWALL is Senior Lecturer at Harvard University's John F. Kennedy School of Government

MARTHA MERRILL UMPHREY is Professor of Law, Jurisprudence and Social Thought at Amherst College

Law and War: An Introduction

LAWRENCE DOUGLAS

AUSTIN SARAT

MARTHA MERRILL UMPHREY

On September 30, 2011, some two weeks after the tenth anniversary of the 9.11 attacks, a Hellfire missile fired from an American predator drone in a remote region of Yemen killed Anwar al-Awlaki. The killing immediately unleashed a storm of criticism, at least in legal circles. A number of legal experts and political actors decried the killing as a stark violation of constitutional rights, American domestic law, and the international law of armed conflict. Speaking for many, Mary Ellen O'Connell, a professor of law at Notre Dame, decried the attack as dangerous, immoral, and criminal.[1] What law authorized the CIA to "take out" al-Awlaki?

Many commentators noted that because al-Awlaki was an American citizen, he should have been protected by the Fifth Amendment's guarantee of due process. Even those experts who conceded that terror suspects may be treated differently than suspects in "ordinary" crimes insisted that al-Awlaki's killing raised thorny constitutional questions. The killing appeared difficult to square with the Supreme Court's ruling in *Hamdi v. Rumsfeld*.[2] In that critical decision, the Court held that the designation and indefinite detention of an American citizen as an "unlawful combatant" (or as an "unprivileged enemy belligerent," to use the substitute nomenclature passed by Congress) in the absence of any mechanism of review constituted a violation of due process. If the executive could not constitutionally detain citizens without supplying some modicum of process, how could it engage in the far more radical act of killing? As presidential candidate Ron Paul observed, a targeted killing of Timothy McVeigh, the Oklahoma City bomber, would have been an unthinkable violation of the Constitution.[3]

Other critics saw the killing as a violation of international law. Jameel

Jaffee of the ACLU observed that al-Awlaki was killed in northern Yemen, far from any battlefield.[4] While the law of war permits the killing of soldiers and officers in a battlefield or war zone, it does not authorize the killing of one's own citizens in an area far removed from any armed conflict based on secret evidence. Such an act resembles less the killing of a belligerent during wartime and more an extrajudicial killing of a terror suspect. And an extrajudicial killing is ultimately nothing other than a state-authorized assassination, forbidden by both domestic and international law. Ron Paul was perhaps the only political figure to push this argument to its conclusion, insisting that the president's authorization of al-Awlaki's killing was an impeachable offense.[5]

Equally vociferous, however, were the defenders of the drone strike. Benjamin Wittes, a prominent legal expert, agreed that al-Awlaki was due a measure of process but insisted the Fifth Amendment does not require prospective judicial review of a targeting decision when the suspect is "believed to play an active, operational role" in an enemy force.[6] In passing the Authorization for Use of Military Force (AUMF), Congress gave the president the legal authority to "use all necessary and appropriate force against those nations, organizations, or persons" that "planned, authorized, committed, or aided the terrorist attacks that occurred on September 11, 2001."[7] Because apprehending al-Awlaki and placing him on trial was not feasible, and because the suspect failed to surrender despite knowledge that he was being targeted, Wittes insisted that the administration was authorized by the law of war to treat al-Awlaki as an enemy soldier or leader in a time of war.

A full year and a half before the drone strike, Harold Koh, the State Department's chief legal advisor, offered what now reads as a detailed, prospective defense of al-Awlaki's killing.[8] As the dean of Yale Law School and as an expert on national security law, Koh had been a sharp critic of the Bush administration's conduct in the war against terror. Now against those who believed the "use of lethal force against specific individuals fails to provide adequate process and thus constitutes *unlawful extrajudicial killing*" (emphasis in original), Koh strongly insisted that the "state may use lethal force" when "engaged in an armed conflict or in legitimate self-defense."[9] Appealing to the example of American aviators who "tracked and shot down the airplane carrying the architect of the Japanese attack on Pearl Harbor, . . . also the leader of enemy forces in the Battle of Midway," Koh argued that such targeting was "lawful . . . under international law."[10] Assuring his audience that "our procedures and practices for identifying lawful targets are extremely robust," Koh concluded that "lethal operations" such as the al-Awlaki killing do "not constitute 'assassination.'"[11] Far from unconstitutional, illegal, or criminal, such acts are "conducted in accordance with all applicable law."

In the days following the strike, the *New York Times* reported on a memo prepared within the Obama administration in the run-up to the killing.[12] Although the contents of the memo remain secret and the full evidence against al-Awlaki is yet to be revealed, the *Times* reported that the memo was an elaborate legal document that cited Supreme Court cases such as *Scott v. Harris* (whether the police's high-speed car chase violated the Fourth Amendment) and *Tennessee v. Garner* (whether the police can use lethal force in pursuit of a fleeing suspect when such force poses a significant threat to bystanders). While critics of the administration's actions seized upon the secrecy of the memo, defenders noted its elaborately legal character as evidence of the profound and sober legal analysis that lay at the heart of the executive's action.

In reviewing the colloquy over al-Awlaki's killing, we do not intend to take sides in an ongoing debate. For us what is more remarkable than the specific arguments themselves is the thoroughly juridified nature of the argument. Largely absent from the debate is any discussion of the wisdom or efficacy of the killing. Instead, we find an argument about law: constitutional, domestic, and international. Perhaps most remarkably, we find *both sides* of the argument making appeals to law.

The Cold War created a memorable schism between two schools of international relations. On the one side were the realists, who believed that on the world stage, the interests of order and security trump the interests of justice; on the other were the idealists, who insisted that, like domestic politics, international relations should submit to the logic and regimen of the rule of law.[13] Here we find no such schism. Both sides in the debate about the al-Awlaki killing appeal to the law; they differ not about the relevance or bindingness of legal norms, but only about matters of interpretation: what the law requires and permits in the specific case.

The debate, then, reveals a great deal about the way that America, and many other nations, presently think about waging war. Law has become a crucial element in that thinking. One cannot engage in war without seeking authorization from the former. Whether the law ultimately functions as a tool of restraint or of empowerment, it has become inescapable. The waging of war and the doing of law are inextricably bound.

The intimate connections between war and law would have been unintelligible to earlier generations of statesmen and legal theorists. The very term "the law of war" would have smacked of the oxymoronic, as law and war were long considered oppositional terms, the one excluding the other. This was perhaps nowhere more clearly the case than in Hobbes's *Leviathan,* arguably the most influential work in Western political theory.

In a stunning heuristic that anticipated modern game theory, Hobbes argued that a state of nature would necessarily devolve into a state of war—not because men are naturally aggressive and appetitive, but because men are naturally self-protective and fearful of the behavior of others likewise engaged in self-protection. In a state of nature, locally rational behavior—acts designed to promote one's survival—lead men inevitably to other actions, such as preemptive strikes, that turn the world into a horrifically irrational state of chaos. This is the world that Hobbes simply calls "war." It is not, in Hobbes's formulation, a state of constant killing. Rather, "as the nature of Foule weather, lyeth not in a showre or two of rain; but in the inclination thereto of many dayes together: So the nature of War, consisteth not in actual fighting; but the known dispostion thereto."[14] Given the ever-present possibility of renewed violence, the state of war is one of relentless misery, deprivation, and want. And it is a state completely without law.

While Hobbes speaks of a law of nature existing in a state of nature, his conception of natural law is remarkably thin and places no restraints on human bloodletting in a state of war. To the contrary, anything and everything are permissible in Hobbes's state of war, as the man who acts with unilateral restraint becomes nothing more than the architect of his own destruction. For Hobbes, the law of nature acts, then, less as a curb on conduct than as a maxim of prudence, urging men to escape the state of war, if possible. For all intents and purposes, then, the state of war is a legal vacuum. The state of war is utterly lawless.

Indeed, for Hobbes, law is the necessary and sufficient condition to extinguishing warfare. And yet the making of law is not simply one of the functions of the state; the state is the precondition of law. Without the state, there can be no law in the Hobbesian scheme: "Where there is no Common Power, there is no law."[15] It is the sovereign that enjoys the monopoly of force requisite to make law and covenants binding on its subjects. The strong relationship between sovereign power and law thus carves Hobbes's world into strict and separate categories. Where there is war, there is no law; and where there is law, there is no war. To put it even more sharply: where there is war, there are no limits to the violence a person may do; where there is law, there are no limits to what the state can proscribe. The two define mutually exclusive zones.

Although Hobbes appears to treat the state of nature as a heuristic, the international arena remained for him a powerful example of the continuing reality of the state of nature. Sovereigns confront each other on the international stage precisely as persons confront each other in the absence of a sovereign. Indeed, for Hobbes, it was the relations between the former that illuminate the plight of the latter, not the other way around.[16] Thus it becomes meaningless to speak of any external legal limits on a sovereign's war-making powers. Such limits could be enforced only by some supergovernment, in which case that power would itself be *sovereign*. Nations can, of course, enter into treaties, but these lack a truly legal character in the absence of a power capable of enforcing their terms. They are like promissory agreements entered into in the state of nature: followed when mutually advantageous, broken when not. Perhaps it comes as no surprise to find an exemplary expression of this view in the words of Adolf Hitler, who in a speech to his generals on November 23, 1939, reminded them of Germany's nonaggression pact with the Soviet Union, but declared: "Agreements are to be kept only as long as they serve a certain purpose."[17] In the absence of an overarching global sovereign, each state finds itself in a state of nature vis-à-vis all others. From this perspective, international law is a contradiction in terms.

It is difficult to exaggerate the influence of this Hobbesian picture on the further development of legal theory. For one thing, it established a tradition, not entirely benign, of sharply distinguishing the internal police powers of a state from its external war-making powers, a point made visible in the work of two of the most important legal theorists of the twentieth century, both profoundly influenced by Hobbes. In *The Pure Theory of Law*, Hans Kelsen, a refugee from Nazi-occupied Vienna, described the development of increasingly centralized nation-states in terms of the extension and penetration of law into every aspect of civic life. As law proliferates and becomes ubiquitous, it works to prohibit the use of all force between persons in civil society. In Kelsen's words, "[T]he use of force is prohibited by making it the condition of a sanction, . . . itself a use of force."[18] The fundamental basis of the legal system, then, is the creation and enforcement of the distinction between the delict (prohibited private force) and the sanction (authorized legal force). This process reaches perfection in the centralized nation in which, to quote Kelsen's breathtakingly simple formulation, "The use of force of man against man is either a delict or a sanction."[19]

Kelsen's highly positivistic account casts fresh light on the purposes of criminal law. Legal prohibitions against murder can be seen as something other than the deontological condemnation of the quintessential *malum in se*. Rather, as an act that invites "self-help"—namely, retaliatory acts of revenge—murder challenges the state's monopoly on force. The state must punish the murderer to eliminate the prospect of retaliatory violence and blood vengeance, and so defend its monopoly on force.

For Kelsen, then, the centralized state is defined by a totalizing project of law. Like Hobbes, Kelsen sees law ultimately as an instrument that aims at the "pacification of the legal community."[20] While Kelsen acknowledges that the inevitable persistence of violence in civil society means that "one cannot very well assert that the state of law is necessarily a state of peace," he insists that "the development of the law runs in this direction."[21] His positivism thus establishes a strong conceptual relationship between the proliferation and centralization of legal power and the establishment and enforcement of conditions of peace.

Contrast Kelsen's Hobbesian understanding of state power with Carl Schmitt's. Schmitt, the preeminent legal apologist for Nazi Germany, embraced Hobbes's understanding of sovereign power as absolute and illimitable. Like Hobbes, and Bodin before him, Schmitt insisted that the sovereign could not be bound by the laws he makes. And, like Hobbes, he understood sovereignty not in institutional terms (the structures of governance), but in functional terms (the powers of governance). This is made clear in his famous definition of the sovereign as "he who decides on the exception."[22] For Schmitt, the exception—the *Notstand*, or state of emergency—is "that which cannot be subsumed."[23] It "defies general codification" under any normal legal configuration, as no legal rule can specify the condition of its nonapplication.[24] Kelsen's vision of a social reality controlled by a totalizing project of law thus made no sense, Schmitt insisted, as the most essential exercise of sovereign power *by definition* resisted juridification. It is because the state of emergency resists juridification and articulation through rules that its invocation signifies the purest instance of the exercise of sovereign power. Indeed, for Schmitt, we can locate where sovereign power resides by identifying who enjoys the power to decide when to suspend the normal application of law (and when to reintroduce it).

Again, our point here is not to settle the debate between Kelsen and Schmitt. Rather, it is to suggest that together the two theorists offer a complex but ultimately complementary picture of the Hobbesian tradition as it came to conceptualize the relationship between law and war. For Schmitt, the paradigmatic instance of emergency is war. It is war that imperils the sovereign; it is war that threatens the very existence of the state. And yet because war represents an existential threat, it presents the sovereign with the opportunity for the pure exercise of power, the chance to command any and all acts necessary for its survival. This contrasts with Kelsen's view from within: in the ordered confines of the centralized state, law reigns supreme, and all acts of private force are treated as delicts. And so we are left with a picture of a nether external condition of war, in which law is absent and all acts of violence are permitted; and an internal world of law, in which all violence is codified, regulated, and policed. In war, the exceptional state, there is no law; in times of peace, there is only law. In both cases, the sovereign's powers are plenary.

The Hobbesian notion that war submits to no law has, of course, been sternly rebutted by generations of legal thinkers. The idea that morals, if not laws, control the waging of war dates back thousands of years. Herodotus describes rules of war recognized by both the ancient Greeks and Persians.[25] One finds similar norms expressed in the Hindu code of Manu ("let him not strike with weapons . . . barbed, poisoned, or the points of which are blazing with fire").[26] In 1474, Peter von Hagenbach was tried and executed in Austria for wartime atrocities committed during the Siege of Breisach.[27] But the Hobbesian view found its sternest conceptual challenge in the writings of his contemporary, Hugo Grotius.

It is perhaps an exaggeration to call Grotius, the great Dutch jurist, the father of international law. Grotius's thinking was part of a tradition built on the earlier work of Bodin and which found richer exposition in the later work of Vattel. But Grotius's magnum opus, *De Jure Belli ac Pacis* (*On the Law of War and Peace*), published in 1625, some twenty-six years before Hobbes's *Leviathan,* remains a watershed work. In it, Grotius challenged the position "which some people imagine" that "in war all laws are in abeyance."[28] Against this view, Grotius insisted on the existence of a "law of nations" that existed separate from and independent of "the law of nature and the law of particular countries."[29] Anticipating the Hobbesian critique, that a system of law based on mutual consent and lacking the force of sanction was no law at all, Grotius insisted, "[L]aw, even though without sanction, is not entirely void of effect":

> For justice brings peace of conscience, while injustice causes torments and anguish, such as Plato describes in the breast of tyrants. . . . But, most of all, in God injustice finds any enemy, justice a protector. He reserves His judgements for the life after this, yet in such a way that He often causes their effects to become manifest even in this life, as history teaches by numerous examples.[30]

As a legal theorist, Grotius lacks Hobbes's clarity of thought. As the quotation above reveals, Grotius, despite his own claims to the contrary, often conflates law with morality, international law with natural law. When he observes that "even the most powerful peoples and sovereigns seek alliances" either "for purposes of trade" or "even to ward off the forces of many foreign nations united against it,"[31] he appears to overlook the distinction between a politically expedient agreement and a legally binding norm. Still, Grotius's argument that "there is a common law among nations, which is alike for war and in war"[32] created a necessary counterweight to the Hobbesian position, and in so doing, exercised a tremendous influence on the development of legal thinking on war in two regards.

Firstly, Grotius insisted, "[W]ar ought not to be undertaken except for the enforcement of rights."[33] Lamenting that "I observed that men rush to arms for the slightest of causes, or no cause all," Grotius argued that for wars to be justified, they must be undertaken with the "scrupulousness" of "judicial processes."[34]

As a second matter, Grotius argued that the conduct of war had to follow law. Moved by the devastations of the Thirty Years' War, which had run less than half its course at the time of his writing, Grotius observed: "Throughout the Christian world I observed a lack of restraint in relation to war, such as even barbarous races should be ashamed of . . . . [It] is as if, in accordance with a general decree, frenzy had openly been let loose for the committing of all crimes."[35]

Insisting on a law "valid alike for war and in war," Grotius thus introduced the distinction between *jus ad bellum* and *jus in bello*. The former, which became known as just war theory, came to concern itself with specifying the conditions under which the recourse to war was permissible; the latter, which became known as the law of war, sought to articulate the means by which law may be permissibly waged. Grotius insisted that both matters fell within the ambit of international law.

Since the days of Grotius, the development of a meaningful law of war has obviously achieved far greater success in the domain of *jus in bello* than *jus ad bellum*. By the time of the promulgation of the "Lieber Code," a manual enumerating "serious breaches of the law of war" that was distributed to field commanders of the Union Army during the American Civil War,[36] it was believed that such norms expressed the content of customary international law. Such customary law found codification in the Hague conventions of 1899 and 1907, which established the "general rules of conduct for belligerents in their relations with each other and with populations."[37] While the Hague conventions sought to establish the legal parameters controlling acts between and against belligerents, the Geneva Conventions of 1949 and 1970 articulated the legal protections of noncombatants, POWs, and other persons *hors de combat*.

By contrast, the attempts to articulate a coherent *jus ad bellum* foundered. Just war theorists attempted to identify the lawful reasons for going to war—self defense, the redress of injuries, and punishment of an offense—but their attempt to locate such norms in customary international law or to frame them through a convention met with little success. The Kellogg-Briand Pact of 1928 sought to prohibit war as "an instrument of national policy" but notably failed to define aggressive war and the sanctions for its waging.[38] Recognizing these failures, J. L. Brierly wrote in his canonical work of 1928, *The Law of Nations*, "[I]nternational law came frankly to admit that all wars are equally lawful."[39]

All this changed with Nuremberg. The trial of the major Nazi war criminals before the International Military Tribunal (IMT), 1945–46, marked a sea-change in the relationship between law and war. As the first international criminal tribunal in human history, Nuremberg represented an emphatic rejection of the Hobbesian-Schmittian theory of the absolute and illimitable powers of sovereignty in the matter of war-making. Nuremberg first punctured sovereign prerogatives by revolutionizing the international community's treatment of the question of responsibility. Despite its somber adumbration of offenses, the Hague conventions had remained silent on the matter of sanctions. Nuremberg, by contrast, assigned "individual responsibility" for the violations of international law under its purview.

The principle of individual responsibility was effectuated by two key provisions of the IMT's Charter: Article 7 held that "the official position of defendants . . . shall not be considered as freeing them from responsibility"; this provision effectively punctured the immunity that previously had shielded heads of state and ministers from answering for their conduct in foreign or international courts.[40] Article 8, in turn, held that "the fact that the defendant acted pursuant to [an] order of . . . a superior shall not free him from responsibility . . ."[41] Taken together, these two provisions essentially created a jurisprudence of war crimes, enabling the imposition of penal sanctions on individuals found guilty of violating international law.

Nuremberg also sought to establish what Brierly, just a few years earlier, had dismissed as a Grotiusian pipe dream: the creation of a workable international jurisprudence of *jus ad bellum*. Often overlooked in more recent treatments of the IMT, the case of the Allied prosecution did not in the first instance focus on war crimes, violations of *jus in bello*; rather, the gravamen of the case was the "crime against peace"—the launching of an aggressive war, a violation of *jus ad bellum*. As we noted above, it was Kelsen who observed that drawing a distinction between the lawful and unlawful use of force is the most basic internal function of a state's legal system. At Nuremberg, the prosecution insisted that an operation fundamental to domestic law should not be ruinously complicated for international law. As Robert Jackson, who led the Allied prosecution during his leave of absence from the U.S. Supreme Court, rhetorically put it, "[It] was, under the law of all civilized peoples, a crime for one man with his bare knuckles to assault another. How did it come that multiplying this crime by a million, and adding firearms to bare knuckles, made it a legally innocent act?"[42] Building on just war theory, Nuremberg insisted that an unjust war was more than a moral wrong—it was an illegal, or rather, a criminal act:

> Any resort to war of any kind is a resort to means that are inherently criminal. War inevitably is a course of killings assaults, deprivations of liberty, and destruction of property. An honestly defensive war is, of course, legal and saves those lawfully conducting it from criminality. But inherently criminal acts cannot be defended by showing that those who committed them were engaged in a war, when war itself is illegal.[43]

Taken as a whole, Nuremberg marked an astonishing repudiation of the idea that law and war are separate and autonomous spheres of activity. To the contrary, Nuremberg insisted that every aspect of the waging of war—from the decision to launch hostilities, to conduct on the battlefield and the treatment of civilians—would be subject to legal scrutiny from the empyrean reaches of an international institution that stood above the domestic legal system of any specific nation-state. Clearly the most vulnerable legacy of the Nuremberg experiment was the effort to create a workable jurisprudence of *jus ad bellum,* as crimes against the peace disappeared from the jurisdictional mandate of the two ad hoc international tribunals established in the 1990s to deal with international crimes perpetrated in the Balkans and Rwanda.[44] Nonetheless, the establishment of the International Criminal Court (ICC) in 2002, a permanent institution meant to supplant the use of ad hoc courts such as Nuremberg and, more recently, the International Criminal Tribunals for Yugoslavia and Rwanda, has renewed the efforts of international jurists inspired by the dream of Grotius to shape a coherent definition of the crime of aggression. Indeed, these labors appeared to bear fruit in the summer of 2010 when a review conference of the ICC drafted and adopted a definition of the crime of aggression, which could pave the way for the court's exercise of jurisdiction over this incrimination.[45]

Nuremberg remains the most visible symbol of the juridification of war, but it hardly stands alone. Taking the American experience as an example, we can point to the incorporation into federal law of international incriminations against war crimes and torture; the articulation of elaborate codes of military conduct and justice, such as the Uniform Code of Military Justice (UCMJ); the promulgation of elaborate procedures to permit the trial of alien terror suspects before military commissions; and the articulation of elaborate rules of engagement in theaters of battle.[46] All of these developments can be seen as placing war and its waging under the aegis of legal oversight. If at one point in Western history, war represented the ultimate evacuation of law, it has now become thoroughly saturated with law, so much so that the decision to kill a single apparent belligerent in a remote region in the Middle East unleashed a debate that directly involves the president of the United States. And as we have noted, at the heart of this debate was not an argument over what is strategically wise but over what is legally permissible.

The remarkable juridification of war raises, of course, a profound question: what has it achieved? For Grotius, the application of law to war was envisioned as a means of limitation, restraint, and humanization. *Jus ad bellum* was understood to reduce to a minimum the instances in which nations would make recourse to war, while *jus in bello* was meant to reduce the brutality of conflict itself, shielding both belligerents and noncombatants from the worst excesses of war. Law, then, was understood as a necessary and perhaps sufficient tool toward the aim of humanizing war.

At the most general level, the essays collected in this volume explore whether this aim has been achieved or is achievable. Has the advent of "lawfare"[47] tamed warfare or has it simply shifted the form and manner of its waging? The question, not surprisingly, resists a simple answer, and our five contributors all push toward somewhat different answers, some operating on a historical register, others on a more normative level. What they share is an interest in interrogating the assumption implicit in the Grotiusian project: that the insertion of law into war is a necessarily salutary development. While none of our contributors defend the Hobbesian/Schmittian position that rejects as incoherent the effort to juridify acts of war-making, they all question the belief, most explicitly expounded by Jackson at Nuremberg, that sees law as the cornerstone of any bulwark against aggression.

This ambivalence is perhaps most explicitly thematized in our first chapter, "Limits of Law: Promoting Humanity in Armed Conflict," by Sarah Sewall. At first glance, Sewall's chapter appears to tell a familiar story about the tension between "law on the books" and "law in practice." Law's efficacy, Sewall insists, will always be measured by its capacity to restrain actual practice. If too wide a gap opens between norm and practice, the very integrity of law will be eroded, as regulations turn farcical. This, Sewall fears, will be the consequence of the growth and proliferation of new laws of armed conflict. Instead of offering meaningful restraint, these laws will simply create occasions for weak enforcement and noncompliance.

On closer inspection, however, Sewall's argument reveals itself to be narrowly tailored to the specific problems raised by the fraught effort to submit war to legal regulation. Sewall notes—as do Gabriella Blum and Samuel Moyn in their contributions—that the law of armed conflict is built on a paradoxical relationship to violence. At its most basic level, the law of armed conflict (LOAC) authorizes persons to commit the very act, which, *pace* Kelsen, describes the paradigmatic delict from the perspective of domestic law: the purposeful, premeditated killing of another person. In this regard, the law of armed conflict serves not only as a restraint but also as an authorization, or, to borrow David Kennedy's language, as "war generative."[48] If for Hobbes, acts of brutal warfare always stood outside of legal restraint, LOAC stands for an equally remarkable proposition: that acts of astonishing violence and horrific destruction can be deemed lawful and legally authorized.

As Sewall (and Blum) remind us, three key norms underlie the line LOAC draws between lawful and unlawful acts of killing: necessity, distinction, and proportionality. "Necessity" stands for the idea that even an extensive destruction of persons and property will not be considered a crime under *jus in bello* so long as such destruction is justified by military necessity; "distinction" requires that belligerents target only combatants and not civilians; and "proportionality" insists that "harm to noncombatants is not excessive in relation to its military benefits."[49]

These interrelated principles obviously raise thorny, if not intractable, problems of interpretation. Sewall notes that in Operation Desert Storm, the U.S. Air Force assessed proportionality in terms of the "overall campaign, not target by target."[50] Is that the proper calculus? The principle of necessity raises similar problems, as it appears to justify potentially calamitous "collateral damage" in attacks that confer great military advantage.[51] Indeed, arguments of necessity have been invoked to justify the dropping of nuclear weapons on Hiroshima and Nagasaki, inasmuch as the bombings arguably accelerated Japan's surrender.[52] If infinitely plastic, then the norms of LOAC offer little meaningful restraint, or rather, provide a legal cover to the most extreme depredations of war.

At the same time, Sewall reminds us that the reality that gave birth to LOAC has been rapidly changing in a manner that raises concerns about its continued relevance. As we noted above, the dream of jurists going back to Grotius was that law could restrain and humanize the allegedly illimitable power of the sovereign in waging war. The Nuremberg paradigm, which helped realize this dream, likewise used international criminal law as a means of punishing atrocities committed by sovereigns. As such, LOAC has been predicated upon a number of foundational distinctions—between war and peace, combatant and civilian, international combat and domestic policing. The changing nature of warfare in the twenty-first century, particularly in the struggle against terrorist organizations and local insurgencies, has volatized these distinctions.[53] These instabilities are nowhere more visible than in the debates over al-Awlaki's killing—whether the targeting should be legally understood as a military operation or as a police chase, and whether the target himself was to be viewed as a combatant or as a civilian, as a soldier or as a criminal. This shifting complex reality, Sewall insists, cannot be juridically subdued by simply expanding the available categories and protections of LOAC, as the categories themselves no longer accommodate the rapidly changing field of practice. Here the gap between norm and practice has opened not because actors choose to ignore the norm, but because the norm no longer corresponds to any *possible* practice.

Similar concerns inform Gabriella Blum's chapter, "The Individualization of War"; indeed, Blum provides a broad conceptual account of the phenomenon described by Sewall. Blum asks us to understand the expansion of the law of war in terms of a shift from "collectivism" to "cosmopolitanism." In this account, from the end of the nineteenth century and through much of the twentieth, the legal regulation of war operated on the level of the "collective"— that is, through a "state-oriented set of obligations—which viewed war as an intercollective effort."[54] More recently, however, the law of war has moved toward embracing the commitments of "cosmopolitan individualism,"[55] a theory that understands rights as vested in individuals "regardless of national affiliation or territorial boundaries."

Like Sewall, Blum argues that this shift has worked to unsettle and destabilize the foundational distinctions upon which the law of war was predicated. As an example, Blum describes changing understandings in the meaning of proportionality, the "just allocation of risk between combatants and civilians."[56] Under the classic collectivist approach, soldiers are allowed "not only to prefer compatriot civilians to enemy civilians" but also their own well-being over that of enemy civilians. From this perspective, "the nationality of the civilian is . . . a determinative factor in risk allocation."[57] Contrast this with the commitments of cosmopolitan individualism. From this perspective, soldiers "bear an equal duty to risk their lives for the sake of enemy civilians as they do for compatriot civilians"; or, to put it somewhat differently, "[It] is the duty of soldiers to risk their lives for civilians, while pursuing military tasks, just as it is the role of police officers to risk their lives for the sake of civilians when they pursue criminals."[58]

This shift—from the collectivist to the cosmopolitan—does not signal simply a sharpening of the calculus of proportionality; rather, it signals a fundamental change in the law of war, as it effectively erases the distinction between combat and policing. Indeed, war begins to look all the more like a police action, controlled by similar norms. This is not a change that Blum finds entirely salutary. For one thing, Blum fears that the "higher bar of compliance" may deter liberal democracies from deploying force "even when such force is justified."[59] More to the point, she fears that treating war like policing creates the risk of treating policing as war: "[O]nce certain practices become legitimated under a paradigm of 'international policing,' they risk spilling over and being legitimated under a paradigm of domestic policing as well."[60] This, of course, is precisely what we've seen in the controversies over detention practices, the use of military commissions to try terror suspects, and the targeted killing of terrorists/fugitives such as al-Awlaki.

Similar concerns animate Laura Donohue's chapter, "Pandemic Disease, Biological Weapons, and War." Broadly historical in its perspective, Donohue's chapter also tells a story of the blurring of categories. From the founding of the Republic through the end of the twentieth century, the legal authority to respond to the threat of pandemic disease dramatically shifted from the police powers of the states to those of the federal government. The events of 9.11, however, triggered a fresh shift in thinking, as the threat posed by disease has more recently come to be seen through a "national security framework" and "through a lens of war."[61] Or, to use the language we encounter in Sewell and Blum, the line between police powers and military action has been rendered fluid and unstable.

Donohue worries that as categories continue to blur, the consequences will be difficult to foresee and control. Were a pandemic to strike the United States, the initial chaos would make it all but impossible to determine whether the outbreak was caused by natural factors or by a purposive act of biowarfare/terrorism. In either case, the response would require the coordinated efforts of institutions of civilian governance and the military. Closing airports and harbors, shutting down railroads, establishing and perhaps enforcing quarantines—a complex mobilized response deploying the full panoply of state force would erase the distinction between police powers and military action, between health policy and national security concerns.

We can already catch a glimpse of the consequences of such an elision by considering the structural similarities between practices of quarantine and detention. As opposed to incarceration, a punitive act imposed on a person after a formal finding of guilt for acts already committed, quarantine and detention present themselves as regulatory acts designed to safeguard against future harms.[62] While the system of criminal justice is prepared to absorb false negatives in order to minimize the chance of generating false positives (incarcerating factually innocent persons), both quarantine and detention are prepared to accept false positives in the hope of eliminating false negatives—carriers capable of spreading deadly diseases or terrorists capable of carrying acts of mass destruction. The striking similarities between the practices and purposes of quarantine and detention make clear the remarkable conflation that Donohue lays bear: just as disease comes to be seen through the prism of war, war comes to be seen through the prism of disease. And far from subduing or pacifying war, the proliferation and expansion of federal law has simply created new practices of justified force, new structures to defend the prerogatives of national security.

Our final two chapters also call into question the capacity of law to humanize war, to act as a meaningful tool of restraint. In "From Antiwar Politics to Antitorture Politics," Samuel Moyn takes as his point of departure the debates concerning the legality of many of the Bush administration's executive acts in waging its self-designated "war on terror. " Liberals, on the one hand, often decried Bush practices as illegal if not directly criminal. Waterboarding, extraordinary rendition, indefinite detention—all were vilified as acts of shocking lawlessness, with few precedents in our nation's history. On the other hand, conservatives bemoaned the hypertrophy of law which allegedly interfered with a vigorous executive response to a national emergency; such conservatives looked back with nostalgia to a simple time when presidents, such as FDR, could act aggressively without worrying about niggling, vexatious legal red-tape.

According to Moyn, both pictures distort the historical record, an argument he develops through a close historical study of the debates concerning the legality of the war in Vietnam. Moyn identifies Vietnam as a watershed in American legal history. Although American statesmen and jurists were the prime movers behind the creation of the Nuremberg trial, America would have to wait until Vietnam to struggle meaningfully with our own nation's fraught relationship to war and law. Here Moyn alerts us to an important irony. Whatever else we might think about the legality of Bush's actions in the "war against terror," they look awfully tame compared with the horrific things America did in Vietnam. And yet if we examine the contemporaneous debates about the legality of the war in Vietnam—at least in the years before the My Lai massacre—we find a fresh anomaly. These debates, to recall the language of Grotius, largely focused on *jus ad bellum* not on *jus in bello*. Vietnam was an illegal war, not because of the napalm, the carpet-bombing, the mistreatment of POWs, but because it was undeclared and aggressive: a war of imperialist domination. Here we see the clear vestiges of Nuremberg thinking in debates about Vietnam.

As Moyn points out, it wasn't until after My Lai and the publication of Telford Taylor's *Nuremberg and Vietnam* that jurists began to train their attention on means and methods of war "decoupled . . . from the legality of the war itself."[63] That Taylor should play such a central role in this shift was, perhaps, inevitable, for it was Taylor, who as chief prosecutor of the twelve "successor" trials staged by the Nuremberg Military Tribunal (NMT), oversaw the shift away from the IMT's emphasis on aggressive war toward the NMT's focus on war crimes and crimes against humanity.[64]

And yet Moyn regards this shift with ambivalence. Noting that debates about Bush-era policies focused almost exclusively on issues such as torture and cruel and inhumane interrogation practices, Moyn insists that "the intense focus on *jus in bello*" creates the risk of "humanizing war," as jurists fail to recall the chief ambition of the IMT: to insist that international law places "constraints on going to war in the first place."[65] As Jackson argued at the time of Nuremberg, if there is no war, there are no war crimes.

At the same time that Moyn implicitly supports the original vision of Grotius—that law can meaningfully restrain war only through a combination of *jus ad bellum* with *jus in bello*—he expresses a final ambivalence about the ultimate efficacy of law. In the wake of Vietnam (and Watergate), Congress legislated the "most significant constraints on executive power ever put on paper in American history."[66] Yet the passage of such constraints was made possible by a massive popular movement against the war and executive arrogance. And in the absence of a strong political movement that pushes for their respect and enforcement, these legal constraints "are not likely to be defended for long."[67] Law, Moyn suggests, may be a necessary constraint on the war, but it is never sufficient. For law to act as a meaningful restraint, it must always be supported by broad expressions of political will.

Our final chapter, Larry May's "War Crimes Trials during and after War," is likewise concerned with the relationship between *jus ad bellum* and *jus in bello*. May's chapter is the most explicitly normative in this book, as he attempts to offer a unified response to two seemingly disparate questions: When should war crimes trials be staged? Who can be held liable for violations of *jus ad bellum*?

Schooled on the Nuremberg precedent, we tend to think of war crimes trials as *post hoc* phenomena, staged in the aftermath of war. But as May points out, this need not be the case; like Moyn, May finds a potent example in the My Lai massacre and the trial of William Calley that ensued. Despite its anomalous features, the Calley trial stands as an example of a war crimes trial staged in the midst of ongoing hostilities. As the struggle against global terror has destabilized the very distinction between conditions of war and peace—a point emphasized by Sewall and Blum—we might expect to see more Calley-like trials in the future, proceedings staged during war, if only because it has become increasingly difficult to say when hostilities end.

The question that concerns May is whether such trials are a good idea. Do they promote the idea that law can act as a meaningful restraint on war? The fact that of the eight Marines implicated in the massacre of twenty-five unarmed Iraqi men, women, and children in Haditha, Iraq, in 2005, only one was convicted of any crime, and this lone conviction followed a plea to a single count of dereliction of duty, should not make us sanguine.[68] In the midst of ongoing hostilities, it is exceptionally difficult for domestic civilian or military courts to find their own soldiers guilty of violations of *jus in bello*.

In seeking to address this concern, May, like Moyn, shifts our attention to *jus ad bellum*. At Nuremberg, crimes against peace were understood as leadership crimes.[69] As opposed to war crimes, which could be perpetrated by soldiers in the field, only those exercising leadership positions could be held responsible for crimes of aggression. In the decades since Nuremberg, the rise of the human rights framework of cosmopolitan individualism, so ably described by Blum, has lent support to the ideas that "soldiers have duties to civilians as fellow humans beings."[70] This human rights rationale, May argues, potentially supports accusations "of violations of the morality of law for what were previously viewed as normal acts of war, namely the killing of one soldier by another soldier."[71] Or to put it somewhat differently, the rise of cosmopolitan individualism makes thinkable the idea that soldiers could be held responsible for participating in wars of aggression. This, however, presupposes that soldiers *know* of the illegality of the war they are participating in; and it is here that May returns to the idea of war crimes trials conducted during hostilities. Such trials, as May imagines them, might not be for violations of *jus in bello* but for violations of *jus ad bellum*, and would serve an important declaratory function to soldiers in the field. For once a court had declared a war "aggressive" and therefore criminal, soldiers of the aggressing force would have effectively been served notice that they are accessories, if not principals, in a crime.

Whether such an extraordinary legal declaration would meaningfully restrain the waging and conduct of war is a question that, as May recognizes, resists a clear answer. Like the other chapters in this book, his piece ends on a note of ambivalence, born of an appreciation of the ever-fraught relationship between law and war. If we have come to reject the understanding of Hobbes that saw law and war as ineluctably separate, we have also come to question the coherence of Grotius's dream that saw war tamed and humanized by the instrument of legal control. Now and for the foreseeable future, law and war will remain inextricably linked, bound by a common preoccupation with the legitimacy of the most extreme acts of force and violence that arise from and seek to tame social conflict. Whether law serves as a means of restraint or simply as a tool of authorization will turn, in no small measure, on the answers that jurists provide to the dilemmas sketched in this volume.

Notes

1. See Mary Ellen O'Connell, "Obama's 'Targeted Killing' Is Worse than Bush's Torture"; http://www.guardian.co.uk/commentisfree/cifamerica/2012/jan/20/why-obama-targeted-killing-is-like-bush-torture.

2. See 542 U.S. 507 (2004).

3. "Ron Paul Condemns Al-Awlaki's Killing"; http://www.npr.org/blogs/thetwo-way/2011/09/30/140950953/ron-paul-condemns-al-awlakis-killing.

4. "ACLU Criticizes Killing of Anwar al-Awlaki, a U.S. Citizen, Calling It a 'Dangerous' Precedent"; http://www.pbs.org/wnet/need-to-know/the-daily-need/aclu-criticizes-killing-of-anwar-al-awlaki-a-u-s-citizen-calling-it-a-dangerous-precedent/11813/.

5. See "Ron Paul Condemns Al-Awlaki Killing."

6. Benjamin Wittes, "On Due Process and Targeting American Citizens"; http://www.pbs.org/wnet/need-to-know/the-daily-need/aclu-criticizes-killing-of-anwar-al-awlaki-a-u-s-citizen-calling-it-a-dangerous-precedent/11813/.

7. "Authorization for Use of Military Force," September 18, 2001, Public Law 107-40 [S. J. RES. 23]; http://news.findlaw.com/wp/docs/terrorism/sjres23.es.html.

8. Harold Koh, "The Obama Administration and International Law"; http://www.state.gov/s/l/releases/remarks/139119.htm.

9. Ibid.

10. Ibid.

11. Ibid.

12. Charlie Savage, "Secret U.S. Memo Made Legal Case to Kill a Citizen," *New York Times*, October 9, 2011, A1.

13. See Gary Bass, *Stay the Hand of Vengeance: The Politics of War Crimes Tribunals* (Princeton University Press, 2001).

14. Thomas Hobbes, *Leviathan,* ed. Richard Tuck (Cambridge University Press, 1996), 88–89.

15. Ibid., 90.

16. Richard Tuck, *The Rights of War and Peace: Political Thought and the International Order from Grotius to Kant* (Oxford University Press, 2001).

17. Hitler quoted by Robert Jackson in opening address for the prosecution, *Trial of the Major Nazi War Criminals before the International Military Tribunal, 14 November 1945–1 October 1946,* 42 vols. [hereafter cited as IMT]. Nuremberg, 1947, vol. II, 144, IMT: "Law of Case."

18. Hans Kelsen, *Pure Theory of Law* (Peter Smith, 1989), 36.

19. Ibid., 42.

20. Ibid., 38.

21. Ibid.

22. Carl Schmitt, *Political Theology: Four Chapters on the Concept of Sovereignty,* trans. George Schwab (University of Chicago Press, 2005), 5.

23. Ibid., 13.

24. Ibid.

25. Aryeh Neier, *War Crimes: Brutality, Genocide, Terror and the Struggle for Justice* (Times Books, 1998), 13.

26. *Code of Manu,* ch. VII, §90; www.hinduwebsite.com/sacredscripts/laws.

27. William Schabas, *An Introduction to the International Criminal Court* (Cambridge University Press, 2001), 1.

28. Hugo Grotius, *De Jure Belli ac Pacis,* trans. Francis Kelsey (Oxford Clarendon, 1925), 235.

29. Ibid., 234.

30. Ibid., 234–35.

31. Ibid., 235.

32. Ibid.

33. Ibid.

34. Ibid.

35. Ibid.

36. *Lieber Code of 1863,* §II, para. 33; http://www.civilwarhome.com/liebercode.htm.

37. Preamble, *Convention with Respect to the Laws and Customs of War on Land (Hague II), 29 July 1899*; http://www.yale.edu/lawweb/avalon/lawofwar/hague02.htm.

38. Gerhard Werle, *Principles of International Criminal Law* (Asser Press, 209), 477–79.

39. J. L. Brierly, *The Law of Nations: An Introduction to the International Law of Peace,* 5th ed. (Oxford University Press, 1955), 35.

40. IMT, vol. I, 12.

41. Ibid.

42. Jackson, ibid., vol. II, 145.

43. Ibid., vol. II, 146.

44. Lawrence Douglas, "Crimes of Atrocity, the Problem of Punishment and the *situ* of Law," in *Propaganda, War Crimes Trials and International Law,* ed. Predrag Dojcinovic (Routledge, 2012), 269–94.

45. See, generally, Claus Kreß and Philippa Webb, eds., "Aggression: After Kampala," *Journal of International Criminal Justice* 10, no. 1 (special issue, March 2012).

46. John F. Murphy, *The United States and the Rule of Law in International Affairs* (Cambridge University Press, 2004).

47. The contemporary usage is usually credited to Charles Dunlap, Jr., "Law and Military Interventions: Preserving Humanitarian Values in 21st Century Conflicts,"

paper prepared for Carr Center for Human Rights, Harvard University, November 29, 2001.

48. David Kennedy, *Of Law and War* (Princeton University Press, 2006), 32.

49. Sarah Sewall, "Limits of Law: Promoting Humanity in Armed Conflict," this volume, 29.

50. Sewall, "Limits of Law," 20.

51. See http://www.crimesofwar.org/a-z-guide/military-necessity/.

52. Gar Alperovitz, *The Decision to Use the Atomic Bomb* (Vintage, 1996).

53. See, for example, Benjamin Wittes, *Law and the Long War: The Future of Justice in the Age of Terror* (Penguin, 2008).

54. Gabriella Blum, "The Individualization of War: From Collectivism to Individualism in the Regulation of Armed Conflicts," this volume, 48.

55. Ibid., 12.

56. Ibid., 22.

57. Ibid., 23.

58. Ibid., 22.

59. Ibid., 38.

60. Ibid., 39.

61. Laura K. Donohue, "Pandemic Disease, Biological Weapons, and War," this volume, 90.

62. See, generally, R. A. Duff, *Trials and Punishments* (Cambridge University Press, 1991).

63. Samuel Moyn, "From Antiwar Politics to Antitorture Politics," this volume, 178.

64. Lawrence Douglas, "From IMT to NMT: The Emergence of a Jurisprudence of Atrocity," in *Unearthing the Subsequent Nuremberg Trials: Transitional Justice, Trial Narratives and Historiography*, ed. Kim Priemel and Alexa Stiller (Berghahn, 2012).

65. Moyn, "From Antiwar Politics to Antitorture Politics," 50.

66. Ibid., 52.

67. Ibid., 51.

68. Charlie Savage and Elizabeth Bumiller, "An Iraqi Massacre, a Light Sentence and a Question of Military Justice," *New York Times*, January 28, 2012, A17.

69. See Kevin Jon Heller, *The Nuremberg Military Tribunals and the Origins of International Criminal Law* (Oxford University Press, 2011).

70. Larry May, "War Crimes Trials during and after War," this volume, 206.

71. Ibid., 13.

Limits of Law: Promoting Humanity
in Armed Conflict

SARAH SEWALL

Introduction

International Humanitarian Law (IHL)[1] seeks to balance the principles of humanity and necessity in the conduct of war. Many states and nongovernmental organizations aim to promote civilian protection in war by "strengthening" the principle of humanity in positive law. This group of actors, which I will call the progressive community,[2] devotes itself to refining interpretations of existing laws and creating new law. However, this focus on raising the standards of positive law may not be the most effective route toward enhancing civilian protection.

Placing higher expectations on the international legal regime could even be counterproductive, because IHL is already becoming less relevant to armed conflict in the twenty-first century. There are three principal reasons why this is so. First, some powerful states that employ force frequently do not share the progressive view of the law. The United States is the most important global actor that clings to a "traditionalist" approach. In practice, the law is rarely a constraint on U.S. actions (although this is not necessarily problematic from the perspective of reducing civilian casualties). Second, many states and nonstate actors that use violence do not follow, and indeed openly flout, the most fundamental IHL principles. While this is not a new phenomenon, it is becoming more significant as states' monopoly of violence erodes and new technologies enable nonstate actors to threaten harm of great magnitude. Third, emerging powers—especially China—lack clear policies toward IHL even as their military roles appear poised to expand.

This essay begins by outlining the challenges of noncompliance in order to show that the edifice of IHL is not as robust in practice as progressives seem to assume. Challenges to IHL suggest the need to shore up compliance with the regime's fundamental rules, rather than ratcheting up the standards of compliance.

The chapter's focus, though, is explaining the gap between the U.S. traditionalist view of the law and that of the progressives. This gap is not well understood by Americans, who are routinely reassured that the U.S. military abides by the laws of war and then perplexed as outside critics dispute U.S. claims. I discuss the two general perspectives on the law and illustrate their implications through two examples: defining military objectives and taking precautions to protect civilians. In both cases, the United States rejects progressive standards yet routinely takes *additional* measures to protect civilians for reasons that are independent of the law. It is the norm of minimizing civilian casualties, however, not the law, that prompts these additional measures. Indeed, normative argument divorced from law offers progressives an alternative means of pushing advanced military powers to enhance civilian protections.

Yet the most fundamental IHL challenge remains enforcement of the most basic protections for civilians. Even the United States is uneven in enforcement of the basic rules of war. The history of American prosecution of service members for IHL violations illustrates this vexing challenge. Progressives should place less emphasis upon raising legal requirements for protecting civilians than upon enforcing minimal standards.

Finally, I explain why a continued progressive push to tighten existing standards of IHL in the name of protecting civilians has several downsides, principally widening the gap between the demands of law and global compliance. This increases the practical costs of compliance for adherents, and may reduce their ranks, including rising powers whose support will be crucial for the future of IHL. More capable military actors such as the United States and Israel, which already question the evolving direction of the law, may further distance themselves from IHL's development. The net result may well be undermining whatever salience IHL retains for armed conflict in the twenty-first century.

I conclude that the progressive community should focus on practical impact—promoting compliance with IHL and punishment for those who violate it—rather than pursuing ever more agreements on paper.

Challenges to IHL

Several developments in international politics cast doubt on the continued salience of the existing rules governing the use of force. First, states—the building blocks of IHL consent and compliance—are eroding in relevance and span of control.[3] But states have been the bulwark of the law. Insurgents and terrorists have remained outside the law from its earliest days, as the debate about Additional Protocol 1 reminds us.

The demise of states suggests that the number of noncompliant actors will grow. Insurgents and illegal groups perceive the law as serving the interests of the strong and see little additional cost for adopting whatever violent means they deem necessary. Armed groups such as the Taliban in Afghanistan and M23 in the Congo routinely violate multiple IHL principles, most notably by purposefully targeting civilians during their military activities.[4] Rebellious forces conceivably could gain control of states and then come to view IHL in a different light. Yet many groups using force today—from drug cartels to Al Qaeda—care little about becoming a state, and care even less about the rules that govern relations among states. Thus the demise of states, and the expanding, globally linked actors that threaten states, pose challenges for the future of the law of armed conflict.

Second, the compliance of states is also uneven. Some states publicly reject the law, while others quarrel about whether their actions comply with its standards. The former is a fundamental challenge to the regime itself. Some states, especially those already isolated from the international community, openly flout the underlying tenets of LOAC, often for the same reason that guerrillas do—they are relatively weak militarily and expect little benefit or legitimacy from compliance.

Asymmetric tactics—which generally entail IHL violations—are often adopted by weaker parties, including states. There is not much to be done about the differences in military power between the United States and some of the so-called rogue states. Yet in 1991 Saddam Hussein did not resort to widespread IHL violations, while Iraqi forces in 2003 flagrantly did so. The armed forces of Serbia in 1999 under Slobodan Milosevic also violated IHL. This dynamic weakens IHL's overall relevance.

Actors' responses to allegations of legal violations provide another barometer of IHL's power. When belligerents do not bother even to justify their actions pursuant to IHL, the law is revealed as less relevant. For example, Sri Lanka's armed forces killed tens of thousands of civilians during their final assault on the Liberation Tigers of Tamil Eelam (LTTE) insurgents. The UN Secretary General's Panel of Experts on Sri Lanka found credible allegations of a "wide range of serious violations of international humanitarian law" by both sides.[5] The Sri Lankan government dismissed such charges as biased rather than seeking to justify its actions as consistent with IHL.

Widespread violations of IHL by state and nonstate actors undoubtedly help to explain why civilians became significantly more vulnerable in war than combatants during the twentieth century.[6] If a goal of IHL in the twentieth century was to make war more tolerable, then from the civilian perspective, it is clearly failing.

A third challenge for the IHL regime is the high degree of uncertainty regarding how changing international power dynamics and technologies may affect IHL. The Western powers that so heavily shaped and legitimized the law are gradually waning in their relative influence and power as the economies and militaries of other states expand. The attitudes of emerging powers are crucial factors that will help determine the future of IHL.

China's views, in particular, are worrisomely opaque. Some commentators have suggested that the Chinese government regards armed conflict as "unrestricted warfare," freed of constraints of IHL.[7] The paucity of official Chinese comment on this point, especially regarding the use of new technology, creates great uncertainty and can lead to worst-case assumptions by those who warily regard Chinese power. The associate risk is a regional or international race-to-the-bottom mentality by those who fear violations by key actors. As international power realigns, it is not clear that the rising powers will share the underlying human rights commitments or perceptions of self-interest that provide incentives to continue IHL compliance. Shifts in global material power create additional questions about whether IHL will remain relevant in practice.

Uncertainty is compounded when new technologies create—or are perceived to create—gaps in the law. At the moment, the international community is seeking to understand how cyber capabilities relate to existing IHL, with some suggesting that they fall easily under its rubric, while others assert the need for new rules to regulate this new type of "force."[8]

A final major stress on IHL is the growing price of upholding the law in the face of adversary noncompliance. The demise of reciprocity is doubly threatening for the legal regime. It's not simply that the many actors do not uphold the law. The second-order effect is that noncompliance increases costs for those attempting to uphold the law. This is no longer a localized risk. The potential diffusion of weapons of mass destruction to nonstate actors increases the threat posed by noncompliant actors, be they terrorists, freedom fighters, or internationally recognized nations. New methods of conflict, such as cyber warfare, further increase the likelihood that IHL-rejecting states or armed groups may be able to place law-supporting states at risk. This is a fundamental change in the power equation of law compliance, and it does not bode well for the law's future.

Overall, then, IHL is being undermined by greater noncompliance and by the rising costs that states face in adhering to the law while other parties do not. Given these challenges, the progressives' focus on tightening civilian protection requirements in the law appears misplaced. It not only fails to address noncompliance; it also fuels divisions among the United States and other important powers about the law's requirements.

IHL

Origins and Balance

As philosopher Michael Walzer reminds us, the law's purpose is not to abolish war, or to make it impossible to fight.[9] Even as war remains hell, the law of war seeks to balance military necessity and humanity.[10] Within the law, several broad principles uneasily coexist. These include "military necessity" (only force that is necessary can be used), "distinction" (between combatants and noncombatants), and "proportionality" (that harm to noncombatants is not excessive in relation to its military benefits).[11]

The law's protections for noncombatants were not conceived by humanitarians and presented to the states to codify as black letter law. Rather, the law's civilian protections grew out of the customary practices of states. These practices were grounded in religious and moral ideals, as well as assumptions about self-interest and utility. But the positive law that emerged in the nineteenth and twentieth centuries codified behavioral rules to which states had already committed themselves in *practice*.

Thus, the law's logic privileged the successful conduct of war—it could not prioritize other goals and remain a code for war (rather than peace). The law also had to reflect the possible. Law that could not be followed within the context of war would lose its meaning and import altogether. The law reflected consensus among its adherents—which remains vital for international law in particular, as there is as yet no centralized enforcement power for global rules. Law that parties would rarely follow would have limited relevance. The progressive effort to prioritize the principle of humanity challenges each of the above tenets.

In balancing necessity and humanity, IHL forbids certain actions, such as the *intentional* targeting of civilians. Yet IHL provides significant scope for unintended effects. It privileges the war fighter's intent and often requires weighing the protection it accords noncombatants against other values or goals (primarily the ability to wage war effectively). To put it crassly: civilians may be unintentionally but predictably killed under certain circumstances, a concept the U.S. military calls "collateral damage."[12] Despite the principle of distinction, IHL in practice provides "qualified"—not absolute—protection for noncombatants.

The progressive community's approach continues to alter the law's balance, pushing it further toward humanity. What has been called the "philosophy of IHL" fundamentally seeks to expand civilian protection within the law.[13] Humanitarians consider the law's contextual and subjective standards and its balancing of necessity and humanity to be weaknesses because they dilute civilian protections. Yet the law's balance and flexibility have proved useful as it seeks to engage a larger and more diverse group of belligerents than existed in the nineteenth century as the law first began to take shape. The law's flexibility and balance have also allowed the law to sustain its relevance despite significant noncompliance and stunning material changes.

There are tradeoffs between promoting higher or "tighter" standards and ensuring the compliance with more basic standards. If compliance with current standards were high, if consensus about the compatibility of greater humanity with victory were strong, there would be a wider margin within which to continue advancing civilian protection in the law. But a host of reasons, many noted above, render the law more fragile and therefore caution against continuing to raise its demands.

Traditionalist and Progressive Views

In order to show how progressive reinterpretation of the law creates a higher standard—and entails costs—this section of the essay explains the orientation of the progressive view and the "traditionalist" view held by the United States. Both progressives and traditionalists agree on the law's underlying principles. But this masks an underlying struggle about the proper balance between military necessity and humanity and the extent of noncombatant protections specified in the law.

The difference between agreeing in principle upon the importance of IHL principles (for example, military necessity, civilian protection, the proportionate use of force), and disputing what these principles require in practice evokes what Frank Michelman has called "the chimera of universally accepted canons."[14] Within the United States, he notes, there is broad agreement on such principles as: no cruel and unusual punishment; no groundless or arbitrary deprivation of life or liberty; and no denial of equal protection of the laws. Competing views of IHL suggest a parallel dichotomy. The law's fundamental canons include the principles of military necessity, the distinction between civilians and combatants, and the proportional use of force.[15] But these IHL canons hide interpretive disputes that reflect first-order divisions. The divisions are ethical, and they are also cultural, organizational, and historical.

Traditionalist View

The United States remains the leading global actor that routinely uses force while it trumpets the centrality of law to its conduct of military operations. Its actions and positions therefore bear centrally on the legitimacy of the law.

The United States has a minimalist, conservative interpretation of IHL that heavily relies upon state practice. This is not inconsistent with respect for the law. Nor is this characterization a criticism of U.S. military operations, because U.S. technical abilities and operational design have pioneered new ways to limit civilian harm.[16] The United States emphasizes its commitment to reducing civilian harm in war, although it generally does not see its actions as reflecting a *legal* requirement.[17] The United States sees a significant gap between the "floor" of legal requirements and a higher "norm" of minimizing civilian casualties.

U.S. views toward law reflect the peculiarities of the American way of war and American views toward international law generally. Broader national, political, and cultural influences also shape U.S. attitudes.[18] The U.S. has sought to retain flexibility in the law, and balks at new restrictions on weapons or interpretations of law that further limit the role of a commander's intent and his subjective judgment.

The current philosophical divide within IHL began to emerge in the 1970s, as the humanitarian impulse began altering IHL's balance of necessity and humanity, seeking to expand civilian protections. The U.S. largely resisted progressive efforts to make the law more precise, absolute, and binding.

Tilting toward Humanity

Until the late 1970s, the U.S. view of the law of armed conflict had generally evolved along with that of the broader community of nations. Beginning in the second half of the nineteenth century, states created Hague Law (pertaining largely to the means of warfare) and the Geneva Conventions (the 1949 Conventions related primarily to the protection of persons). The U.S. position began to diverge from the progressive mainstream of international thought with the 1977 Additional Protocol 1 (AP1) to the Geneva Conventions. The United States has since resisted several progressive efforts to make the law more supportive of the principle of humanity. However, the fundamental reason the United States decided not to embrace the protocols was only partly related to humanitarianism.

The U.S. objected most to what it cast as the protocol's legitimization of the use of violence by nonstate actors. AP1 upended the sovereign state's lawful monopoly of violence without imposing concomitant enforcement responsibilities about how guerrillas might employ force. The treaty sought to enhance enforcement of rules by expanding their writ to actors "outside the tent." But the gamble did not fully account for the enduring asymmetry of means that could render rule-compliance the functional equivalent of handcuffs. Arguing that the protocol had been politicized and would have counterproductive effects, President Ronald Reagan refused to submit it for ratification.[19]

A lesser point of contention for the United States was AP1's incorporation of certain human rights concepts to "strengthen" civilian protections.[20] States had added clarifying language to long-standing provisions and defined the principle of proportionality. The new provisions induced U.S. military fears of a creeping infiltration of human rights, civilian, and peacetime standards into LOAC—both substantively and procedurally. General U.S. skepticism toward the protocols began to wane only later; in 1987 the United States finally announced that it considered many of the civilian protection provisions to be customary law.[21]

The 1977 Additional Protocols marked the beginning of a rift between "traditionalists" like the United States and "progressives" who sought accommodation to changing social views (human rights) and material facts (the persistence of guerrilla movements). These progressives led the next thirty years of expansion and reinterpretation of both international law and the civilian protection norm. In particular change was advocated not by the superpowers that relied most upon the use of force, but by middle powers, including virtually all European nations.

The United States remained engaged in international negotiations regarding the future of IHL. Yet it ultimately became a bystander or an active opponent of the legal codification of much of humanitarian norms through international law and institutions. The United States declined to join the land mines ban, the International Criminal Court, or the Convention on Cluster Munitions.[22] In each case, the United States warned that the legal innovation was ill advised and could impose unpalatable constraints on American military freedom of action and ultimately American power. A handful of great and emerging powers, as well as some non-European allies such as Israel, frequently stood with the United States.

Progressive View

The broad thrust of progressive efforts is to make IHL more specific and objective thereby enabling a broader range of actors to understand and apply it to military operations. Substantively, the progressive approach tilts law away from a balancing of military necessity with civilian protection and toward the human rights standards that apply during peacetime.

International humanitarians emphasize the principles of humanity and dictates of public conscience over actual practice. As Rudolf Dolzer notes, their favorite IHL provision (originating in the Martens clause and adapted in AP 1) emphasizes that civilian protection stems from "the principles of humanity and from the dictates of public conscience " as well as established customary practice.[23]

The emphasis on belief rather than practice troubles traditionalists. Some believe that progressive views reflect hostility toward the use of military power.[24] States that don't plan or want to employ force appear to have fewer incentives to protect military necessity as they promote humanity in law. As a result, traditionalists saw the progressive states as willing to handicap military necessity in the name of humanity.[25]

The fault lines between these two perspectives become most visible in the translation and application of specific IHL provisions. The next section illustrates how these views shape understandings of specific provisions of law.

Devil in the Detail: IHL Provisions

The gap between U.S. views of IHL and those asserted by the progressives is best illustrated through examples. For the purposes of our discussion, the most fundamental aspect of law is the principle of distinction, which holds that only military objectives may be targeted. Other key humanitarian protections, such as the principle of proportionality, the requirement to take precautions to protect civilians before using force, logically hinge upon the lawfulness of the target. The U.S. view of military objectives differs from that of the progressives, but has a complex relationship to humanitarian outcomes. It is more permissive in what it considers a military objective, yet it often uses its more flexible interpretation for the purpose of reducing civilian harm.

Defining a Military Objective

The Geneva Convention's Additional Protocol 1 defines military objectives more broadly than simply troops and tanks. Military objectives are objects that, by their nature, location, purpose, or use, make "an effective contribution to military action" and whose destruction or neutralization in the circumstances ruling at the time "offers a definite military advantage."[26] Objectives must meet the criteria outlined in both the first and the second clauses or "prongs." Civilian objects, in contrast, are all those things that are not military objectives.[27]

The central question is in what circumstances objects other than self-evidently military targets (for example, forces and equipment) are lawful military objectives. The less direct the contribution to military action, the greater the controversy about its status as a lawful military objective. In general, the United States assumes what has been called "a large interpretation"[28]— meaning expansive—of the definition of military objectives, a position that proves especially controversial in the context of strategic air targeting. The progressive community has a more narrowly defined view of the law.

Both generally agree that objects that inherently serve both military and civilian purposes (such as electricity or transportation grids) are military objectives. Indeed, these are referred to as "dual use" objects.[29] Attacks on such objects must also meet the "second prong" of the definition of military objectives (that is, whether their destruction offers a definite military advantage) and other IHL requirements.[30] An issue of greater controversy is when a civilian object becomes a military objective.

i. Potential use

The two IHL perspectives have different standards on this point. Progressives argue that an object's military contributions must be actual or reasonably expected—not simply possible. U.S. military actors believe that asserting "some plausible future military 'purpose' would be sufficient to render a normally civilian media facility a military objective."[31] This leads to disputes. For example, during Operation Iraqi Freedom the United States argued that the Iraqi regime had been known to broadcast songs on television stations as a means of communicating with military forces. The United States consequently concluded that the stations were legitimate military objectives. Human Rights Watch (HRW) objected that there was no evidence that the broadcasts *were* being used to direct the armed forces.[32]

The U.S. *Operational Law Handbook* states that classifying an object as a military objective "is dependent upon its value to an enemy nation's war fighting or war sustaining effort (*including its ability to be converted to a more direct connection), and not solely to its overt or present connection or use*" (emphasis added).[33] The progressive community argues that the United States is too quick to classify civilian objects as military objectives based on conjectured future use. The ICRC argues that the determinant criteria must be fulfilled in the circumstances ruling at the time, because otherwise "every object could *in abstracto*, under possible future developments, e.g., if used by enemy troops, become a military objective."[34]

ii. War-sustaining

A related controversy revolves around the requisite directness of an object's "effective contribution to military action" in order to be considered a military objective. The U.S. definition pointedly departs from the language in AP1. The United States considers military objectives to include those that may effectively contribute to "the enemy's war-fighting or *war-sustaining* capability" (emphasis added).[35] The U.S. military's Joint Publication 3-60 reinforces this approach by defining civilian objects as "all civilian property and activities other than those used to support or *sustain* the adversary's war fighting capability" (emphasis added).[36]

How does a "war-sustaining" contribution differ from a contribution to military action? Some outsiders see them as fundamentally different categories. Critics of the U.S. view argue that "[it]seems that the category of objects with a 'war sustaining capability' is broader than and includes objects making an 'effective contribution to military action.'"[37] An ICRC expert concludes that the U.S. position "means to abandon the limitation to military objectives and to admit attacks on political, financial (e.g. the main export industry, the stock market or taxation authorities) and psychological targets, as long as they include the possibility or the decision (which are two different things) of the enemy to continue war. Those who suggest a large interpretation of the concept of military objectives mention that targeting of bank accounts, financial institutions, shops and entertainment sites may prove in the long run more destructive than attacks on dual-use targets."[38] He argues that AP1 effectively excluded "*indirect* contributions and *possible* advantages; without this restriction, the limitation to 'military' objectives could be too easily undermined."[39]

Indeed, the U.S. advanced this "large" interpretation during the Kosovo War as it explored attacking the factories and other economic interests of Milosevic's key political allies.[40] Planners believed that harming such economic interests would translate into political pressure on Milosevic to end the war. A plain reading of the AP1 does not allow targeting the economic interests of civilians where those interests do not contribute to adversary military action. However, where the United States was able to posit a link to war sustainment, the letter of the law could be met—despite the fact that Kosovo was not perceived as a lengthy total war in which industrial production was a critical factor.[41]

American military lawyers would dispute the characterization of this interpretation as "large." They argue it is a long-standing U.S. view, and they note the U.S. historical record of targeting war-sustaining objects.[42] The U.S. *Operational Law Handbook* provides little consolation for humanitarian critics. The handbook explains: "The connection of some objects to an enemy's war fighting or war-sustaining effort may be direct, indirect or even discrete. The United State accepts a more attenuated connection between object and contribution than that supported by humanitarian organizations and many other states.[43]

These are just two respects in which the traditionalist and progressive views differ in defining military objectives. Disagreement attends other key civilian protection provisions as well.

Precautions

The progressive and traditionalist communities differ in understandings of IHL requirements to take precautions to protect civilians before launching military attacks. The general U.S. view is that the law requires intent and effort, but not maximum effort, to reduce civilian harm. In the name of humanity and civilian protection, progressives promote a maximalist approach.

Since it is almost always possible in retrospect to identify additional actions that might have been taken to verify a target or reduce the humanitarian effects of attacking a target, it is almost always possible to argue that a belligerent has failed to take reasonable or feasible precautions. In the past decade, charges that the United States has failed to take adequate precautions to protect civilians has become an increasingly common criticism of the U.S. use of force.

Force protection figures centrally into this debate, as many additional precautions increase risks to belligerent forces. Progressives seem to expect belligerents to take more risk as a matter of law. The United States does not view IHL as necessarily requiring increased risk assumption (indeed it considers force protection an element of military necessity). From the U.S. perspective, feasible and reasonable efforts to minimize noncombatant deaths will meet the law's standards, and these need not require increasing risk to U.S. service members.[44]

Thus, NATO's decision to reduce the flight deck for aircraft during the Kosovo campaign was essentially a policy call (although made by military commanders), not a judgment of law. Indeed, in this case even the International Criminal Tribunal for the Former Yugoslavia did not find that the flight deck per se was unlawful.[45] Nor did it consider NATO's actions to demonstrate "the degree of recklessness in failing to take precautionary measures which would sustain criminal charges."[46] This reinforced, at least in that tribunal, the notion that combatants have no legal obligation to assume greater risk by flying within reach of enemy air defenses in order to improve target discrimination. NATO chose to require its pilots to assume greater risk because the operation was being heavily criticized for causing civilian casualties. This illustrates why norms, rather than law, can be important in advancing protection for civilians.

Traditional and progressive disagreement about military objectives, precautions, and other aspects of law will continue to persist, regardless of how the law develops on paper or in the minds of other actors. International judicial mechanisms lack enforcement power. The long-standing U.S. political allergy to perceived infringements upon national sovereignty makes "foreign" judgments highly controversial.[47] The United States remains wary of the ICC and is unlikely to join the court in the medium term; the robust U.S. judicial process would ensure that American service members never faced an ICC judgment in any event. Traditionalists will retain their views of IHL.

Therefore, progressive shaping and reinterpretation of law will not necessarily lead the United States to alter either its views or its behavior. Instead, continued reinterpretation will widen the gap between what traditionalists say the law requires and what others insist that the law means. Greater disagreement about the law, particularly when it involves the leading global actor, does not strengthen the law's legitimacy or influence.

Law versus Norm

Particularly for states that take the law seriously, agreeing to new legal restrictions is a sober business. IHL imposes costs for belligerents, particularly if adversaries fail to reciprocate compliance. Thus states that rely heavily upon the use of force—notably the United States and Israel—are particularly wary of legal commitments. Even if a state is willing to extend the principle of humanity in certain conflicts, it may hesitate to commit to do so in every conceivable future conflict. As a matter of law, it may insist upon preserving wide scope for military action (even if it chooses in a particular case to meet or exceed the standards that progressives demand).

The United States is such an actor. Although the nation insists upon minimalist interpretations of IHL, it often fights according to a higher standard of civilian protection than it believes is required by law. "In point of fact," a senior military lawyer explained, "the law is more permissive [of civilian casualties] than is politically tolerable in many 21st century conflicts."[48] These "political restrictions" come in the form of strategic guidance and rules of engagement. Therefore even as the U.S. military rejects "progressive" internationalist interpretations of the law as overreaching and wrong, it accepts (sometimes grudgingly) requirements to conduct itself pursuant to higher humanitarian standards.

The expectation that powerful states will minimize civilian harm is a norm that exists alongside IHL.[49] This norm, which I call the norm of minimizing civilian casualties, emerged in the aftermath of the Cold War, fueled by the human rights movement, the growing transparency of war, and military capabilities that demonstrated the possibility of reducing numbers of civilian deaths even in major armed conflict. The expectation that parties will avoid harming civilians in war differs from the IHL principle of noncombatant immunity. In law, the principle of noncombatant immunity is balanced uneasily with other principles of the law, as explained above. But the norm is unencumbered by the need to balance humanity and necessity. In the norm, the humanitarian goal stands alone.

The norm differs from the law in other important respects. First, the norm judges results, not intent. The law emphasizes a commander's intent and beliefs prior to taking military action, rather than evaluating the act by its consequences. Second, the norm applies an elastic—not a universal—standard that demands more of more capable parties. Third, while it is not clearly defined, the norm can be measured. Fewer civilian casualties are better, and zero harm is the only unquestioned success. These factors make the modern norm a challenging standard to meet. It is the norm that explains why the United States develops weapons designed to limit collateral damage, computer programs to predict civilian casualties, and otherwise seeks to realize humanitarian objectives in its conduct of war.[50]

While the United States rejects progressive standards as a matter of law, it is nonetheless comfortable adopting them as a matter of self-interest. The norm has power because other states and publics care about civilian deaths, and U.S. interests can be affected—directly and indirectly—as a result. So, for example, if the United States wants to sustain a military coalition or attain overflight rights for a bombing raid, it may need to reassure its partners that its use of force will avoid killing civilians. Allies can demand civilian protection if they are going to stay in your coalition or provide basing rights or otherwise support an American political agenda. Civilian protection can also make operations more effective (as posited in U.S. COIN doctrine). Further, protecting noncombatants can be an expression of national identity and the result of popular normative expectations ("We're the good guys"). Norms, which are manifest in the consequences of violations, have pushed the United States to minimize civilian harm in war and otherwise uphold the humanitarian intent of IHL. The U.S. example shows that the law is not the only route to promote humanity in war; norms, politics, and self-interest can also be harnessed to enhance civilian protection.

Normative pressures will not be effective in shaping behavior every case. They are likely to work best when states have a stake in their identity as moral actors (are predisposed to value the argument) and when the progressive states that care about the norm are able to provide concrete incentives for compliance (providing or withholding goods that the state values). Informal social sanctions may have more concrete power than that lodged in the "vanishing point" of international law. They won't work on all actors, though, especially the outliers and rogues already unmoved by the idea of the law itself. Yet for the more advanced military powers (which are the only realistic targets of progressive legal efforts anyway), norms may accomplish most of what the law, in theory, would be able to achieve—and without the negative backlash that accompanies raising legal standards.

Enforcement

Given blatant noncompliance by many global actors and substantive disputes about standards among other states, progressives' efforts to improve protection by reinterpreting and rewriting law seem oddly out of step with the realities of modern conflict. The law's balance has shifted toward humanity on paper, but in most conflicts the balance has not shifted in practice. Civilians caught in war often lack the most fundamental protections of law. They seek IHL basics, not its refinements. Since extant law so often fails them, it is difficult to see why expanding law would most effectively advance their needs.

Enforcement of the most basic IHL principles, nor their refinement, is a more pressing humanitarian challenge. This is the significance of the International Criminal Court—its charter is to prosecute the worst war crimes (and genocide and crimes against humanity) where states cannot or will not do so. The new court is a product of the very progressive internationalist movement that I have criticized for focusing on raising humanitarian standards in positive law. What makes the ICC a triumph, though, is its goal of enforcement. There remains some disagreement about whether the court's substantive writ—laboriously negotiated among states—exceeds customary law.[51] But the court's goal was less to expand or refine rules than to ensure their relevance. Instead of expanding the gap between what the law promises and provides, the ICC helps close that gap.

This is not the place to discuss the court's many limitations or to assess fully its contributions to date. I will simply note that the court has indicted some thirty individuals, thereby setting critical (if sometimes inconsistent) precedents about IHL's power and reach. It has also (and more controversially) played a role in ongoing conflicts by indicting political and military leaders while they are still engaged in armed conflict. The court over time will help strengthen the law by spurring states to help it enforce violations of the most heinous crimes.

Progressive actors devote comparatively little effort to enforcing IHL tenets despite the frequent and often egregious violations, which have helped increase the proportion of civilian casualties in armed conflict. States, NGOs, and academics seem to find it easier and more fulfilling to pursue new agreements, with the satisfaction of a treaty in the end (and the recognition it reflects upon its advocates). In the name of protecting civilians, they interpret provisions of the law at conferences, in papers, and for the public. Some advocacy groups, such as Human Rights Watch and Amnesty International, and regional or international organizations, play a critical role documenting armed conflict and highlighting the violations they identify. Yet the focus remains defining the law, not enforcing it. Few progressive actors consider it a core responsibility to monitor or assess national military justice systems. In short, progressives do not devote sufficient effort to ensuring justice for combat-related crimes.

This is not simply an issue for nations with weak judicial systems or militaries of low professional standards. The United States, despite its historical commitment to the rule of law, its robust integration of lawyers and law into the operational force, and its distinctive Uniform Code of Military Justice, can fall short on enforcement of IHL tenets. First, it is not clear that the U.S. effectively presses criminal charges against service members for IHL conduct violations in combat.[52] In the last decade, the U.S. military has deployed hundreds of thousands of troops to two major counterinsurgency campaigns. Only a handful of widely reported instances have led to prosecutions, despite persistent allegations of potential IHL violations.

These facts raise questions that ought to occupy the progressive community. Is the military justice system committed to identifying and prosecuting potential combat-related crimes—or are the cases we know of just a small fraction of those that should be pursued? Was the 2005 incident at Haditha, Iraq, in which U.S. Marines raged house-to-house, sequentially shooting some two dozen children, women, and an old man in a wheelchair, the only case of its kind? The killings came to light not through the chain of command, but after inquiries from a dogged journalist. The case revealed widespread official suppression of information about the massacre. More disturbingly, officials in the chain of command insisted that the deaths of some dozen civilians did not strike them as unusual. Improved leadership attention and enhanced reporting requirements would likely make a similar case now stand out, but it is difficult to know how many incidents escape official attention.

There are questions, too, about disciplinary approaches and the definition of a "successful" prosecution. In the American military, some alleged violations are handled as administrative matters, with nonjudicial punishments. When law of war violations are pursued through the full legal process, they are typically prosecuted not as war crimes but as their paler equivalent violation under the Uniform Code of Military Justice. And the punishment that accompanies the convictions can appear puzzling. In 1968 U.S. soldiers murdered hundreds of Vietnamese villagers at My Lai, but only one soldier was convicted; Lt. William Calley served symbolic jail time and three and half years of house arrest for the many murders. Some forty years later, most of the Marines involved in the Haditha killings were acquitted or saw charges dismissed. Only Staff Sgt. Frank Wuterich was convicted—on a single count of negligent dereliction of duty—receiving a reduction in rank and a pay cut for his role in the murders. From the perspective of civilian victims, can this look like justice? What does the U.S. record of prosecutions suggest about the institutional commitment to ensuring compliance with IHL?

There are many reasons—including the politics of second-guessing those in combat and the difficulty of gathering evidence from a war zone—why military justice can be so elusive. Claims of self-defense or necessity seem to carry great weight. Where civilian deaths are independent of combat operations, as a case of rape, or killing civilians for "sport," they can be more easily recognized as crimes and prosecuted. But where civilian deaths can be plausibly connected to combat operations, it appears notoriously difficult to punish the perpetrators.

The Haditha case indisputably lies at the heart of civilian protection in IHL. To some, it may not seem like an open and shut case. But Haditha is an elemental test of the U.S. commitment to the most basic civilian protections in armed conflict. If what happened at Haditha does not merit jail time, what combat-related IHL violations would? What signal does the disposition of the case send to U.S. forces? What does it say about the role of law in war? Progressives may be concerned about the more esoteric points of law, but enforcement should be the priority of actors that care about the law. If war crimes like Haditha escape punishment, it matters little how the finer points of LOAC evolve on paper.

The Case for Legal Modesty

The law's power and influence in war are often misunderstood not just by progressives but also by the service members who respond to it. American forces, particularly in the lower and enlisted ranks, sometimes perceive law and the involvement of lawyers as powerful, but negative—an impediment to "winning."[53] This is a zero-sum and utilitarian view, one in which humanitarian constraints only prolong war and increase its human costs to civilians, adversaries, and American service members. Progressive states and organizations likewise assume the law is powerful, promoting it as a primary constraint on military action. They see this as a positive outcome that protects noncombatants.

But the law's effect is more complex than either view. Even as the reach of operational law expands on paper, IHL is becoming less practically relevant for military forces for a variety of material and ideational reasons. The ranks of rejectionist actors grow. Rising powers without a history of IHL involvement are likely to reshape the practice of war. Noncompliant actors view IHL compliance as increasingly difficult to achieve, and therefore less worth any effort or respect. Moreover, these rogue states and nonstate terrorists are gaining access to technologies and tactics that can threaten compliant states, making the latter less willing to comply on new, evolving, and uneven fields of battle. The middle powers seeking to expand the law's reach are among the most reluctant to use force and therefore shielded from the protections they promote. The United States, which sees the law as minimalist and permissive, regards political guidance and operational concerns as more restrictive influences upon Rules of Engagement (ROE) and strategy to minimize civilian casualties.[54]

In this context, preserving agreement on the most elemental IHL standards remains both a challenge and essential. It makes little sense to spend limited resources reaching international agreements to ban the use of new weapons while those who purposefully slaughter civilians enjoy impunity. Enforcement of key LOAC principles demands a renewed push from the states that have assembled the IHL edifice. The ICC will help fill the enforcement vacuum for the most horrific LOAC violations, but it can only handle a limited docket. Moreover, it is based on the principle of complementarity with functioning national courts. Yet even the most professional and sophisticated national armed forces may fail to identify and effectively prosecute combat-related war crimes. The paucity of consequences for violators of the most basic rules mocks efforts to promote more restrictive interpretations of those rules.

Civilian protection in war is crucially important. Yet the law's relationship to war is becoming increasingly tenuous. The challenge is less to expand law's nominal reach than to deepen understanding, expand acceptance, and promote enforcement of its most basic standards. As we have seen, defining these principles has become more difficult as progressives interpret and create laws that exacerbate disputes among largely law upholding states. These efforts drive a deeper wedge between those who make the rules and those who are expected to comply with them. This is an indulgence that war's victims can ill afford.

Actors concerned with strengthening civilian protection should continue to advance a humanitarian agenda by strengthening normative expectations of human-rights supporting states. But it is unnecessary, and it may even prove counterproductive, to ask ever more of a body of law that already faces widespread noncompliance and weak enforcement. Ongoing work to "strengthen" the law of armed conflict may reflect the identity and institutional interests of norm-promoters, but it skirts more fundamental challenges facing the law and war. It does little to serve the noncombatants that nominally motivate humanitarian efforts, and it might ultimately unravel the underlying normative consensus about the utility of law for regulating violence in international politics.

Notes

1. IHL is alternatively called the Law of Armed Conflict (LOAC) in the United States.

2. This community includes Canada and many European middle powers that have been at the forefront of forging new IHL agreements, organizations such as the International Committee of the Red Cross and Human Rights, and academic international law experts. Rudolf Dolzer calls this progressive constellation of states, scholars, and nongovernmental organizations (NGOs) the "international humanitarian law community." See his dissection of the communities battling to define the law of armed conflict in Rudolf Dolzer, "Commentary," in "Legal and Ethical Lessons of NATO's Kosovo Campaign," ed. Andru E. Wall, *International Law Studies* 78 (2002): 355.

3. The trend is unlikely to reverse itself. See National Intelligence Council, *Global Trends 2030: Alternative Worlds*, December 2012.

4. The Taliban has periodically issued instructions to its fighters to avoid harming civilians, suggesting some sensitivity to the issue despite widespread violations of such orders.

5. United Nations, Report on the Secretary-General's Panel on Accountability in Sri Lanka, March 31, 2011; http://www.un.org/News/dh/infocUS/Sri_Lanka/POE_Report_Executive_Summary.pdf.

6. Adam Roberts, "Lives and Statistics: Are 90% of War Victims Civilians?" *Survival: Global Politics and Strategy* 52, no. 3 (2010).

7. Qiao Liang and Wang Xiangsui, *Unrestricted Warfare* (Beijing: PLA Literature and Arts Publishing House, February 1999).

8. For more on cyber issues, see William A. Owens, Kenneth W. Dam, and Herbert S. Lin, eds., *Technology, Policy, Law, and Ethics Regarding U.S. Acquisition and Use of Cyberattack Capabilities* (Washington, DC: National Academies Press, 2009). Although unmanned drones (remotely piloted vehicles) raise concerns, I consider the IHL issues to be familiar (principally about proportionality given associated civilian deaths). Drone use certainly raises *jus ad bellum* and ethical issues, however.

9. Michael Walzer, *Just and Unjust Wars: A Moral Argument with Historical Illustrations* (New York: Basic Books, 1977), 45.

10. Michael N. Schmitt, "Military Necessity and Humanity in International Humanitarian Law: Preserving the Delicate Balance," *Virginia Journal of International Law* 50, no. 4 (2010): 795, 976. Dolzer also notes the need for balance between civilian concerns and necessity. He writes, "The concern here is a fragmentation in the outlook on humanitarian law that may occur when [principles] are seen in isolation." Dolzer, "Commentary," 356

11. Adam Roberts and Richard Guelff, eds., *Documents on the Laws of War* (New York: Oxford University Press, 1982), 9–10.

12. The terms *noncombatants* and *civilian* are used interchangeably in this essay, despite significant contemporary definitional debate about each of these words. Civilians can lose their protected status by directly participating in hostilities. Not all persons protected in war are civilian; the 1949 Geneva Convention IV includes combatants who are hors de combat in the category of protected persons. See Roberts and Guelff, *Documents on the Laws of War*, 302.

13. Marco Sassoli, "Legitimate Targets of Attacks under International Humanitarian Law," International Humanitarian Law Research Initiative; http://www.hpcrresearch. org/sites/default/files/publications/Session1.pdf.

14. Frank I. Michelman, "Integrity-Anxiety?" in *American Exceptionalism*, ed. Michael Ignatieff (Princeton: Princeton University Press, 2005), 269.

15. Torsten Stein, "Coalition Warfare and Differing Legal Obligations of Coalition Members under International Humanitarian Law," in Wall, "Legal and Ethical Lessons of NATO's Kosovo Campaign," 321–22.

16. The large-scale U.S. or U.S.-led use of force today causes relatively few civilian casualties by historical standards. This observation is not meant to imply that the United States limits civilian harm as much as it possibly can, or that the U.S. use of force always comports with IHL.

17. U.S. military actors often insist that their civilian casualty mitigation efforts exceed legal standards. Proceedings of the National Security and Human Rights Program (NSHRP), a decade-long series of off-the-record workshops involving military

and human rights actors that I conducted under the auspices of the Carr Center for Human Rights Policy.

18. For example, Frank Michelman has argued that the United States is particularly concerned with maintaining continuous and legitimate rules through stable interpretation. Michelman, "Integrity-Anxiety?" 264–66.

19. See George H. Aldrich, "Prospects for United States Ratification of Additional Protocol I to the 1949 Geneva Conventions," *American Journal of International Law* 85, no. 1 (January 1991): 1–20.

20. Wall, "Preface," to "Legal and Ethical Lessons of NATO's Kosovo Campaign," xvi.

21. See Michael J. Matheson, "Remarks on the United States Position on the Relation of Customary International Law to the 1977 Protocols Additional to the 1949 Geneva Conventions," reprinted in "The Sixth Annual American Red Cross Washington College of Law Conference on International Humanitarian Law: A Workshop on Customary International Law and the 1977 Protocols Additional to the 1949 Geneva Conventions," *American University Journal of International Law and Policy* 2, no. 2 (Fall 1987): 419–27.

22. President William J. Clinton signed the treaty establishing the court, but his successor, President George W. Bush, "unsigned" the Rome Statute in May 2002.

23. Dolzer, "Commentary," 356.

24. As W. Hays Parks commented, "The Europeans are so concerned [about U.S. views] because they don't like war, and they've been far removed from armed conflict for a half century. They see U.S. as gunslingers." Interview by author, Washington, DC, December 21, 2009.

25. NSHRP Proceedings.

26. Geneva Convention Additional Protocol 1, Article 52.2.

27. Where there is doubt about an object normally used for civilian purposes (such as a school), "[It] shall be presumed not to be so used." Geneva Convention Additional Protocol 1, Article 52.3.

28. Sassoli, "Legitimate Targets of Attacks under International Humanitarian Law," 6.

29. The term is sometimes criticized as creating an impression that the targets should be protected because of their importance to civilians. W. Hays Parks, "Asymmetries and the Identification of Legitimate Military Objectives," in *International Humanitarian Law Facing New Challenges,* ed. Wolff Heintschel von Heinegg and Volker Epping (Berlin: Springer, 2007).

30. Progressive criticism of attacks on dual use objects typically reflects concern about the proportionality of the attack—that is, the effects on civilians, rather than the legal status of the targets. The destruction of infrastructure during Operation Desert Storm was widely criticized for this reason.

31. Human Rights Watch staff argued that "some hypothetical military use" of a

civilian object is insufficient as a matter of law to render it a military objective. Dinah PoKempner, Marc Garlasco, and Bonnie Docherty, "Off Target on the Iraq Campaign: A Response to Professor Schmitt," *Yearbook of International Humanitarian Law* 6 (2003): 122.

32. Human Rights Watch, Off Target: The Conduct of the War and Civilian Casualties in Iraq, 2003, 49.

33. *Operational Law Handbook 2005*, ch. 2, §IX.A.4.

34. Sassoli, "Legitimate Targets of Attacks under International Humanitarian Law," 3.

35. 1995 NWP 1-14M, §8.1.1. The Air Force Pamphlet on Targeting similarly specifies, "The key factor is whether the object contributes to the enemy's war fighting or war sustaining capability." AFP 14-210, Section 1C, §1.7.1. The Navy handbook further states that "economic targets of the enemy that indirectly but effectively support and sustain the enemy's war-fighting capability may also be attacked." NWP 1-14M, §8.1.1. (The example cited is raw cotton, which was targeted during the Civil War because it was a source of revenue for the South.)

36. JP 3-60, Appendix A, §4(a).

37. University Centre for International Humanitarian Law Geneva, Expert Meeting, "Targeting Military Objectives," May 12, 2005.

38. Sassoli, "Legitimate Targets of Attacks under International Humanitarian Law," 6.

39. Ibid., 3

40. William Arkin and Robert Windrem, "The Other Kosovo War," InfoSec News, August 30, 2001; http://www.msnbc.com/news/607032.asp?cp1=1.

41. Ibid.

42. Such as targeting cotton during the Civil War.

43. The "attenuated" reasoning chain, when taken to its extreme, echoes Al Qaeda's justification for attacking the World Trade Center (that is, that the attack would undermine the West's political resolve in what the terrorist organization perceived as an ongoing conflict).

44. Nonetheless, the United States may adopt greater precautions for normative, operational, or political reasons. This argument is expanded in Sarah Sewall, *Chasing Success: The Air Force and Civilian Harm*, forthcoming from Air University Press.

45. International Criminal Tribunal of the Former Yugoslavia, "Final Report to the Prosecutor by the Committee Established to Review the NATO Bombing Campaign against the Federal Republic of Yugoslavia," para. 56.

46. Ibid., 70.

47. For example, the United States refused to participate in the 2003 International Court of Justice proceedings and later blocked enforcement of the court's judgment against the U.S. for mining harbors in Nicaragua.

48. Major General (Ret.) Charles Dunlap, interview by author, Washington, DC, December 4, 2009.

49. See Sewall, *Chasing Success.*

50. U.S. uses of force are nonetheless often controversial, because of both civilian casualties and alleged IHL violations.

51. China, for example, has argued that the court's substantive writ exceeds customary law. Lu Jianping and Wang Zhixiang, "China's Attitude towards the ICC," *Journal of International Criminal Justice* (July 2005).

52. A combat-related crime—in which risk might plausibly be asserted by the defendant—differs from crimes unrelated to combat operations (for example, Staff Sgt. Robert Bales's 2011 murder of sixteen people in Afghanistan, or the 2006 rape and murders in Mahmoudiya, Iraq).

53. This is one of several popularized (and erroneous) "lessons" of Vietnam.

54. As one senior U.S. military lawyer told me, "In actual execution, military people think in terms of [Rules of Engagement], and the source of those rules is political. Most military lawyers understand that ROE must comply with international law, but it's not that hard to comply with international law, frankly."

The Individualization of War: From War to Policing in the Regulation of Armed Conflicts

GABRIELLA BLUM

In his 2000 centennial article in the *American Journal of International Law*, Theodor Meron celebrated "The Humanization of Humanitarian Law," demonstrating the many ways in which international law has evolved to push the humanitarian concerns of individuals from the margins of states' interest toward the center of international attention.[1] Meron was undoubtedly correct in his systematic description of this legal evolution. In fact, in the eleven years since his article was published, the focus on the individual in the legal regulation of warfare has intensified. Others, too, have followed in Meron's footsteps to herald the influence of human rights norms, the development of international criminal law, and the spread in time and space of humanitarian norms as touching on the fate of individuals in times of conflict.[2] Some have lamented that this process has not gone far enough.[3] There are, as always, also skeptics of the humanization of humanitarian law argument, either on positive or normative grounds.[4]

In this essay, I argue that the "humanization of international humanitarian law" marks a shift from collectivism toward cosmopolitan individualism in the regulation of wartime conduct. In other words, wartime regulation has evolved from a predominantly state-oriented set of obligations—which viewed war as an intercollective effort—to a more individual-focused regime; and consequently, these wartime obligations are owed not only to other parties to the conflict but, at least in aspiration, to the entire international community. Moreover, the individuals with which wartime regulation now concerns itself, at least in aspiration, are not necessarily those belonging to a "party to a conflict" but may be anywhere in the world, including individuals who used to be considered "enemy civilians" and are now as innocent in the eyes of the law as one's own civilians. While both collective and individual concerns have driven wartime regulation from its early incarnations to the present day, the centrality of the former has given way to the steady rise of the latter. In this sense, wartime regulation is increasingly aspiring to make war look more like a policing operation, in which people are expected to be treated according to their individual actions rather than as representatives of a collective.

As I follow this shift from collectivism to cosmopolitanism, my stance is not entirely celebratory. This is neither because I reject the enterprise of placing the welfare of individuals front and center, nor because I adopt a Schmittian view of a world divided into friends and enemies. Rather, it is because I believe that the growing individualization of wartime regulation has wide-ranging normative and pragmatic consequences, many of which have remained underappreciated, even by those who have taken a more skeptical stance regarding the shift. These consequences derive in part from a tension in current international law between the growing recognition and importance of individuals, and the parallel recognition of states as the only full repositories of rights and obligations—even further, perhaps, that states are *necessary* for safeguarding the rights and protections promised to individuals, without which they become more vulnerable to both internal and external harm. Essentially, without a true commitment to cosmopolitanism—which our current world is far from espousing—any unqualified commitment to the welfare of individuals is bound to run up against our commitment to collective political structures. Until we reach a true age of cosmopolitanism, individualism must to some extent revert back to nationalism, thereby limiting and obscuring the entire enterprise of the individualization of wartime regulation.

This essay sets out to illuminate some of the legal, political, and cultural consequences of this tension, using some of the most heated contemporary debates over the conduct of war as a prism. In its latter part, the essay also suggests what may be some of the unappreciated consequences of the turn from collectivism and individualism in the regulation of armed conflict. A definitional caveat: "collectivism" and "nationalism" come in many shades. I use the terms here loosely to stand for the centrality of the state or a defined community as the bearer of rights and obligations, and as the mediator through which individuals are endowed with rights and obligations. When speaking of "individualism" and "cosmopolitanism," I imagine two elements:

first, a recognition of the status of individuals as direct bearers of rights and obligations; and second, the universal application of those rights and obligations regardless of national affiliation or territorial boundaries.

Part I of this essay demonstrates the shift from nationalism to individualism in the regime that applies to wartime conduct. Notably, the description is not confined to hard legal norms in the form of treaty or customary law, but includes social and political norms that direct states' behavior during times of armed conflict. This is because I believe that law, politics, social norms, and morality all interact and shape one another to guide wartime conduct, especially as regards some actors—specifically, liberal democracies.

Part II demonstrates how various contemporary debates over particular doctrines and practices of war both reflect and refract the overarching question of the collective or individualized nature of war. Among these debates are the distinction between the *jus ad bellum* and the *jus in bello*; the application of the principle of proportionality in the *jus in bello*; the project of international criminal law; reparations to victims of war; and detention of terrorists. By framing these issues as implicating (among other things) the individual or collective nature of war, the tradeoffs that exist between a cosmopolitan or national view of war are highlighted.

Part III concludes by speculating about some of the broader implications of the move from a nation-centered law to a more universal, individual-centered regime of wartime conduct, or from a war model of regulation to one of policing.

I. Demonstrating the Shift

Collective Undertones

Historically, the laws and customs of warfare developed as unilateral undertakings or bilateral agreements between warring parties—and, expectedly, came to conceptualize warfare and its limitations vis-à-vis the concerns of sovereign states. Constraints on legitimate warfare were driven by a mix of self-interest in discipline and professionalism among warriors, a mutual interest in reciprocally containing and constraining warfare, and humanitarian concerns for those affected by conflict. Predominant in the Western tradition was just war doctrine, which in its early origins aimed to provide a theological, conscience-based justification for Christian soldiers to participate in wars. Under this doctrine, sovereigns were both the only "right authority" with the power to wage a just war and those who determined the conduct of a just war. The requirement that war be waged only if so approved by the highest authority was meant to ensure the concentration of war-making power in the hands of the sovereign, denying any right to private wars among his subjects. Concentrating military power in the hands of the sovereign was not only a way to safeguard political stability but was also designed to bring all exercise of violence under the rule of law. Agreements on war and peace were thus signed by sovereigns in their own individual names and were enforced domestically by each sovereign on his own people. The sovereign was the embodiment of the state, and the people were partly his property, partly his very extension.

The modern codification of the laws of war began in the mid-nineteenth century, through a series of multilateral treaties (although the Lieber Code, unilaterally promulgated by President Lincoln during the American Civil War, was an important precursor to these treaties). Several multilateral treaties were concluded, mostly to regulate means and methods of warfare, but increasingly, also, to accord protections to the most vulnerable groups, including civilians in occupied territories and prisoners of war. The four Geneva Conventions of 1949 deepened and expanded these protections, and the 1977 Additional Protocol 1 codified and further developed protections for all civilians affected by war, both in occupied and unoccupied territories. Some regulation of noninternational armed conflicts began with Common Article 3 of the Geneva Conventions and then expanded in Additional Protocol 2.

These treaties were negotiated among states, and their provisions, up until 1977, were commonly phrased as applicable to the "High Contracting Parties." Rules thus bound those who had agreed to be governed by them in their mutual relationships, leaving them free of such legal bounds vis-à-vis those who had not accepted the rules.[5]

In terms of the content of the rules, most wartime treaty provisions aimed to regulate the relationship between a warring party on the one hand, and the enemy's nationals on the other—the latter distinguishing between the discrete categories of combatants and civilians. An additional set of provisions applied to neutral states and nationals. Very few, if any, prohibitions applied to the relationship between a state and its own nationals. This was in line with the traditional concept of sovereignty as a shield from external intervention in a state's own internal affairs.

Geographical boundaries and national affiliation were thus the fault lines that determined the applicability and scope of wartime regulation: individuals were given protections according to their nationality (citizen, enemy citizen, neutral party's citizen) and status (civilian or combatant). All protections were mediated through the bargaining states and depended on states' consent. Even with the expansion of humanitarian norms during the twentieth century, and as the laws of war reemerged under a new, paradoxical, name—international humanitarian law (IHL)—negotiated provisions remained focused on parties' obligations vis-à-vis enemy nationals, objects, and property, with very little regulation of the duties of care that a government owed its own nationals.[6] Moreover, under the doctrine of belligerent reprisals, which was in effect until 1977, states were allowed to violate treaty or customary norms in retaliation for earlier defection by the enemy. The actual protections accorded to any enemy national therefore depended on her own government's earlier actions toward those whom it had considered to be enemy nationals. Individual soldiers and civilians were thus left at the mercy of their government's choice to comply with or violate agreements. This was in line with the traditional view of sovereignty: subjects (citizens) as the extension of the sovereign (state).

A "protected" person under the Fourth Geneva Convention, 1949, was thus defined as "not a national" of the party in whose hands one found oneself.[7] And protected persons were to be safeguarded by a "protecting power." The latter could, in principle, be a neutral state, but more commonly, it was the International Committee of the Red Cross (ICRC). The protecting power was meant not only to serve a monitoring role but also to advocate in behalf of the enemy nationals who would otherwise remain voiceless. This arrangement, once again, was tied to the issue of allegiance and national identity; driven by the belief that the principle of diplomatic protection, under which the state is the international advocate of its people, could not persist in situations of interstate enmity, and required the intervention of a third party.

The project of international human rights law (IHRL), in its modern incarnation after World War II, sought to fill the gap left by IHL. It pierced the veil of sovereignty and regulated the relationship between a government and its own nationals within any given state. Still, IHRL was initially understood as a distinct and separate body of law, operating in different temporal and geographical dimensions from IHL. Human rights laws regulated peacetime, not war; they applied within the territory of the state, endowing (or recognizing) rights in citizens and residents, and only to a much lesser extent, gave rights to those outside the state's territory. The International Court of Justice (ICJ), in its 1996 Advisory Opinion on the Legality of Nuclear Weapons, ruled that IHL was *lex specialis*, and that in cases of legal conflict between the provisions of IHL and those of IHRL, the former would prevail.[8]

The collectivist, allegiance-based impulse of IHL was evident even in the regulation of noninternational armed conflict—which, in its purest form, takes place within the territory of one state among citizens of that state. Take, for instance, the case of a government fighting rebels: despite all parties being citizens of one state, government forces are nonetheless allowed to conduct wartime activity in a manner that treats the rebel group as an "enemy." It may directly target combatants belonging to the rebel forces, and even inflict collateral damage on civilians surrounding the rebels (that is, its own citizens), even where such targeting or collateral damage would probably be unlawful under an IHRL regime.[9] That the collective-based notion of allegiance plays a role even when the conflict is an internal one became evident with the effort that has been made over the past couple of decades to mirror the regulation of international armed conflicts in noninternational armed conflicts and effectively create one common regime for both:[10] as the ICTY observed in the *Tadic* case, a meaningful test for who should be considered as "protected" under the law in the case of a civil war cannot be nationality, but ethnicity or a group membership: "the Convention's object and purpose suggest that *allegiance to a Party* to the conflict and, correspondingly, *control* by this Party over persons in a given territory, may be regarded as the crucial test."[11]

Another facet of the national or communal underpinnings of IHL is the type of obligations to which the parties are held. The vast majority of the relevant treaty provisions broadly command, "Do no (or little) harm"; very few prescribe affirmative duties. Among the latter are the obligation to take precautions in attack so as to minimize harm to civilians, the obligation to give advance warning to civilians before attacks if possible, and the obligation to supply prisoners of war (POWs) with basic provisions. In fact, a major development of IHL in the twentieth century has been the codification and further development of limitations on harm that parties could lawfully inflict on one another. There has been little further development, however, in affirmative duties of care, outside the context of occupied territory: there is no obligation to offer assistance to enemy nationals, either civilians or combatants (other than those who are in the hands of the enemy party), in food, shelter, or medical treatment, or in any other way, to equate the treatment of one's own nationals with that of one's enemy's citizens.[12] The only obligation in this regard is not to impede humanitarian assistance that is offered to the enemy's civilians by other parties.[13]

The collective undertones of the laws of war are also evident in the arrangements that govern reparations for wartime harm, once the war is over. Historically, victors exacted reparations from the vanquished, partly as compensation for the war effort and any harm they suffered, and partly as deterrence against future violence. Reparations were state-focused, made by one sovereign to another, without any standing for individuals. A paradigmatic case was the 1918 Treaty of Versailles and its "War Guilt Clauses" that ordered Germany to cede territory to its neighboring countries and pay huge amounts of reparations to those who had defeated it.

In modern times, the right to reparations has disassociated from military victory, conditioned instead on wrongdoing: reparations are now due for war crimes or other atrocities committed by one party against the other. Still, as a matter of practice, receiving reparations is unusual and is mostly limited to cases of internationally imposed arrangements—and thereby, effectively, to military victory. Such was the case, for example, when Iraq was ordered to pay reparations to several countries for its invasion of Kuwait and the ensuing Gulf War.[14] While the rights of the victim state to reparations from the perpetrator state is well established, the rights of individuals to claim compensation from a wrongdoing enemy remain far weaker, in both law and practice—and again, are mostly contingent on specific arrangements.[15] This is another manifestation of the diplomatic protection principle (and, more broadly, state sovereignty): the claims of individuals are to be mediated through their state, which is the protector and advocate of its people.

The Shift toward Cosmopolitan Individualism

A combination of ideological, strategic, and political forces have driven the shift from communalism to individualism in the regulation of wartime behavior. It would be impossible to show which of these forces was most influential, either independently or in connection with a particular issue. Sometimes, military regulations that began as strategic self-interest were later incorporated into the law; at other times, legal norms shaped moral sensibilities, which were then translated into strategic and tactical conduct. These driving forces have been most influential over liberal democracies, and much of the analysis below thus focuses inevitably on the norms that govern— or purport to govern—liberal democracies.

Where state, sovereign, and people were one unified entity to thinkers of the Middle Ages, the early modern and enlightenment scholars sought to set the three apart. By laying the foundations for a positive international law, Hugo Grotius opened the way to recognizing universal rules of war that would apply in all wars. A century later, Emer de Vattel and Immanuel Kant distinguished more clearly between the enemy sovereign and the enemy population, making the *jus in bello* independent from the *jus ad bellum* and thus limiting the collective nature of war and warfare. Consequently, the fate of individuals would no longer depend on their association as "subjects" of the ruler but on their own contribution to the war: combatants would be targetable, while civilians would be spared, regardless of who was to blame for the war in the first place.

As noted earlier, from the mid-nineteenth century onward, a wave of treaties were negotiated to extend to both combatants and civilians protections from the scourge of war. And while regulation remained centered on the context of enmity and the obligations owed one's enemies, over time, the concern for the suffering of individuals elsewhere and everywhere across the lines has grown more noticeable. If Carl Schmitt believed that the political world is fundamentally divided into "friends" and "enemies,"[16] IHL, in a counter-Schmittian move, sought to downplay the concept of "*enemy* nationals" and highlight the protections that individuals must be accorded *as* individuals, or as rights-bearing human beings. This move was most recently and most prominently adopted by the United States in its contemporary military doctrine, at least as it applies to counterinsurgency operations. If the 1956 Military Manual referred in several places to "enemy civilians," the 2005 Counterinsurgency Manual refers only to "civilians," forgoing any association of these civilians with "enemies."[17]

The strongest expression of the move toward cosmopolitan individualism—

effectively, the recognition that human beings are all of equal worth and dignity—has been the abolition of the principle of reciprocity and the outlawing of almost all forms of belligerent reprisals. As codified in Additional Protocol 1 and reflecting (or evolving into) customary international law, parties at war are now bound by universal obligations, whether or not they have formally accepted or consented to these obligations. Parties are not allowed to contract out of obligations, and their duties persist even in the face of perpetual defection by their enemies. A party therefore cannot harm POWs or target civilians or damage cultural objects even if its enemy engages in all these practices. The underlying rationale for this development is that the right to be protected from harm belongs to the individual person, and not to her state or government to bargain over. In fact, even if she wants to, the individual person cannot contract out of or waive the protections accorded to her under the law.

As the figure of the individual loomed larger, nationality and geography have become increasingly overshadowed by universal commitments to the equal worth and human dignity of each individual life. Under the International Law Commission's Draft Articles on State Responsibility (DASR), all countries in the world are "injured parties" in cases of [grave] IHL violations, even if those countries have no immediate stake in the particular conflict.[18] Moreover, none of the otherwise recognized justifications for breach of obligations, such as consent, force majeure, necessity, or distress apply to grave IHL violations.[19] The traditional diplomatic protection of citizens from foreign harm by their own states has thus been replaced by a universal commitment of all states to all individuals around the world.

A further major step in the individualization of wartime regulation was taken with the evolution of human rights norms in the post–World War II era, described by some as a true "revolution," or in Samuel Moyn's words, "the last utopia."[20] As earlier mentioned, the two fields of law—IHL and IHRL— were originally thought of as distinct and parallel. Over the last two decades, however, there has been a growing trend toward viewing them as synchronic and complementary (even if, in direct cases of conflict, IHL trumps IHRL), or in other words, as "converging." Under the convergence view, IHRL applies wherever a government has some degree of control—but not necessarily complete control—over foreign territory and nationals; its rationale thus shifts governments' responsibility from their own citizens to all those directly affected by their actions. The move, in other words, is from nationality to humanity.

More broadly, the spread of democracy, human rights norms, and a liberal "culture of life" all codified the rights of individuals to be free from violence, domestic or international. Western-liberal sensitivity to pain and suffering and what Charles Taylor has termed a growing "universal benevolence"[21] reinforced pacifist undertones—present to some extent since early Christianity, but never a victorious strain and perpetually overrun by countercurrents across the Western world, especially in Europe following World War II.[22] Modern aversion to war strengthened, in turn, the individualized view of legitimate violence: if war was ever to be tolerated, it would have to be not only a last resort but also as narrowly tailored as possible to be directed only against those most deserving of it. When carried out, it must distinguish with the utmost precision between the innocent and those who must be "neutralized," "frustrated," and, only begrudgingly, "killed."

The individualization of the laws of war has been apparent not only in terms of who is endowed with rights, but also in terms of who owes obligations. Developments in IHL and IHRL were complemented by a revival—at first, measured and constricted, and then, bold and expansive—of the project of international criminal law. Individual perpetrators of war crimes and crimes against humanity, like the more limited class of pirates before them, were now *hostis humani generis*—the enemies of all mankind, indicted by and in the name of "the people of the international community."

With criminalization came universalism: the regime of "Grave Breaches" under the 1949 Geneva Conventions and their 1977 Additional Protocols gave all states the right (indeed, the obligation) to prosecute those who had committed grave war crimes, regardless of national affiliation.[23] Although the juridical concept of universal jurisdiction was put to only limited practice in the decades following World War II, when focus was mainly on German war criminals, from the 1990s onward, there has been a surge in the willingness to exercise universal jurisdiction by Western European and other Western countries, covering the conflicts in Rwanda, Eritrea, the Middle East, Argentina, El Salvador, and more.

The paradigmatic expression of a truly universal criminal law was the project of international criminal tribunals, first, with the dedicated Tribunals for the Former Yugoslavia and Rwanda, and then, with the establishment of the International Criminal Court. The ICC project itself was intended to make the project of international criminal law even more universal, under the aegis of a transnational, rather than national, institution. Although the principle of complementarity mandates that the ICC will step in only if the national courts are either unable or unwilling to prosecute, these conditions themselves—"unable" and "unwilling"—must be measured according to some international standard.

The criminalization and universalization of grave violations of IHL thus transformed the laws of war from a set of essentially bilateral commitments of governments toward one another into a victims-oriented regime that gives a voice and standing to victims of such violations wherever and whoever they might be, regardless of their national affiliation or their government's standing.

Beyond a growing ideological, moral, and aesthetic commitment to the well-being of individuals, the greater individualization of wartime regulation has also been driven by a noticeable change in the nature of the military threats faced by states. States no longer enjoy a monopoly over the use of significant military power. Technology has made some weapons, including those of mass destruction, more widely available, less expensive, and more destructive than ever before. Globalization, openness, and interdependence have increased vulnerability to external and internal threats. Consequently, individuals and groups of individuals are nowadays capable of dealing physical blows on a magnitude previously reserved for regular armies. This is true not only for ideologically driven terrorists or insurgents but also for the modern incarnation of the mercenaries of the Middle Ages: money-driven private military companies. The law of war thus finds itself in a paradoxical state of trying to regulate the behavior of those who have no legitimate standing in its eyes (in large part, because they are not states), and who have no particular interest in obeying it.

At the same time, technological innovation also allows for more precise identification and targeting of distinct individuals and objects. With capabilities come expectations, and there is a growing pressure on well-equipped forces of liberal democracies to avoid any and all civilian casualties by using more precise and discriminatory technology. Even though expectations sometimes exceed capabilities—and go beyond what the laws of war actually mandate—

capabilities have made the normative commitment to individualization more forceful in principle and more realizable in practice.

The combination of a greater normative commitment to individuals and the technological ability to distinguish among individuals has contributed not only to focusing harm on individuals who are threatening (and who are largely also viewed as "guilty"), but also to voluntarily undertake to promote the welfare of those individuals who are innocent. Liberal democracies now increasingly provide humanitarian aid in food, shelter, medical care, and more to civilians in territories in which they are conducting combat operations—all traditionally provided by the ICRC and other international aid societies, but rarely before by warring parties themselves. Building hospitals and schools is now seen to be as much part of the war effort as targeted killings. Even though the duty to make reparations arises only in cases of violations of IHL (and even there, the duty toward enemy states is more strongly established than toward individuals), some countries have instituted processes of ex gracia compensation for individual civilians who have been harmed in the course of *lawful* military operations.[24]

Although most of this positive assistance is clearly driven by a self-interested effort to win over the allegiance of the local population, it nonetheless creates norms and expectations for future conduct in other arenas. More generally, the lines between self-interest and accepted norms are all the more blurred as states must weigh their domestic and international reputation, as well as the "hearts and minds" of those they target. It is for this reason that the present-day American counterinsurgency doctrine demands U.S. soldiers to assume greater risk to themselves in order to minimize civilian casualties in Afghanistan; and it is for this reason that it was the U.S. Department of Defense—not the ICRC or Human Rights Watch—that had embarked on research and development of nonlethal weapons, with the effort to minimize death on the battlefield and allow for effective policing operations.

II. Tensions between Community and Humanity

The picture painted so far of the trend toward individualization and cosmopolitanism is painfully incomplete. One might even mistake it for a depiction of a world without widescale violence, whose sole business and pleasure it is to concentrate on the well-being of individuals whoever they are and wherever they may be.

That is clearly not the world we live in.

Since the end of World War II, there have been more casualties among civilians than among combatants. The incidence of international armed conflicts has declined overall, but that of noninternational armed conflicts, in which civilian casualties are widespread, has been on the rise. The same states that are concerned about the loss of their monopoly over the use of force, especially vis-à-vis violent nonstate actors, are relying on military contractors. They are also producing and exporting massive quantities of small arms, knowing that they lack any control over where these arms end up. Only a handful of states, Costa Rica the largest among them, have given up their military forces. Explicit pacifist voices are still rare among mainstream politicians, policy-makers, and even academics.

The rise and spread of media have universalized the experience and realization of pain, however indirectly, giving an unprecedented number of people access to images from all over the world, and empowering people not only to consume news but also to produce it—and through it, as the Arab Spring demonstrated—effect true political change. And still, for all its potential as a tool for arousing empathy, media attention to wartime suffering is still marginal when the war affects some foreign land. Its effect on viewers is also uncertain: images of the genocide in Rwanda were available early on, but prompted no meaningful international reaction. World attention is not evenly spread: some suffering garners more attention and action than others, and not all deaths make it to the front page of the *New York Times*, not even when the death toll is in the thousands.[25]

Universal jurisdiction invites dozens of requests for arrest warrants, but only a small number of cases—mostly from areas of conflict over which there is little international controversy—are seen to their conclusion.[26] Human rights treaties have been widely ratified, but the practical effects of ratification on states' human rights practices are still being debated among experts.[27]

This discrepancy between the legal trend toward universal individualization and the endemic and widespread contrary practices that still prevail suggests that the "humanization of IHL" faces significant hurdles. Some of these hurdles derive from structural and political deficiencies, such as failed or fragile states, nondemocratic ideologies, or a general lack of empathy in people or governments. But even strong, functioning liberal democracies often exhibit gaps between their stated commitment to the general welfare of individuals and actual military practice—which suggests that something else is at play. This gap, I claim, derives from the intuitive commitment of individuals to their nation or collective, evident in both peacetime and wartime, at the obvious and inevitable expense of others. In other words, a commitment to individualism without a true commitment to cosmopolitanism necessarily circles back to nationalism, thereby limiting and obscuring the entire enterprise of the individualization of wartime regulation.

To demonstrate this point, I turn next to several issues of heated contemporary debate, all related to the regulation of war: the distinction between the *jus ad bellum* and the *jus in bello*, the *jus in bello* principle of proportionality, the project of international criminal law, reparations for war victims, and the detention of terrorists. My purpose here is not to resolve these debates or weigh in on their normative merit, although I offer my own point of view on some. Rather, it is to demonstrate how these debates, implicitly but essentially, revolve around the tension between the rights of the nation and the rights of individuals.

Jus ad Bellum and Jus in Bello

As earlier noted, ever since Vattel and Kant, the laws of war have operated on the notion that *jus in bello* was both distinct from and independent of *jus ad bellum*. As a direct derivative, the principle of equal application of the law, or the parity principle, dictates that soldiers' immunities and obligations shall not depend on whether they are fighting a just or an unjust war: all soldiers may engage in lawful warfare against their enemies and all must respect the limits of lawful warfare. A soldier is thus immune from prosecution for his lawful belligerent activities, and he can stand trial only for any war crimes he has committed, regardless of whether the war he is fighting is just or unjust.

The equal application principle has come under growing pressures from both lawyers and philosophers challenging its moral foundation as well as practical utility.[28] There are many facets to this debate, far more than can be addressed here. As a general matter, however, the debate implicates the degree to which any population, and in particular, the armed forces of that population, can and should be held accountable for national policies.

Crucially, arguments in favor of collapsing the distinction between the two strands of the law—the *ad bellum* and the *in bello*—rest on a view of combatants as *individuals*: rather than mere instruments or agents of an all-powerful sovereign, combatants must be considered, first and foremost, as individual men and women, capable of and responsible for independent decision-making. If a soldier believes that her government's use of force is illegal, she must refuse to take any part in it; and if she nonetheless takes part, whatever her personal views are, she must be held accountable for fighting an unjust war. It is only if the soldier was conscripted and has no option but to fight, that she bears little, if any, responsibility.[29]

Opponents of this view maintain that an individualistic view of soldiers would undermine any notion of discipline and organization within the armed forces, making even the waging of just wars impossible. Under this view, the *collective* enterprise of war must be preserved in order to make war possible in the first place. Opponents can also invoke conscription: while it is true that most liberal democracies have forgone mandatory military service, international law has stopped short from forbidding conscription as a violation of human rights. This legal stance evinces the recognition of states' essential interest as part of their bargain in the social contract in raising and maintaining armies, armies that would become useless if they did not follow the orders of the government.

This facet of the debate over the distinction between *jus ad bellum* and *jus in bello* therefore stands for both individualization and universalism. Soldiers are undoubtedly both individuals-citizens and citizens-agents of the collective, but which are they more in the context of just war theory: Individual bearers of their own rights and obligations, regardless of their government's decision-making? Or, within bounds, merely neutral instruments of their government's decision-making?

The recent effort to make the crime of aggression an indictable offense under the statute of the ICC, to some extent, splits the difference. The general understanding seems to be that aggression is a crime for which only political leaders and high commanders should be held accountable, not regular soldiers. It is thus a step toward the individualization and universalization of responsibility, albeit to a limited degree. Still, this compromise might reflect pragmatic considerations (in the same way that only the most egregious and responsible perpetrators of other crimes under the ICC may be indicted) more than any principled stance about the lack of responsibility of soldiers participating in unjust wars.

Proportionality in the Jus in Bello

IHL prohibits any intentional or indiscriminate targeting of civilians. It permits, however, the unintended (even if foreseen) harm to civilians that is inflicted in the course of legitimate attacks, provided this harm is not excessive in relation to the military advantage that is to be expected from the attack.[30] At work here is the principle of proportionality, the violation of which is now recognized as a war crime under the ICC Rome Statute.[31] Furthermore, attacking forces must employ all feasible precautions to minimize civilian harm;[32] and where two options for gaining the same military advantage are possible, the one that is expected to inflict fewer civilian casualties must be pursued.[33]

The exact assessment of permissible collateral damage is difficult to perform, and the vagueness and malleability of the principle of proportionality—as of its moral origin, the principle of double effect—have long been lamented. Against the background of contemporary conflicts, in which most hostilities take place in civilian populated areas, the application and judgment of proportionality has been the subject of growing controversies.

A particular point of contention has been the just allocation of risk between combatants and civilians, or, in other words, the degree to which combatants must assume risk to themselves in order to protect civilians in the combat zone. For instance, the military can sometimes choose between deploying ground troops and relying on airpower. Ground operation exposes the soldiers to greater risks from enemy fire, while air power—so it is generally assumed, even if sometimes erroneously—exposes civilians to greater risks of collateral harm. In general, the reliance on more firepower shifts the risk from the combatants onto the local civilians. Should soldiers ever be allowed to do that? Must the military always send in ground troops? What is the correct life-life tradeoff between *our* soldiers and *their* civilians?

The question of how to allocate risk between our own combatants and the civilians on the enemy's side implicates both the individualization of war and the move to greater cosmopolitanism in its regulation: the increased status of the individual civilian as bearing rights vis-à-vis the enemy state (thereby checking even legitimate military necessity of the state), and the decreasing relevance of nationality or citizenship in determining the scope and degree of these rights.

Two opposing strands in contemporary scholarship address the question of risk allocation, their main point of contention being the cosmopolitanism aspect of risk allocation. One strand, which I term the "role school," holds that it is the duty of soldiers to risk their lives for civilians while pursuing their military tasks, just as it is the role of police officers to risk their lives for the sake of citizens when they pursue criminals, and just as it is the role of firefighters to endanger themselves in rescuing those who are caught in flames. Under the role school, soldiers bear an equal duty to risk their lives for the sake of enemy civilians as they do for compatriot civilians. In other words, under the role school, there can be no differentiation among civilians on the basis of nationality, and soldiers are under a duty to protect all civilians equally.[34]

The opposing strand, which I name the "allegiance school," holds that soldiers are recruited by and in behalf of their country. While they must take care not to harm enemy civilians, their duties are first and foremost owed to their country and their fellow citizens. Under the allegiance school, therefore, soldiers are allowed not only to prefer compatriot civilians to enemy civilians in designing military operations, but they are also allowed to prefer their own well-being (that is, "force protection") to that of enemy civilians, so as to ensure that they can continue the task of protecting their country and fellow citizens.[35] Rather than police forces or fire fighters, the relevant analogy for the allegiance school may be the Secret Service, whose agents must sacrifice their lives to protect the president (or whomever they are entrusted with protecting), but not for any other person. By analogy, soldiers must risk their lives to protect their fellow citizens, but not every citizen around the globe.

One way of considering the merits of each side of this debate is by comparing legitimate warfare with legitimate policing: As a general matter, it would be fair to say that proportionality implicitly permits armed forces to inflict more harm on civilians than domestic law enforcement in liberal democracies would allow (consider, for instance, the conventional prohibition on shooting at a criminal suspect in the midst of a crowd but for extreme and rare exceptions, a prohibition that would be somewhat relaxed in a scenario of war). This laxer standard could be a derivative of one (or both) of two assumptions: the first is that the effective prosecution of war entails greater amounts of firepower than effective policing, and thereby inevitably inflicts more civilian casualties; if this is the reason, then wherever it is possible to refrain from using greater amounts of firepower, that option must be pursued. Another possible explanation, however, is that in the crime context, the first commitment of the government is to public safety, and it would make no sense to kill innocent people in order to capture a criminal. But in war, the first commitment is to military necessity—even if balanced by humanitarian limitations—for which reason it is permissible to kill people unintentionally, even if they are innocent.

Moreover, in the case of policing, it is territorial boundaries—rather than nationality—that define the scope of police officers' obligations: they must risk their lives for the sake of all local residents (including foreign tourists), but not for those who are endangered in foreign countries (including fellow nationals who are visiting those foreign countries). In the case of war, nationality is more significant: soldiers will risk their lives to protect or rescue fellow citizens captured by the enemy, wherever they are held. At the same time, the fact that the military will take further measures and assume extra risk to rescue fellow citizens who are taken hostage by the enemy says very little about the baseline obligation that soldiers generally owe to either compatriot citizens or foreign civilians.

Seen in this view, both the role school and allegiance school must struggle between individualism and nationalism and explain why and how each of these commitments matters—as applied to soldiers, compatriot civilians, and other civilians. When one looks at the subscribers to these opposing schools, an interesting sociological phenomenon presents itself: some prominent advocates of the role school are progressive American scholars, while many among the allegiance school are Israeli. There are, of course, differences and debates within both national camps, and scholars from other countries also weigh in on the debate. But one explanation for this seeming American-Israeli divide may be found in the different conflicts fought by the two countries: the contemporary wars fought by the United States do not affect the American society in any direct way. American civilians have not been directly harmed by these wars (other than the terrorist attacks of September 11, 2001), there is no military draft, and no special tax was imposed to finance the wars (though the wars undoubtedly consume a significant part of the country's budget, invariably affecting citizens' welfare). The end of conscription after Vietnam contributed to the notion of war as a government operation, much in the same way that operating prisons or maintaining seaports is a government function. Americans, by and large, do not view themselves as being in direct conflict with the ordinary citizen of either Afghanistan or Iraq.

In this vein, the American Counterinsurgency Doctrine (COIN) now holds that Iraqi and Afghan civilians must be protected even at the expense of American forces' protection. The term "enemy civilian," which appeared in the 1956 Army Field Manual, is nowhere to be found in the COIN document. There is only the "civilian"—generic, unattached, innocent. While COIN's prescription about risk to soldiers is a self-interested strategic instruction rather than a legal or ethical one, the strategy itself stands for the idea that civilian casualties alienate the local population (as well as domestic or international observers), and that in the types of war fought by the United States in these arenas, the individualization of war—or, essentially, policing—is also the dominant strategy for any attainable victory.

For Israel, war is national and communal (Jewish vs. Arab). Conscription makes (almost) everybody's sons and daughters soldiers. The Israeli-Arab, and mainly the Israeli-Palestinian, conflicts are driven by nationalist, religious, and ethnic divisions. They are intercommunal, atavistic struggles. The conflict, when it flares up into active hostilities, directly impacts Israelis and Palestinians— their physical safety, property, and day-to-day life. In this environment, no individual is merely an individual, but a member and an extension of his or her community, which is in constant struggle against the other community. The ideal of the generic civilian has far less resonance in this state of affairs, inviting instead a consideration of the "enemy civilian." Naturally, civilian status must still be a determinative factor in weighing deliberate or indiscriminate harm, and all civilians must be protected at all times from such harm; this is the uncontestable prescription of international law. But when weighing comparative risks among soldiers and civilians for purposes of proportionality assessment, a question which the law is far less clear about, the association of the civilian with the "enemy" invites soldiers to prefer their fellow citizens' lives as well as their own lives to that of the enemy civilian.

Undoubtedly, it is not only the type of war fought by both countries that distinguishes progressive American from Israeli scholars; both the United States and Israel define themselves as liberal democracies, but Israel also defines itself as the homeland of the Jewish people. It is this collective identity that is its most important characteristic, its raison d'etre, and which explains, at least to some degree, the difference in attitudes toward the "enemy civilians."

International Criminal Law

The evolution of the project of international criminal law (ICL) signifies a major development in the regulation of armed conflicts, indeed, in the eyes of some, the most significant development to date: the transformation of state-centered obligations, confined to the realm of interstate relationship and notorious for their weak compliance and enforcement, into individual crimes—enforceable and punishable in practice. Moreover, ICL has shifted attention from the abstract, self-serving concept of "military necessity" onto the plight of victims and the atrocities committed in its name.

As earlier noted, ICL is also a cosmopolitan project, seeking to ensure that all victims of wars, regardless of geography or nationality, could find justice, either under universal jurisdiction of domestic courts or transnational criminal courts. Dormant for fifty years after the Nuremberg Trials, ICL was revived, at first with the establishment of the dedicated International Tribunals for the Former Yugoslavia and Rwanda, and then with the establishment of the International Criminal Court, the spread of universal jurisdiction in national courts, and the creation of several new national and hybrid accountability mechanisms.

At once celebrated and criticized, international criminal law is the de facto individualization of accountability for wartime crimes. If the concept of states' crime and punishment was once endemic to international law, it has now been formally excised, to be replaced by the more benign concept of state responsibility. Criminal liability, instead, has been channeled to individuals: only individuals can be deemed guilty and subsequently punished. Only individuals, not states, can be assigned moral blame and be required to account for their crimes with a criminal sanction.

ICL is thus another step in the individualization of war, only, unlike human rights, it is a step taken not only for the sake of the victim but also for the sake of the broader society to which the perpetrators belong: instead of indicting the entire community, guilt is channeled to a few individual leaders and commanders. But this exact individualization of accountability masks the collective responsibility of the community that allowed the criminals to perpetrate their crimes in the first place. War, after all, is collective violence. What distinguishes war crimes from ordinary crimes is the collective context in which they take place. A wartime rape is different from an "ordinary" rape exactly because it is used in a context of intercommunal violence; because it means not only to destroy the victim's body and soul but because it is intended to do so as a weapon of war. It is violence by a collective, for a collective, against members of another collective. The individualization of war through the individualization of crimes effectively cleanses the wider population—on behalf of which the perpetrator has acted—of guilt, at least in its practical manifestation. For the individual perpetrator, a criminal trial adjudicates only one thin slice—the particular crime committed—of what is invariably a multifaceted and complex conflict, often spanning decades of social, ethnic, religious, and economic rivalry.

The debate over the indictment of individual leaders or commanders for war crimes is not new; it has been raging at least since the end of World War II. Karl Jaspers urged his readers to distinguish between the metaphysical, moral, or political guilt of the German nation on the one hand, and the legal guilt, with its associated consequences, of its leaders on the other hand, even as others called to hold the entire German nation guilty in the legal sense. While the collective "punishment" of the German people was formally avoided with the Marshall Plan, West Germany did make substantial monetary reparations, which were effectively borne by its entire population.

When it comes to crimes perpetrated by leaders of democratic countries, the commitment to individual responsibility runs up against another liberal democratic principle, which is popular sovereignty. If we take popular sovereignty seriously, the leaders of any democratic society are not the source of power, nor the ultimate subject of responsibility. Political authority lies with the people, and that authority logically yields responsibility. Individual leaders may very well be guilty of war crimes, but they would not be the only guilty party in a perfect system of accountability: those in whose name crimes had been committed would also be held responsible, as a society, even if not as individuals, and even if not to the same degree as its representative leaders.[36] Of course, even where the groups in whose name crimes have been committed are not democratic structures, responsibility spreads far wider than the individuals indicted for war crimes.

It is possible, of course, that for practical purposes, it would be wise to distinguish between guilty leaders and responsible societies for the sake of restoring peace and security and allowing the perpetrators and victims to coexist in the long term. But such necessity is debatable as an empirical matter and might not hold true in all cases. Moreover, there are also sound pragmatic arguments that favor collective accountability: holding groups responsible is a more efficient way of policing (as the group is better situated to control its individual members than any external actor), a more effective way of securing accountability (the group cannot escape justice), and a more equitable and profitable source of reparations (as the group can make larger compensations than any one individual).[37]

It would be impossible to do justice here to the full scope of the debate over collective and individual responsibility. For present purposes, it would suffice to point at the fact that the project of international criminal law, while laudable in its effort to hold the perpetrators of the most heinous international crimes accountable, may have made it too comfortable to overlook the accountability of others who share, at the very least, some degree of moral responsibility for those crimes.

Reparations for Victims of War

There is currently no consensus on whether states have a duty under international law to make reparations to individual victims of IHL violations (as distinguished from reparations to enemy states). In some cases, dedicated ad hoc mechanisms have been established in order to secure such reparations for particular conflicts.[38] More generally, however, attempts by international fora to promulgate a clear and general duty to compensate individual victims of war crimes have all remained in the realm of soft law.[39] What is clear, however, is that no legal obligation to compensate exists where civilians were harmed in the course of legitimate operations of war—that is, where no violation of the laws of war occurred.[40]

Nonetheless, since the Korean War, the United States has maintained a system of "solatia" payments (or other types of condolence payments) as a show of sympathy to civilians harmed in the course of U.S. combat operations, even where the harm was brought about by lawful military activity. Payment has also been offered to those harmed as a result of enemy attacks where the harmed civilian was working with the U.S. forces.[41] Despite early disagreements on the matter, the decision was ultimately made to make solatia payments available in Afghanistan and Iraq as well. As earlier noted, other foreign forces have followed the American model and are offering *ex gracia* condolence payments to civilians harmed as a result of the foreign forces' operations in those theaters.[42]

No such payments have ever been offered, for instance, by the Israeli government to Palestinian civilians, even though some compensation was made to foreign nationals who were hurt by IDF operations in Gaza or the West Bank. Russia has similarly never offered compensation to any Chechen civilians, nor did it comply with the European Court of Human Rights judgment that awarded compensation to Chechen civilians after finding Russia had violated its human rights obligations. To the best of my knowledge, no NATO country has compensated civilians harmed by NATO's military operations in the Balkans in the 1990s.[43]

The decision to make or withhold reparations to individual victims is undoubtedly a matter of self-interest of the relevant country in the relevant theater of war. But what this self-interest mandates is a direct derivative of either the individualistic or collectivist view of the conflict at hand. Where a conflict has stronger collective undertones, we can expect any reparations policies, if at all, to be far less generous.

Consider also decisions by countries to compensate their own nationals for harm suffered in war. As earlier noted, international law permits each individual country to decide if and how it chooses to compensate its citizens for wartime harm. Israel, for instance, offers compensation to any Israeli who suffered bodily or property harm as a result of an act of war or terrorism directed against Israel. The United States does not generally offer such compensation, but for exceptional cases (such as the 9/11 victim fund), although this may simply be due to the scant number of American civilians harmed by war or terrorism. Here we find once more at work the collective and collectivizing nature of war that drives some countries to compensate their citizens for war-related harm—a recognition that the individual has suffered *for* her nation and fellow citizens, and that she need not be seen to bear the costs of the conflict alone.[44]

More recently, a group of Libyan rebels who were harmed by NATO friendly fire announced that they would expect compensation from NATO. A Libyan rebel commander was quoted as saying, "[We] are not questioning the intentions of NATO, because they are supposedly here to help us and protect our civilians. ... Mistakes do happen[,] and those who make the mistakes should admit their mistakes and compensate for them." There is no indication that NATO is about to offer such compensation. And yet, the mere claim by the rebels—who are neither citizens of NATO countries nor the victims of any apparent war crime, only beneficiaries of NATO's efforts—signifies the normative change that has occurred in placing human rights and the plight of individuals (in this case, individual *combatants*), front and center in wartime regulation.

Detention of Suspected Terrorists

Few issues have generated as much scholarly and policy debate as the question of the legal regime governing the detention of terrorists, particularly the post-9/11 detention of terrorists (or suspected terrorists) by the United States at Guantanamo Bay.

The simplest depiction of the debate asks which framework should apply to the detention of terrorists who are captured outside the battlefields of Iraq or Afghanistan: the laws of war or domestic criminal law—or, alternatively, whether these combatants demand a new, hybrid body of law that borrows from both regimes. Consequently, detention policies implicate the questions of whether there is such a thing as a "war on terrorism"; if so, against whom the war is waged; what its geographical and temporal boundaries are; and whether terrorism, if not at all war, must be treated like any other crime, domestic or transnational.

The choice between the two paradigms is crucial and highlights the political, strategic, and practical difficulties in classifying terrorism under one or the other. In war, every combatant is an enemy, and is identifiable as such by the uniform he wears. The enemy combatant is subject to direct incapacitation through killing or capture, not because he is guilty of any crime but because she poses a threat. The threat he poses exists in principle, by his mere association with an enemy force, even if the threat does not present itself at any particular moment (hence, in war, the sleeping, naked, or noncombat soldier is targetable at any time).

A captured enemy combatant may be detained as a prisoner of war until the end of hostilities. Unless the combatant had committed war crimes, he cannot be tried for participating in the war. At the end of hostilities, captured combatants who are held as POWs must be released, as by definition they no longer pose any threat. The party to whom they belong essentially vouches for their future peaceful conduct.

Criminals, conversely, are not identifiable by any insignia or external markings. They are presumed innocent and immune from any sanction unless their individual guilt can be proven through the law enforcement process. The punishment of individuals under criminal law is generally justified on the mixed consideration of the individual's moral guilt (just desert) and the threat he or she poses to society (deterrence or incapacitation).

Terrorists generally do not wear uniforms. Sometimes, there is a leadership that can account or vouch for their actions or bargain on their behalf; at other times, there is none, or the relationship between the terrorist and the group is a tenuous one. Unlike the case of the enemy soldier, the threat that any single terrorist poses cannot be deduced from any external assessment; instead, his affiliation to a terrorist group or his involvement in terrorist activities must be ascertained on a case-by-case determination.

The human rights community, by and large, challenges the wartime detention model and the quasi-POW holding of those terrorists captured outside Afghanistan (and previously, Iraq). Its position is that, if captured, suspected terrorists must be subject to the ordinary U.S. criminal law system; only if they are found guilty as charged may they be held under a court-pronounced sentence. All others must be released. The U.S. government, on the other hand—consistently across presidential administrations—holds that the war extends beyond any active battlefield and follows Al Qaeda members and supporters wherever they are. Consequently, all captured terrorists may be subject to a quasi-wartime detention, and criminal trials, whether civilian or military, are the government's prerogative but not its duty.

While the debate over the detention of terrorists is primarily over the war or crime model of terrorism, it can also be viewed through the prism of the collective and individual models of conflicts. For the American government, Al Qaeda is a collective that is threatening as a collective, and that must be fought wherever it is found. It is group membership, rather than any geographical boundary, that determines who the enemy is, and any member of the group, as well as anyone who closely associates with the group, is presumed dangerous. The critics of the American position submit, conversely, that if there is a war at all, it is confined to Afghan territory; and anyone captured outside the immediate theater of war must be presumed innocent unless and until proven otherwise.

With individualization, threat thus turns into guilt: rather than detaining the terrorist as an agent of a threatening collective, much like the detention of an enemy soldier as an agent of his state, critics of the U.S. position hold that the individual terrorist's guilt under domestic criminal law must be proven by due process and cannot be assumed by association.

Somewhat paradoxically, the Israeli Supreme Court, unlike its American counterpart, has ruled that no terrorist may be held in preventive detention based on group membership alone; instead, it requires that the individual guilt/ threat of each detainee, meaning his direct and active involvement in terrorist activity, must be ascertained and proven as a precondition for his detention.[45] This was the ruling even though the Court recognized that such detention is taken within an ongoing armed conflict between Israel and terrorist organizations. The Court has thus taken a more individualized view of wartime regulation, even though the general Israeli view of the conflict emphasizes the collective.

There are at least two possible explanations for this discrepancy between American and Israeli detention policy and regulation. One explanation lies, paradoxically, in the more collectivist view of the conflict by Israel. Precisely because of that collectivist view, the Israeli Supreme Court may have feared that membership in a terrorist organization might turn out to be an overinclusive test for purposes of detention, especially considering that many Palestinian groups have civic and political functions alongside militant components. While any member of Al Qaeda may be thought of as, by definition, a terrorist, the same cannot be said about any member of Hamas (nor necessarily, for that matter, any member of the Taliban).

Another explanation has to do with the distinction between the legal attitudes to law enforcement and belligerency in both countries: in the United States, the distinction between what is permissible under law enforcement and what is permissible under the laws of war is stark. Protections afforded to suspects and defendants under the law enforcement model do not vary according to the type of suspect and/or offense; security offenses are thus by and large addressed through the same rules and processes as any type of crime, subject to close judicial scrutiny. That scrutiny has been largely absent, or at best lethargic, when it came to reviewing the exercise of war powers by the executive, including with regard to detention. In Israel, a country under a formal state of emergency since its inception, special criminal procedures allow the police and prosecutors more latitude in dealing with those charged with security offenses than with ordinary criminals. At the same time, and because war is not an exceptional state of affairs, courts are less deferential to the executive than their American counterparts with regard to the exercise of war powers. As a result, the Israeli courts, while recognizing the overall paradigm of a war on terrorism, have pushed for a more individualized application of wartime detention powers, essentially driving the war model to look more like the laxer law enforcement paradigm as applied to terrorists.

Whatever explains the original difference between the two models of detention, even the United States now has, partly in response to slow but persistent pushback by the courts, more individualized features, including individual review of grounds for detention and the release of those deemed no longer sufficiently threatening to warrant detention, even as the war on terrorism continues.[46]

III. Implications

The examples of issues that implicate collectivism versus individualism are a few among many possible others. One could easily describe in similar terms the debates over the permissible scope of targeting combatants, the precise contours of "direct participation in hostilities" that permit the targeting of involved civilians, the appropriate degree of conversion between IHL and IHRL, or of other contemporary debates over wartime regulation. All of these questions ultimately implicate the collective nature of war and a degree of an alternative commitment to individual cosmopolitanism.

Naturally, a commitment to either nationalism or to individualism has broad and far-reaching implications, well beyond the sphere of wartime regulation. The meaning of sovereign equality, the primacy of states as international actors, questions of redistributive justice and obligations owed to others—these are only some of the wider issues implicated by the move from collectivism to individualism. Still, in what follows, I restrict my observations to the implications of this move in the context of violent conflict alone.

Overall, the trend toward individualism has had positive effects on the welfare of individuals, as far as conflicts involving liberal democracies go. Western public opinion tolerates far less cruelty than it used to and places greater checks on governments in their wartime conduct. And yet, the individualization of warfare also harbors some dangers: for the ability of liberal democracies to wage wars (for self-interest or in the interest of others) effectively; for the potential incidence of violence (political or criminal); for domestic policing within liberal democracies; and for interstate relationship more generally. These are the implications I would like to focus on in these concluding observations. Some of my claims may seem overbroad and debatable. They need not be taken as attempts to predict the future with accuracy. Rather, they are intended to suggest possibilities—what might be at stake in preferring an individual-oriented regulation of war.

The first obvious implication of the individualization of war has to do with the very definition of war. With the move toward a greater focus on the treatment of individuals qua individuals, there will be growing pressures to treat more types of wars as policing actions rather than armed conflicts in their traditional legal sense. Once in a world of policing action, the fate of each individual must depend, much as in domestic law enforcement situations and to the extent feasible, on that individual's actions rather than her affiliation or association. Individuals, rather than societies or even classes of people, would be deemed "good" or "evil," and handled accordingly.

This is already, to a large degree, the American counterinsurgency doctrine, but there is reason to expect that it is one that would not remain limited to counterinsurgency operations. Mutatis mutandis, it may come to apply to more traditional, state-to-state scenarios as well. Or put differently, there may no longer be "traditional" scenarios altogether. Note the reluctance of American leaders to characterize the NATO-led military operation in Libya as "war," a reluctance undoubtedly shaped by myriad domestic and international considerations, but nonetheless emblematic of the general aversion to "war." A similar aversion to the concept—"war"—existed in Israel with regard to the 2010–11 war in Gaza (officially named in Israel, "Operation Cast Lead").

In addition, a policing model will not necessarily be limited to coercive action. If it is necessary to correct against deviance, or to think about "rehabilitation," there may be growing expectations of positive duties incurred by the policing party toward the policed population. Despite the obvious self-interest driving in the current extension of positive assistance in conflict areas, as a historical matter, some traditional IHL obligations that were followed as a matter of self-interest (such as not harming enemy POWs) were later incorporated into the law of war as absolute legal obligations. Some calls to favor individual human security, including through the supply of positive assistance, are already noted on the international plane.[47] Victory, in other words, would no longer be framed in terms of national security alone, but also in terms of overall human security. And building hospitals will become as much a part of warfare as are targeted killings.

While at first glance we should be hopeful about treating more of war like policing, thus bearing the promise of less pain and suffering, there are possible drawbacks to be contemplated.

One significant risk is that a policing or quasi-policing model resonates more with liberal democracies that are committed to the ideals of individualism than with nondemocracies. It thus places higher standards of compliance and expectations for compliance with the laws of war from parties who are committed to liberal democratic ideals and who have the means of enforcing these ideals than from those who are not. Such differing expectations are likely to come from outside observers as well as from domestic constituencies.[48] Again, this difference is not unique to the field of war; but war offers a particularly pronounced context for it. The uneven application of the law might prompt nondemocratic entities or those generally not committed to similar norms to engage liberal democracies violently as a way of extracting costs that derive from a stricter compliance by the latter with humanitarian rules. Such violent engagement could result in unjust achievements for the attacking forces as well as the ultimate harm of more individuals. It might also drive such actors to practices that are more dangerous to local civilians, such as shielding or blending within the local population. Clearly, there are still many sound reasons to adhere to a humanitarian ideology even in the face of defection by others, and even at the cost of being somewhat constrained in war waging and prosecution. Nonetheless, the uneven application of a law that has a claim to universality inflicts a price that must be acknowledged

At the same time, the higher bar of compliance might deter liberal democracies from using force, even when such force is justified and warranted under a *jus ad bellum* test. Unless one holds that all wars are inherently evil and must be forbidden, this may be a real risk to the welfare of individuals who are threatened by unjust aggressors. One type of case in point may be humanitarian interventions, which, under the projected scenario, may be even more discouraged than they naturally are, as intervening powers must consider not only risking their own combatants and expending their own resources, but also protecting local nationals as if the latter were their own citizens. The Libyan government's bad-faith attempt to inflate the number of civilian casualties inflicted by coalition airstrikes played exactly to the unrealistic expectations of zero civilian casualties. It further sought to turn humanitarian concerns from a justification of the coalition's actions to an indictment against them.

Another potential risk of treating war as policing is that it may invite treating more of policing as war. Once certain practices become legitimated under a paradigm of "international policing," they risk spilling over and being legitimated under a paradigm of domestic policing as well. Some domestic policing is increasingly incorporating a collectivist mindset: material support statutes in the United States,[49] as applied by courts, now cover wide swaths of people, effectively making any association with Al Qaeda or with related elements a major federal crime. In this line, James Forman has made the observation that "[in] calling the fight against crime a war, advocates for harsher measures told us we must accept that some innocents will suffer."[50] And it is not enough to argue that the problem begins and ends with illegitimately defining certain crimes such as terrorism as "war"—and that if we remain true to a criminal paradigm, much of the debates (for example, overdetention or targeting) could be easily resolved within the traditional law enforcement paradigm. War is what we see and what we define as such. It has no objective test other than "scale and effect."[51] At certain times and in certain places, terrorism *is* a warlike phenomenon. Drug cartels, pirates, and transnational criminal networks may at some times and in some places turn out to pose a warlike threat. In those cases, it is not at all clear that traditional policing can effectively meet the threat. And just as in the case of political or ideological nonstate actors, the greater constraints on what liberal democracies are allowed to do to meet the threat might offer greater incentives for transnational criminal actors to employ warlike methods to advance their goals.

Moreover, the greater the push to protect individual rights and privileges in traditional settings of law enforcement, the greater would be the pushback to operate outside law enforcement and in the ethical zone of war. It may very well be that one reason there have been far more targeted killing operations during President Obama's term than during his predecessor's administration is that detention has become so complicated and fraught with legal challenges. The growing pressure to expand the category of "civilians taking direct part in hostilities," so as to allow for the capture or targeting of those who are not clearly combatants but nonetheless support hostile activity, is another manifestation of the pushback against growing constraints on war.

If the risk of individualizing collectivism is that it ends up collectivizing individualism, this phenomenon also manifests itself in the groupings of individuals according to nontraditional features: instead of territory or citizenship, groups would be identified according to ethnicity, religion, or ideology. Already we see this move in speaking about "Global Al Qaeda" or "radical Islam." Terrorist detainees, almost all Muslim, fall exactly within this category of individuals-collectives. It is unclear that these types of groupings would prove more protective of their individual members than the more traditional collectivizing characteristics.

The state system itself is coming under growing pressures. In the context of war, more than in other contexts perhaps, the competition between the state and the individual may have profound implications on the state and its declining power. Over the past several decades, in a move welcomed by most Western international lawyers and policy-makers, state sovereignty has been reconceptualized as responsibility, rather than immunity. This was a necessary development for those who wished a world in which human rights could obligate states in their relationship with their own citizens. Nonetheless, the erosion of sovereignty as immunity may have serious repercussions for the relationship between the state and other states: if external powers have a claim that the state does not meet its responsibilities in regulating the conduct of its own people, they may have a stronger claim for forcefully intervening in those states to avert danger to themselves. This is essentially the American justification for targeted killings in Yemen or Somalia. At the same time, the erosion of sovereignty might also serve as an incentive for some regimes to behave as if they are leading "failed states," so as to induce more external intervention against domestic rebels or subversive elements; again, Yemen under Saleh's presidency is an example.

Finally, a somewhat tangential implication might have to do with the practice of military conscription: if individual rights and liberties are to dominate the state, the justification for conscription quickly subsides. Reliance on volunteers is expensive and complex, and pushes for greater privatization of force—essentially a resurrection of the mercenary forces of the Middle Ages. Private military companies tend to be less disciplined and potentially more harmful to the local population than regular soldiers.

A final point must also be made: much of the individualization of warfare has taken part in wars that are fundamentally nonexistential for the liberal democracies that are fighting them. Indeed, at times when the threat perception was higher, these democracies ignored or relaxed many of the constraints they had assumed at other times. While it is virtually impossible to imagine a return to mass killing in wars involving democracies of the kind that the twentieth century had witnessed, it remains to be seen how much of the trend toward international policing remains in effect for a liberal democracy facing what it perceives as an existential threat.

Notes

I am grateful to participants of the Tikvah Center workshop at NYU, participants of the "Law and War" series at Amherst, and to David Luban and the research group on "Sovereignty, Global Justice and the Ethics of War" at the Institute for Advanced Studies at the Hebrew University. I am indebted to Yonina Alexander, Brian Itami, Natalie Lockwood, and Joshua Roselman for excellent research and editorial assistance.

1. Theodor Meron, "The Humanization of Humanitarian Law," *American Journal of International Law* 94 (2000): 239.

2. See, for example, Ruti G. Teitel, "Humanity's Law: Rule of Law for the New Global Politics," *Cornell International Law Journal* 35 (2002): 355; Kenneth Watkin, "Controlling the Use of Force: A Role for Human Rights Norms in Contemporary Armed Conflict,"

American Journal of International Law 98 (2004): 1; David Kretzmer, Rotem Giladi, and Yuval Shany, "Introduction to the Symposium on International Humanitarian Law and International Human Rights Law: Exploring Parallel Application," *Israel Law Review* (2007): 306.

3. See, for example, Erik Roxstrom, Mark Gibney, and Terje Einarsen, "The NATO Bombing Case (Bankovic et al. v. Belgium et al.) and the Limits of Western Human Rights Protection," *Boston University International Law Journal* 23 (2005): 55; David S. Koller, "The Moral Imperative: Toward a Human Rights–Based Law of War," *Harvard International Law Journal* 46 (2005): 231. See also Anne-Marie Slaughter and William Burke-White, "An International Constitutional Moment," *Harvard International Law Journal* 43 (2002): 1 (suggesting that the United Nations charter be amended so as to make any attack on an individual civilian a violation of the charter).

4. For both positive and normative skepticism, see Robert J. Delahunty and John C. Yoo, "What Is the Role of International Human Rights Law in the War on Terror?" *DePaul Law Review* 59 (2010): 803; Naz K. Modirzadeh, "Dark Sides of Convergence: A Pro-civilian Critique of the Extraterritorial Application of Human Rights Law in Armed Conflict," *International Law Studies, U.S. Naval War College* 86 (2010): 349.

5. See, for instance, Common Article 1 of the Geneva Conventions, 1949.

6. The few obligations that fell under the latter category included, for instance, a prohibition on erecting military facilities next to civilians so as not to place the civilians in harm's way.

7. Geneva Convention IV, Article 4.

8. Legal Consequences of the Construction of a Wall in the Occupied Palestinian Territory, Advisory Opinion, 2004 I.C.J. 136, 178 (July 9, 2004). See also Legality of the Threat or Use of Nuclear Weapons, Advisory Opinion, 1996 I.C.J. 226 (July 8, 1996).

9. Compare the legal tests of proportionality under a human rights regime, as applied by the European Court of Human Rights in *Isayeva v. Russia* (I and II).

10. Compare Meron, "The Humanization of Humanitarian Law," who believes that it is further evidence of the humanization—that is, the individual focus—of IHL. In my view, it reflects a view of communal allegiance as replacing national allegiance in these types of conflicts.

11. *Prosecutor v. Tadic,* ICTY IT-94-1-A, para. 166 (July 16, 1999) (emphasis added).

12. The one exception here requires equating the treatment of POWs with that of national soldiers in the same area. Geneva Convention III, Article 25.

13. See, for example, Geneva Convention IV, Articles 8, 63, and 140.

14. Security Council Resolution 687 (1991) of April 8, 1991, para. 16. No other country was ordered to pay any compensation to Iraq or Iraqis.

15. The vast majority of the 2.6 million claims received by the UNCC were from individuals. See http://www.uncc.ch/theclaims.htm. On the legal status of an

obligation for reparations, see Liesbeth Zegveld, "Remedies for Victims of Violations of International Humanitarian Law," *International Review of the Red Cross* 85 (2003): 297; Emanuela-Chiara Gillard, "Reparations for Violations of International Humanitarian Law," *International Review of the Red Cross* 85 (2003): 529.

16. Carl Schmitt, *The Concept of the Political* (Chicago: University Of Chicago Press, 2007) 26.

17. Compare U.S. Department of the Army, *The Law of Land Warfare* (U.S. Army Field Manual no. 27-10, 1956), paras. 49, 84, with David Petraeus, *The U.S. Army and Marine Corps Counterinsurgency Field Manual* (U.S. Army Field Manual no. 3-24, 2006) [hereinafter COIN], paras. 1-127, 1-131, 2-1–2-57.

18. See Articles on Responsibility of States for Internationally Wrongful Acts, in "United Nations International Law Commission Report on the Work of Its Fifty-third Session," UNGAOR, 56th Sess., Supp. no. 10, at 43, UN Doc. A/56/10 (2001), at 110–11.

19. These are considered peremptory norms. See ibid. at Article 27.

20. Samuel Moyn, *The Last Utopia: Human Rights in History* (Cambridge: Belknap Press, 2010).

21. Charles Taylor, *Sources of the Self: The Making of the Modern Identity* (Cambridge: Harvard University Press, 1992).

22. On European aversion to war and violence and the transatlantic divide over the utility of force, see Robert Kagan, *Of Paradise and Power: America and Europe in the New World Order* (New York: Alfred A. Knopf, 2003).

23. For example, Geneva Convention IV, Articles 146–47; Geneva Convention III, Articles 129–30; Additional Protocol 1 to the Geneva Conventions, Articles 85–86.

24. See "Addressing Civilian Harm in Afghanistan: Policies & Practices of International Forces, Campaign for Innocent Victims in Conflict" (Washington, DC, 2010) [hereinafter CIVIC Report].

25. See, for example, Howard Ramos, James Ron, and Oskar N. T. Thoms, "Shaping the Northern Media's Human Rights Coverage, 1986–2000," *Journal of Peace Research* 44 (2007): 385.

26. Maximo Langer, "The Diplomacy of Universal Jurisdiction: The Regulating Role of the Political Branches in the Transnational Prosecution of International Crimes," *American Journal of International Law* 105 (2011): 1.

27. See, for example, Oona Hathaway, "Outcasting: Enforcement in Domestic and International Law," *Yale Law Journal* 121 (November 2011): 252; Beth A. Simmons, "Reflections on Mobilizing for Human Rights," *New York University Journal of International Law & Politics* 44 (Spring 2012): 729; Eric Neumayer, "Qualified Ratification: Explaining Reservations to International Human Rights Treaties," *Journal of Legal Studies* 36 (June 2007): 397.

28. For a description and defense of the equal application principle, see Adam

Roberts, "The Equal Application of the Laws of War: A Principle under Pressure," *International Review of the Red Cross* 872 (December 2008): 8; Robert D. Sloane, "The Cost of Conflation: Preserving the Dualism of *Jus ad Bellum* and *Jus in Bello* in the Contemporary Law of War," *Yale Journal of International Law* 34 (2009): 47. For a critique of the principle, see, esp., Jeff McMahan, *Killing in War* (New York: Oxford University Press, 2011).

29. Jeff McMahan, "The Ethics of Killing in War," *Ethics* 114 (July 2004): 725.

30. Additional Protocol 1, Article 57(2)(b).

31. Rome Statute of the International Criminal Court, Article 8(2)(b)(iv), July 17, 1998, UN Doc. A/CONF.183/9, entered into force July 1, 2002.

32. API, Article 57(2).

33. Ibid., Article 57(3).

34. For the role school, see Avishai Margalit and Michael Walzer, "Israel: Civilians and Combatants," *New York Review of Books* (May 14, 2009): 21–22; McMahan, "The Ethics of Killing in War"; David Luban, "Just War and Human Rights," *Philosophy & Public Affairs* 9 (Winter 1980): 160; Paul Christopher, *The Ethics of War and Peace: An Introduction to Legal and Moral Issues* (Upper Saddle River, NJ: Prentice Hall, 1994), 165.

35. For the allegiance school, see Asa Kasher and Major General Amos Yadlin, "Israel & the Rules of War: An Exchange," *New York Review of Books* (June 11, 2009). Iddo Porat, "Preferring One's Own Civilians: May Soldiers Endanger Enemy Civilians More Than They Would Endanger Their Own Civilians?" working paper, available at http://www. clb.ac.il/uploads/Preferring-%20April%2010%20-%20for%20Sheffield%20Book.pdf.

36. For a much more developed version of this argument, see Anna Stilz, "Collective Responsibility and the State," *Journal of Political Philosophy* 19 (2001): 190–208.

37. See Daryl Levinson, "Collective Sanctions," *Stanford Law Review* 56 (2003): 345.

38. See, for example, the Ethiopia-Eritrea Claims Commission.

39. See, for example, "Basic Principles and Guidelines of the Right to a Remedy and Reparations for Victims of Violations of International Human Rights and Humanitarian Law." General Assembly Resolution 60/147 (December 16, 2005).

40. In fact, international law has made some efforts to order domestic compensation for victims of crime, but has made no such effort to order domestic compensation for victims of war. See A/RES/40/34 UN General Assembly Declaration of Basic Principles of Justice for Victims of Crime and Abuse of Power, 96th Plenary Meeting (November 29, 1985).

41. See http://www.gao.gov/new.items/d07699.pdf. Army Regulation 27-20, para. 10-10 states, "Payment of solatia in accordance with local custom as an expression of sympathy toward a victim or his or her family is common in some overseas commands." See also CIVIC Report.

42. The United Kingdom, Australia, Poland, Norway, and Canada have instituted

standing programs for compensation; the Netherlands, Italy, and Germany pay more sporadically, and only for some types of damage. See also CIVIC Report.

43. There are some claims that the United States has made such payments, but I could not verify this.

44. Interestingly, some states compensate their citizens for harm they incurred by violent crime, perhaps espousing a belief that crime is also a threat to the national collective as such.

45. *CrimA 6659/06 A&B v. The State of Israel* [2008] (Isr.).

46. See Samuel Issacharoff and Richard H. Pildes, "Targeting Warfare: Individuating Enemy Responsibility," working paper, on draft with the author.

47. Shannon D. Beebe and Mary Kaldor, *The Ultimate Weapon Is No Weapon: Human Security and the New Rules of War and Peace* (Jackson, TN: PublicAffairs, 2010).

48. On different expectations for compliance, see Gabriella Blum, "On a Differential Law of War," *Harvard International Law Journal* 52 (2011); Marco Sassòli, "Should the Obligations of States and Armed Groups under International Humanitarian Law Really Be Equal?" *International Review of the Red Cross* 93 (June 2011).

49. 18 U.S.C. §2339.

50. James Forman, Jr., "Exporting Harshness: How the War on Crime Helped Make the War on Terror Possible," *New York University Review of Law & Social Change,* 33 (2009): 331–74.

51. See, generally, *Prosecutor v. Tadic,* ICTY IT-94-1-A, para. 166 (July 16, 1999), Case Concerning the Military and Paramilitary Activities in and against Nicaragua (*Nicaragua v. United States of America*), 1984 ICJ Rep. 392 (June 27, 1986).

Pandemic Disease, Biological Weapons, and War

LAURA K. DONOHUE

Over the past two decades, concern about the threat posed by biological weapons has grown. Biowarfare is not new.[1] But prior to the recent trend, the threat largely centered on state use of such weapons.[2] What changed with the end of the Cold War was the growing apprehension that materials and knowledge would proliferate beyond industrialized states' control, and that "rogue states" or nonstate actors would acquire and use biological weapons.[3] Accordingly, in 1993 senators Samuel Nunn, Richard Lugar, and Pete Dominici expanded the Cooperative Threat Reduction Program to assist the former Soviet republics in securing biological agents and weapons knowledge. The Defense Against Weapons of Mass Destruction Act gave the Pentagon lead agency responsibility.[4] Senator Lugar explained, "[B]iological weapons, materials, and know-how are now more available to terrorists and rogue nations than at any other time in our history."[5] The United States was not equipped to manage the crisis.[6]

The actual acquisition of unconventional weapons by nonstate actors augmented concern. In 1984, for instance, the Rajneesh cult in Oregon sought to prevent the local community from being able to vote against its land development plans.[7] The group contaminated local salad bars with *Salmonella typhimurium*, infecting 751 people.[8] In 1995 Aum Shinrikyo released a sarin nerve gas attack on the Tokyo subway, killing twelve people.[9] And in 1998 an American citizen, Larry Wayne Harris, obtained plague and anthrax (a vaccine strain) and isolated several other dangerous bacteria.[10] His aim was to disseminate biological agents on U.S. soil, using a crop-duster, to alert the U.S. government to the Iraqi biological weapons threat, and to create a separate homeland for whites.[11]

These and similar incidents pointed to an alarming trend: from previously a dozen or so investigations per year, in 1997, the FBI opened 74 investigations related to the possible acquisition and use of chemical, biological, radiological, or nuclear materials.[12] The following year, it investigated 181 possible incidents.[13] Eighty percent of the cases turned out to be hoaxes, but a significant number represented unsuccessful attacks.[14] By January 31, 1999, Monterey Institute for International Studies had compiled an open-source data base of 415 such incidents—most of which occurred toward the end of the twentieth century—where terrorists had sought to acquire or use weapons of mass destruction.[15]

All of this was before the attacks of September 11, 2001, and al Qaeda's stated intent to use biological weapons, backed by actual efforts to obtain biological agents.[16] The anthrax attacks in autumn 2001 further underscored the threat, killing five people and infecting eighteen others.[17] In 2002 President Bush stated, "The gravest danger to freedom lies at the crossroads of radicalism and technology. When the spread of chemical and biological and nuclear weapons, along with ballistic missile technology—when that occurs, even weak states and small groups could attain a catastrophic power to strike great nations."[18] New scholarship began focusing on the threat.[19] The consensus was that it was increasingly easier and less expensive to launch a biological attack—using either natural or engineered agents.[20] In order to address the challenge, domestic preparedness needed significantly more attention.

Even as the United States became increasingly concerned about terrorist acquisition or use of biological weapons, scientists and policy-makers began paying more attention to the threat posed by naturally occurring outbreaks of disease. A series of public health incidents catapulted the discussion forward. The first, avian influenza, emerged in Hong Kong in 1997. It infected eighteen people and killed six more.[21] The disease quickly spread, becoming epizootic and panzootic, having been identified on multiple continents in eagles, tigers, domestic cats, and pigs, as well as aquatic and domesticated birds.[22] Although it was not initially transferrable between humans, scientists quickly became concerned that the rapid mutations of the disease that occurred in infected animals and humans could quickly create a more virulent strain.[23] Within a decade, the patterns of mortality had changed: whereas in 1997, most deaths occurred among patients older than thirteen years of age, by 2006 the fatality rate for infants and young children had reached 90 percent.[24] Recollections of the devastation caused by the 1918 Spanish Influenza heightened fear: also avian in origin, within a year it had become one of the three worst pandemics in history.[25] More than 1 billion worldwide had come down with the flu (half the world's population), with between 50 and 100 million succumbing.[26] In other words, the disease had killed more than twice the number killed in World War I, with a mortality rate of only 2.5 to 5 percent. These numbers paled in comparison to the more recent strain of H5N1, where 60 percent of the humans infected with the disease had died.[27] Calls for more stringent quarantine measures emerged.[28]

A second outbreak proved equally disconcerting: in 2003 severe acute respiratory syndrome (SARS), caused by a strain of the same virus underlying the common cold, hit southern China.[29] Within days, it had spread from a hotel in Hong Kong to Hanoi—and as far away as Toronto. Transferred by a small number of "superspreaders," within months some eight thousand people in twenty-nine countries had contracted it, and nearly eight hundred people had died.[30] The sudden proliferation of academic and policy-oriented pieces on how to fight emerging diseases followed.[31]

A third outbreak underscored not just domestic but also international concern. On June 11, 2009, the World Health Organization declared that H1N1 influenza had become pandemic, heralding the first such declaration since 1968.[32] The first cases had been identified in Mexico some two months previously. Although the pandemic proved to be less serious than first feared,[33] its occurrence underscored the potentially devastating effect of the disease.

In keeping with these concerns, an increasing number of federal statutory and regulatory initiatives have been introduced to address the threat posed by both biological weapons and pandemic disease.[34] Simultaneously, the executive branch has issued new policy documents, directing agencies to conduct better research and to make more robust preparations for responding to such threats, and laying out the planned course of action.[35]

Three broad observations about these initiatives follow. First, many of them tend to view biological weapons and pandemic disease through a national security lens, linking the two in terms of institutions, authorities, and approach. The Homeland Security Act of 2002, for instance, created the Department of Homeland Security (DHS), whose primary mission is to prevent terrorist attacks within the United States, reduce vulnerability of the U.S. to terrorism, and minimize damage and assist in recovery from domestic terrorist attacks.[36] But from the beginning, DHS saw its role as much broader. Its website declared that "[in] the event of a terrorist attack, natural disaster or other large-scale emergency, the Department of Homeland Security will assume primary responsibility ... for ensuring that emergency response professionals are prepared." The National Response Plan underscored DHS's dual role: to assist "in the important homeland security mission of preventing terrorist attacks within the United States; reducing the vulnerability to all natural and man-made hazards; and minimizing the damage and assisting in the recovery from any type of incident that occurs."[37] The Public Health Security and Bioterrorism Preparedness and Response Act of 2002,[38] as indicated by its title alone, focused on preparedness for response to public health emergencies as well as biological terrorism. The Centers for Disease Control and Prevention, in proposing broader authorities, noted, "Stopping an outbreak—whether it is naturally occurring or intentionally caused—requires the use of the most rapid and effective public health tools available."[39] Homeland Security Presidential Directive 10 asserted that the traditional public health approach was no longer sufficient for the biological weapons threat: health care providers and public health officials were considered among the first lines of defense. Accordingly, a new biodefense program would combine and strengthen the state's ability to respond to biological weapons *and* natural disease. Similarly, in presenting the 2007 Pandemic Influenza Implementation Plan, White House officials and the Assistant Secretary of DHS underscored that the government intended to treat biological weapons and naturally occurring diseases in similar fashion: "We at DHS are focused on multi-use institutions that we can put into place for whatever emergencies arise."[40] The link between the two is not just happenstance: the stated intent in releasing this document was to redefine public health as a national security priority.[41]

A second observation that can be drawn about the measures that have proliferated is that isolation and quarantine appear to be central to the legal framework and the policy response.[42] Thus the Public Health Security and Bioterrorism Preparedness and Response Act of 2002 streamlines and clarifies communicable disease quarantine provisions.[43] It also makes quarantine applicable at an earlier stage by replacing language that previously required that the disease be "in a communicable stage" with a measure allowing quarantine "in a qualifying stage."[44] The White House expanded the list of quarantinable diseases to include SARS (April 2003),[45] and pandemic influenza (April 2005).[46] In 2003 the Department of Health and Human Services amended its regulations to incorporate any quarantinable diseases listed by executive order, bypassing rulemaking requirements.[47] The Centers for Disease Control proposed new regulations, specifying exact periods of quarantine and the procedure to be followed in the event of its implementation.[48] CDC suggested that "[q]uarantine of exposed persons may be the best initial way to prevent the uncontrolled spread of highly dangerous biologic agents such as smallpox, plague, and Ebola fever. ... Quarantine may be particularly important if a biologic agent has been rendered contagious, drug-resistant, or vaccine-resistant through bioengineering, making other disease control measures less effective."[49] National exercises designed to press on response in the event of biological weapons attack include planning for mass quarantine.[50] Quarantine, indeed, is at the core of the U.S. Pandemic Influenza Strategy Implementation Plan, which was issued by HHS as a blueprint for how agencies will respond in the event that avian influenza becomes human-to-human transferrable. The reason this is remarkable is that, by the document's own admission, scientists generally agree that influenza is one disease for which quarantine is likely to be particularly ineffective—yet the document refers to quarantine 138 times, and in a manner of consequence, detailing the use of quarantine both at ports of entry and in the execution of geographic quarantine (*cordon sanitaire*).[51]

The third observation that can be made about the measures that have been adopted is that, as biological weapons and pandemic disease have folded into the homeland defense realm, growing attention is being paid to the role of the military in enforcing such provisions. HSPD 10, for instance, considers the military to be central to U.S. biodefense.[52] In large measure, this stems from the biological weapons component of the threat. But in enacting the 2002 Homeland Security Act, Congress explained that the federal government could use the military in response to any national emergency, including natural disasters. Following Hurricane Katrina, the 2007 Defense Authorization Act made such authority explicit.[53] Renaming the Insurrection Act "Enforcement of the Laws to Restore Public Order," the new language gave the president the authority to impose martial law in the event of "natural disaster, epidemic, or other serious public health emergency, terrorist attack or incident, or other condition"—without any contact or collaboration with state officials.[54] The shift to federal authority immediately incurred the wrath of the state governors.[55] The new powers had been "quietly tucked into the enormous defense budget bill," the *New York Times* pointed out, "without hearings or public debate. The president," moreover, "made no mention of the changes when he signed the measure, and neither the White House nor Congress consulted in advance with the nation's governors."[56] Senators Patrick Leahy and Christopher Bond spearheaded new legislation that returned the Insurrection Act to its original form. Nevertheless, the incident highlighted a shift in the federal view of pandemic disease and human-engineered biological agents. Use of the military—both Title 32 troops and Title 10 forces—to respond to public health crises has broad support.[57] Even without the statute, the deployment of military in Katrina was largest military deployment in domestic bounds since the Civil War.[58] And the policy documents currently in place support the use of the military to enforce quarantine.[59]

There are practical reasons for the emergence of each of the three areas identified. The association between biological weapons and pandemic disease stems from a common nexus: both involve viral or bacteriological threats to human life. Similar institutions would likely be the first to become aware of the spread of such diseases—that is, hospitals and public health entities are likely to be on the front line of defense regardless of whether the disease is natural or man-made. At the onset of disease, it may be impossible to ascertain whether a disease is naturally occurring, or the result of a concerted attack. The question thus becomes, institutionally, whether it even *makes sense to separate them*—or whether it makes more sense to have the same entities identifying and responding. The consequences of either type of threat also may be largely the same and demand that the state marshal similar resources to respond. In other words, from a mitigation perspective, it matters little whether avian flu is deliberately disseminated or happens to transfer from animals to humans. The same medical response may apply.

As for the use of quarantine and isolation, the government may be limited in the options available. For both natural diseases and for engineered weapons there may not be vaccines—or medication—available to counter the spread. Although medical opinion is divided as to the effectiveness of such measures, there does seem to be consensus about the tendency of quarantine and isolation at least to slow the spread of disease, buying time in the interim for the government and public health officials to craft a more effective response. And for those who view such steps as a last and unlikely resort, it nevertheless makes sense to think through the consequences of such measures prior to their implementation, in the event that they may be needed.

Turning to the use of the military, the armed forces have for decades been engaged in biological weapons research. The military understands many such weapons. It is likely to have a greater capacity to identify engineered diseases and potentially devastating natural diseases that have served as a basis for BW research with precision. It may have access to a broader range of antibiotics, vaccines, and prophylactic measures than civilian agencies. The military has prepared its own personnel to face such weapons in a way that civilian agencies have not. Furthermore, it may be the only institution with the necessary technology, resources, and manpower to be able to effectively counter an attack—or a pandemic disaster.

These practical considerations are important and, indeed, have been deeply influential in the changes that are occurring. But what has become lost in the discussion are many of the constitutional questions and policy concerns that present themselves. That is, once pandemic disease and biological weapons are placed within a national security framework, disease becomes seen through a lens of war. Broader powers, with fewer checks on them, come into play. Rights become constricted, judicial remedies narrowed, and civilian agencies pushed to one side. Federalism falls even further away as a check on national authority. Such a shift may be warranted when the country is at war and civil society itself is threatened; but how does one mediate the response as a framing for all of public health, once it has been placed on a national security footing? That is to say, what happens when the federal government can impose *cordon sanitaire* on cities, regions, or entire states, using the military to enforce it, in response to annual outbreaks of influenza? This is the current state of play.

These developments run counter to history: on the one hand, the country has had long experience with natural disease and its weaponization, and quarantine and isolation have been a common response. But despite the potentially devastating consequences of both threats, for much of the country's history, it was the states—not the national government—which took the lead. This chapter suggests that what we have actually seen is two major shifts: the first, which took place during the early part of the twentieth century, was the federalization of quarantine law as a response to the introduction of natural disease and its transfer between the states. The second, and most recent, is the one identified above—that is, the integration of public health and biological weapons concerns, the use of quarantine and isolation for both, and the potential use of the military to enforce federal law.

This chapter argues that while strong arguments support the first shift, the second is of concern. The history of public health law in general, and quarantine and isolation in particular, sheds light on four constitutional concerns: first, the degree to which Article II claims override the tension between police powers and the Commerce Clause, driving the discussion into the realm of war; second, in looking at a growing role for the military in the realm of public health, what the contours of military deployment on U.S. soil might be; third, the extent to which Commerce Clause authorities more generally may be marshaled in the realm of public health—an area traditionally reserved to the states via the Tenth Amendment; and fourth, whether recent interpretations of the Necessary and Proper Clause militate in favor of an expanded federal role in this area. The chapter concludes its discussion with two policy considerations: whether the increasing emphasis on biological weapons risks allowing the proverbial tail to wag the dog of public health, as well as whether the use of quarantine and isolation ought to be considered as a viable response.

I. Local Quarantine Authorities and the Weaponization of Disease

During colonial times, disease threatened the very existence of the settlements. Land and maritime quarantine authorities were frequently introduced and rarely successful.[60] They tended to be reactive and temporary, responding to reports of sickness abroad with orders forcing ships to moor offshore and preventing people or goods from entering colonial bounds. Harsh penalties for breaking quarantine applied. Massachusetts Bay,[61] New York,[62] the Province of Pennsylvania,[63] New-Castle upon Delaware,[64] Maryland,[65] Rhode Island,[66] South Carolina, and Virginia passed similar measures. England strongly objected: quarantine devastated trade. But the colonies persisted. It was well within their rights to protect colonists—indeed, the colonies themselves—

from the threat. Special measures targeted the deliberate spread of disease, with death without benefit of clergy providing the strongest of penalties that could be applied. During the War of Independence, further reports emerged of the English use of disease as a weapon.

Following the Revolution, the newly formed states incorporated colonial measures into their new statutes and, in some cases, their constitutions. Maryland, New York, Massachusetts, Pennsylvania, Connecticut, Delaware, South Carolina, Rhode Island, and Virginia all introduced quarantine laws, in the process conveying significant authorities to local entities. Towns were so clearly in the lead on all questions of public health, that it was left to them to decide when and to what extent communication and commerce could be severed with any other town, city, region, or state in the United States where contagion raged. Seen as the quintessential manifestation of state police powers, the protection of public health easily trumped any claims to federal Commerce Clause authority.

A. *Colonial Provisions*

Massachusetts Bay provides a good example of how the colonies responded to the threat of disease. In 1647 the General Court received reports that the "plague, or like grievous [in]fectious disease," had broken out in Barbados.[67] The colony responded with an order instituting quarantine against all vessels arriving from the West Indies.[68] No one on board would be permitted ashore, nor could anyone within the colony board such vessels, or purchase anything carried by such ships, absent a valid license.[69] The penalty for violating the order was £100.[70] Once the yellow fever epidemic ended, the order was repealed.[71] Similar response patterns marked subsequent outbreaks of disease.[72]

These measures had a significant (and negative) impact on the flow of trade, which earned England's enmity.[73] The Privy Council soon became concerned that "the uncontrolled manner in which the Colony was exercising its powers was becoming increasingly detrimental to the economic welfare of England and the Empire."[74] When Massachusetts Bay passed a particularly stringent measure in response to an outbreak of yellow fever, the Lords of Trade argued that being able to retain a ship, indefinitely, on the grounds of the presence of any contagious disease fell beyond the pale.[75] The Privy Council agreed. "There is no such act as this," it wrote, "in any other of his Majesty's plantations."[76]

The terms "contagious, epidemical and prevailing sickness" were too broad and "liable to great abuses," even as the penalties inflicted were disproportionately high.[77] "We are therefore humbly of opinion," the Privy Council reported, "that the inconvenience thereby intended to be prevented may be better provided against by order of the Governor and Council from time to time than by any standing Act of the General Assembly."[78] Massachusetts Bay disagreed. It immediately passed a new statute with minor alterations.[79] (Instead of applying broadly to all contagious diseases, the act specified plague, smallpox, and any "pestilential or malignant fever.")[80]

Many of the provisions adopted to counter the threat of disease proved insufficient. The colonies responded not by dispensing with such power, but by broadening their application and introducing increasingly harsh penalties. In 1714, for instance, the Massachusetts Bay General Assembly passed an act targeting vessels arriving from France and other parts of the Mediterranean.[81] Any shipmaster who failed to observe the mandatory forty-day period of isolation would be put to death.[82] Passengers coming ashore without express license from the governor and council would be liable to three years' imprisonment.[83]

Massachusetts Bay also adopted measures enabling it to perform domestic (land) quarantine and isolation. In 1742, for example, a statute targeting smallpox gave towns' selectmen the power to obtain a warrant to remove any persons "arriving from infected Places."[84] For those already residing in the colony, the head of the family became required to report anyone falling ill and to mount a red flag on the "most Publick Part of the infected House."[85] The flag would remain there " 'till the House in the Judgment of the Select-Men is thoroughly aired and cleansed, upon Penalty of forfeiting and paying the Sum of *fifty Pounds* for each Offence, one Half for the Informer, and the other Half for the Use of the Poor of the Town where such Offence shall be committed."[86] Refusal or inability to pay the fine was punishable by whipping, up to thirty stripes.[87] Where more than twenty families contracted the disease, such measures were waived.[88]

Several other colonies considered and adopted similar, extensive quarantine provisions. In New York, for instance, even under Dutch rule quarantine applied.[89] Under English rule, the governor and council issued further orders.[90] The Province of Pennsylvania also made use of quarantine.[91] In 1700 the

General Assembly introduced a statute prohibiting vessels arriving "from any unhealthy or sickly place" from coming closer than a mile from land, absent a clean bill of health.[92] Passengers and cargo could only come ashore with a permit from the local authorities.[93] A £100 penalty applied.[94] In 1719 the General Assembly of Rhode Island and Providence Plantations at Newport passed a law to prevent any vessel carrying smallpox "or any other Contagious Disease" from anchoring within one mile of any landing place.[95] The statute required license to land from the governor, or in his absence, from one or more justices of the peace, with failure to obtain such a license before landing carrying a penalty of £100.[96] If passengers or sailors came ashore, the justice of the peace could confine them "to any such Place, as to him shall seem convenient, for to prevent the spreading of any Infection."[97]

The threat did not just come from abroad: colonies frequently introduced measures to prevent the spread of disease within North America. In 1721, for instance, Rhode Island passed an act requiring all goods, wares, and merchandise from Massachusetts Bay to be transferred to islands offshore, "exposed to the Sun, and Aired and Cleansed, not exceeding ten Days, nor under six days, before they shall be permitted or suffered to be brought into any Dwelling House, Shop or Warehouse in any Town within this Colony."[98] Criminal penalties applied.[99] The law required innkeepers to report ill lodgers and authorized justices of the peace being to remove the sick "to any such Place as they shall think needful to prevent the spreading of the same."[100]

As aforementioned, many of these provisions proved unsuccessful. But instead of dispensing with such measures, the colonies often redoubled their efforts, introducing more powers and harsher penalties. Thus, as smallpox continued to plague Newport, in 1743 the colony repealed and reissued revised provisions.[101] No ship, from any port, with any person ill from any contagious disease would be allowed within a mile of shore.[102] The governor and justices of the peace could send medical personnel to confirm the health of the passengers.[103] The Town Council controlled all communications.[104] Two-thirds of the penalties incurred for breaking quarantine would be given to any informers.[105] All costs associated with addressing sickness on board the vessel—including the cost of ammunition for the town's guns forced to fire at the vessel to prevent it from coming into the harbor—was to be paid for by the vessel itself.[106] As for the health of the town's inhabitants, not only must inns submit health reports (with the justices of the peace empowered to remove anyone ill), but any inhabitant of the town could be forcibly removed from his or her home and placed in the local quarantine facility, "or any other convenient Place, in order to prevent the Spreading of the Infection."[107] Thus emerged the legal groundwork for the use of *cordon sanitaire*. Guards would be placed to prevent anyone from entering or leaving homes or other quarantine areas, absent a town license.[108] A fine accompanied any infractions, with half to be paid to any informers.[109]

The harshest penalties applied to knowing dissemination of disease. The law made it a crime to willfully or purposely spread smallpox within the colony.[110] Anyone found guilty of doing so would be put to death "without Benefit of the Clergy."[111] The attempt to spread disease earned a similarly stringent punishment: all individuals "legally convicted of wickedly endeavouring to spread [smallpox], shall be sentenced to be whipped, not exceeding *Thirty Nine Lashes*, and suffer Six Months Imprisonment, and be kept to hard Labour."[112]

B. The War of Independence

During the Revolutionary War, more than 130,000 colonists died from smallpox—an outbreak attributed at the time to British use of the disease as a weapon.[113] Reports first surfaced that the British were engaged in biological warfare during the siege of Boston. By 1781 further reports emerged of the deliberate spread of smallpox in Virginia.[114] Other accounts followed: the *Pennsylvania Gazette*, for instance, wrote, "Lord Cornwallis's attempt to spread the smallpox among the inhabitants in the vicinity of York, as been reduced to a certainty, and must render him contemptible in the eyes of every civilized nation."[115] Benjamin Franklin noted as much in his *Retort Curteous*.[116] Historian Elizabeth Anne Fenn writes, "It would be easy to dismiss these accusations as so much American hyperbole. But evidence indicates that in fact, the British did exactly what the Americans said they did."[117]

The disease had a significant impact on the colonists' effort to win independence. It decimated the Revolutionary Army at a critical time.[118] The colonies, however, responded not by introducing broader authorities or more stringent penalties, but by taking advantage of what little was known, scientifically, about the disease. In Massachusetts, for instance, new laws authorized justices of the court of general sessions in any county to establish inoculating hospitals.[119] In Rhode-Island and elsewhere, similar measures permitted widespread inoculation.[120]

Following the Revolution, despite the use of smallpox as a weapon, and the devastating impact of the disease, the states—not the federal government—continued to take the lead. Maryland, for example, which introduced quarantine regulations in 1766, continued the act in 1769, 1773, 1777, 1784, 1785, 1792, and 1799.[121] Upon reaching statehood, Maryland transferred quarantine authorities to its constitution. Article 33 empowers the governor to "order and compel any vessel to ride quarantine, if such vessel, or the port from which she shall have come, shall, on strong grounds, be suspected to be infected with the plague."[122] The governor's authority to quarantine appears in the same sentence as the governor's power, with the advice and consent of the council, to embody and direct the state militia, suggesting a close correlation between these authorities as an aspect of state sovereignty as well as state defense.[123] Concerned that even these provisions were insufficient, subsequent legislation expanded the governor's authority. From 1793 the governor's powers in regard to any malignant contagious disease, included the authority not just to prevent ships, goods, or persons from stepping on shore, but to prevent "all intercourse or communication," over land or water, between Maryland and any region where such sickness was present—both in the United States and abroad.[124] The governor thus had the authority to sever domestic relations. Quarantine was so decidedly local, that it overrode the union.

The context mattered: the union initially was not strong, as the failure of the Articles of Confederation was to attest. State measures provided the first and last line of defense. But even decades after the adoption of the U.S. Constitution, states continued to emphasize the autonomy of not just state but also local authorities in the exercise of quarantine and response to disease. Maryland, for instance, made arrangements for the appointment of a local health officer in Baltimore, who had the independent authority to authorize the quarantine of people and goods for up to thirty days.[125] Local ordinances continued this trend, with Baltimore passing measures in 1797, 1798, and 1800, making further provisions for quarantine and the establishment of a lazaretto to perfect the same.[126]

New York, Massachusetts, Pennsylvania, Delaware, Connecticut, Delaware, South Carolina, Rhode Island, and Virginia followed a similar pattern.[127]

Authorities extended well beyond maritime quarantine. In 1797, for instance, Massachusetts empowered selectmen to remove and isolate any sick persons found within the town boundaries.[128] Broad humanitarian contours applied: isolation must be given effect in the "best way … for the preservation of the inhabitants, by removing such sick or infected person or persons, and placing him or them in a separate house or houses, and by providing nurses, attendance, and other assistance and necessaries for them."[129] Like Maryland, Massachusetts drew a line between the state and the rest of the country. Towns could require that anyone arriving from a region in the United States in which contagious disease could be found to notify town authorities within two hours of their arrival.[130] Justices of the peace then had the authority to force any visitors to leave, with up to a $400 fine for lack of cooperation.[131] Any inhabitant of the town entertaining a visitor for more than two hours after the departure warrant had been issued could be fined.[132] Similar authorities, *pari passu*, were given to local authorities to prevent any baggage or goods originating outside the state from entering town boundaries.[133]

It was not just quarantine law that fell within local power. Broad public health concerns lay, too, within their reach. Massachusetts soon established a Board of Health in Boston, which focused on

> [all] such sources of filth as may be injurious to the health of the inhabitants of said town, whether the same shall proceed from stagnant waters, cellars, drains, common sewers, slaughter-houses, tan-yards, fish, fish-houses, fishing-boats, fish-boxes, oysters, oyster-boats, hogs, hog-sties, docks, necessaries, livery and other stables, putrid animal and vegetable substances, vessels, scows, or boats, or any other cause of any nature or kind whatsoever, which, in their opinion, may be injurious to the health of the inhabitants …[134]

Board members could make forcible entry to carry out their duties.[135] To this board also were assigned additional quarantine authorities, within which it had broad leeway.[136]

Some states went further. In 1794, for example, Connecticut introduced a statute allowing towns to exile any sick person carrying a contagious sickness, where such infection "may probably be communicated to others."[137] In the event that a suitable nurse could not be found, a warrant could be issued to *other* towns in Connecticut, requiring them to provide assistance.[138] A heavy fine attached. Where individuals became sick, with any infectious disease, the head of the family became required to fly a white flag, which could be removed only by the selectmen or by a justice of the peace.[139] In the event that contagious disease struck a town, all dog owners became required to "destroy their Dogs or cause them to be killed."[140] Anyone infecting any town in Connecticut, either by land or water, incurred a fine, with the selectmen ascertaining the length and manner of airing of all commercial goods.[141] Connecticut criminalized the transfer of smallpox, with the burden of proof shifted to the person thus accused.[142]

C. Federal Reticence

Throughout this time, public health was firmly in the hands of the states, which, in turn, delegated the authority to local entities to determine when and how to give effect to the provisions.[143] The national government proved reluctant to become involved. Indeed, its initial response was to duck and run: the first federal statute on the topic simply allowed Congress to reconvene outside the capitol where "the prevalence of contagious sickness" or "other circumstances ... hazardous to the lives or health of the members" should occur.[144] It was not until two decades after the Revolution that Congress directly addressed quarantine, at which time it passed a measure subordinating the national government to the states.[145] Repealed three years later, the statute allowed the president to provide assistance in enforcing quarantine, if states first requested it.[146]

Debates in Congress preceding enactment of the measure demonstrated uneasiness at curbing state rights and giving too much power to the federal government.[147] The original bill would have given the executive branch the authority to determine where quarantine stations would be located. The House of Representatives strongly objected. Quarantine lay within the states' purview.[148] Its impact on commerce paled in comparison to the importance of quarantine in maintaining public health, which lay at the heart of state police power.[149] Beyond the principled objections lay practical constraints: states were on the front line of defense, and communication with the national government took too much time.[150] It was for this reason that states had long been "in the habit of regulating quarantine, without consulting the General Government."[151] Life and death depended on speed.[152] And history proved important: states had previously introduced such measures—*quod erat demonstrandum*, quarantine must be a state power.[153] The few who supported a stronger federal role heavily relied on the Commerce Clause in their assertions.[154] They argued that as a practical matter, moreover, the federal government had the authority—and resources—to ensure compliance.[155] But their pleas fell on deaf ears, and the bill passed, absent the offensive language.

The federal government thus embarked on a path that subordinated it to state interests. Thus, when Congress created the first marine hospital in 1796, the institution was left in local control.[156] Three years later Congress repealed the act, giving Treasury the authority to require that U.S. officers assist in executing quarantine laws, consistent with state health provisions.[157] (In recognition of constitutional limitations, the statute explicitly noted that alterations to duties of tonnage would require further congressional approval.)[158] With the federal government in a supportive role, the debates preceding adoption of the bill did not center on state rights.[159] Nevertheless, the statute marked the first forays of the federal government into the quarantine domain, by creating a federal inspection system for maritime quarantine.[160] Under Treasury's auspices, the national government could now obtain information about the spread of disease along the Eastern seaboard.[161] Subsequent orders issued by the Secretary of the Treasury reiterated that Marine Hospital Service Officers, customs officials, and revenue officers were to cooperate in enforcing local quarantine law and regulations.[162]

By the nineteenth century, public health generally, and quarantine in particular, had become firmly established as within the state domain. Accordingly, in *Gibbons v. Ogden*, Chief Justice Marshall described state police powers as:

> That immense mass of legislation, which embraces every thing within the territory of a State, not surrendered to the general government: all which can be most advantageously exercised by the States themselves. Inspection laws, quarantine laws, health laws of every description, as well as laws for regulating the internal commerce of a State . . .[163]

Marshall's articulation summarized the state of play and became its own source of authority. The attorney general subsequently relied on *Gibbons* to explain to the Secretary of the Treasury why the federal government could not itself issue quarantine regulations.[164] State courts concurred.[165] The states steadily expanded their reach into the public health arena, establishing local boards of health and delegating to them when, where, and in what manner quarantine would be given effect.[166]

II. Establishing the Federal Domain

While public health and quarantine remained central to state interests, the commercial implications of domestic and international (retributive) quarantine gradually attracted more federal attention.[167] Debates between contagionists and noncontagionists slowly shifted the conversation. During the Civil War, the Confederate Army harnessed disease as a weapon; but stronger calls for federal control did not immediately follow. Instead, economic concerns played a key role. The formation of the Marine Hospital Service, and its more effective use of quarantine, added weight to a federal solution. Encouraged by judicial opinions, Congress began to legislate in this area. Thus, by the early twentieth century, although some actions had been taken in this realm, the federal government had yet to preempt the states, which continued to exercise their authorities. In the end, direct confrontation between state police powers and potential Commerce Clause claims was avoided through congressional leverage of the Spending Clause. Treasury bought up the ports, thus the authority to exercise maritime quarantine. Gradually these authorities extended the interior as the Public Health Act, and, later, the Stafford Act provided federal authority to impose quarantine.

A. Foreign Relations

European powers, all of whom had long experience with quarantine as a way to stem the introduction of disease, considered the American system to be outdated and ineffective. Ships arriving in the United States from Central and South America, prior to making the voyage across the Atlantic, were not subjected to particularly rigorous inspection; nor did the United States require bills of health or other assurances from ships departing from U.S. shores. The new country's vessels thus soon found themselves subject to stringent measures targeting trade, requiring American vessels, upon arriving in Europe, to remain in quarantine longer than those of other countries. Efforts to convince Spain, England, and others to change these provisions, however, fell on deaf ears. Foreign countries simply did not trust vessels coming from the United States.[168]

Part of the problem with the U.S. approach was, precisely, its localization: the manner in which inspections and quarantine operated varied significantly between ports: different rules, standards, and levels of compliance marked the localized approach to public health. Two problems thus presented themselves to the federal government: the first centered on U.S. foreign relations and the impact the localized system was having on U.S. trade abroad. The second stemmed from the domestic field, as the uneven application of public health measures led to increased trade difficulties within the country as well.[169] Congress began to lament the local system as provincial and unscientific.[170]

> Considering the magic influence of names, it were to be wished that the term quarantine should be erased from the statute books of the Union, and of each particular State. Regulations, precise and explicit, should, in the opinion of your committee, be formed to prevent foul and infectious vessels, with sickly crews, from entering our ports, or proceeding on any voyage in that situation.[171]

A uniform federal system would help to ensure stronger sanitary provisions and alleviate European concern about vessels arriving from the United States.[172]

Two civil reform groups leant momentum to the political interest in federal control. Contagionists, believing that disease transferred by individuals coming into contact with each other, sought a more stringent and uniform federal system.[173] Anticontagionists advocated for better national sanitation and an end to the local (indeed, any) quarantine regime.[174] Either way, a federal solution, predicated on the Commerce Clause, provided the answer. The Committee on External Hygiene explained:

> We consider that quarantine from its close connection with the U.S. Revenue Department, and the important bearing which it has upon commerce (which Congress alone can regulate) and upon travellers soon to be disperse throughout different and distant States of the Union, is a national, rather than a State concern, and we cannot conceive that a uniform system of quarantine can be established throughout the Union unless it be organized . . . as a national institution.[175]

A series of National Quarantine and Sanitary conventions focused on not if, but how to reform the system and to transfer control to the federal government.[176] But such meetings immediately ceased as the country fell into the Civil War.

As during the Revolutionary War, disease became a weapon. Scholars report that the Confederacy tried to spread yellow fever, smallpox, and other diseases among Union soldiers and civilians.[177] Plans ranged from sending infected individuals behind enemy lines and distributing goods carrying contagion, to contaminating water sources.[178] In 1863 this method of warfare prompted the Union to issue an order outlawing the use of such techniques.[179]

Natural outbreaks of disease during the war further illustrated the degree to which states depended on other regions to prevent the transfer of disease.[180] But state rights still trumped. In 1865 the administration brought forward a bill to give the Secretary of War, with the assistance of the secretaries of the Navy and Treasury, the authority to enforce quarantine at all ports of entry, as well as domestic *cordon sanitaire*.[181] Senators were incredulous. Henry B. Anthony (R-RI) questioned the chair of the Commerce Committee on the extent of the proposed authorities. "[All] the powers at their command may be used if necessary," Senator Zachariah Chandler replied.[182] Shocked, Anthony inquired whether the Secretary of War could impose martial law to stem the tide of disease. Chandler answered that they could "use any power requisite to stop the cholera." Anthony objected: "I would rather have the cholera than such a proposition as this."[183]

Historian Les Benedict explains, "Although during the Civil War a growing number of people were demanding vigorous exercise of national authority, most Americans still regarded general police regulation—the ordinary day-to-day legislation affecting crime, health, sanitation, personal property, etc.—to be the responsibility primarily of the states."[184] Many congressional members considered state and national quarantine authority, as in interstate commerce, to be mutually exclusive.[185] Lot M. Morrill (R-ME), maintained, "All sanitary regulations touching the health of this country within the jurisdictional limits of the several States are matters of police regulations."[186] While the Civil War thus may have marked an important step in the evolution of American federalism, it was not immediately reflected in the realm of public health. By the late nineteenth century, however, things started to change.

B. Economic Considerations and the Commerce Clause

Federal initiatives remained highly sensitive to state concerns. The move toward greater federal involvement, when it did come, was not one grounded in war or national security, but rather economic concerns: namely, the impact of disease on trade and the costs of maintaining a robust system. Institutional reforms, which allowed the federal government to have greater insight into the introduction and transfer of disease, and scientific advances, which moved quarantine to a rational-based system, here mattered.[187]

In 1878 Congress introduced a new quarantine act.[188] The statute marked the federal government's first assertion of control over quarantine, yet important limits applied: regulations could govern only the arrival of ships from foreign ports.[189] They could not run afoul of state or municipal authorities.[190] The statute also created a worldwide surveillance system, requiring U.S. officers based overseas to send weekly reports on the health of foreign ports and to immediately inform the supervising surgeon general of the outbreak of any contagious diseases abroad.[191] Congress made further provision for underwriting scientific research on "the origin and causes of epidemic diseases, especially yellow fever and cholera, and the best method of preventing their introduction and spread."[192]

The following year Congress expanded the number of federal quarantine stations and created a national board of health.[193] Again, restrictions emphasized the primacy of the states: the members of the board were directed to cooperate with and to help the local and state boards of health, with their responsibilities limited to matters concerning cholera, smallpox, and yellow fever. This time, however, Congress considerably loosened the purse strings, which was to prove critical in the transfer of authorities to the federal government. The statute allowed Treasury to buy up local ports, in the process assuming responsibility for stopping disease at the borders. Local entities could voluntarily relinquish their authority, in return for financial remuneration and preventing further drains on state coffers. Three years later, Congress freed up money for states to request (and receive) up to $100,000 to assist in the event of an actual or threatened epidemic.[194]

Even as early success stories involving the Marine Hospital Service lent momentum to a new federal role,[195] frustration about the current system grew. State measures were reactive and failed to take into account broader public health needs.[196] The federal government had to wait until states requested assistance—which meant that it was not until epidemics were underway that they could act.[197] Local health laws, focused on local interests, had become corrupted by "the commercial interests of rival ports, the partisan struggles of opposing political factions, and the heedless parsimony with which money has been doled out."[198] Ports of entry lacked incentives to protect inland areas.[199] Sanitary measures fell short: placing immigrants arriving with a multitude of sicknesses in crowded, poorly ventilated, and unsanitary quarters, and then sending them throughout the United States begged credulity.[200]

Proponents of a stronger federal role argued that it would, in contrast, create a uniform approach and ensure that the costs were shared. The result would be better training for immigration officers and, by stopping disease at the borders, the alleviation of barriers to interstate trade. The federal government could shift its resources to ports in need, avoiding the quagmire of local politics.[201] A consensus among leaders in medicine, industry, and politics slowly emerged: the federal government needed to be in charge.[202]

A timely case spurred the courts to consider the contours of state and federal authority. At issue in *Morgan's Steamship v. Louisiana Board of Health* was the right of the state legislators to require vessels entering the Mississippi River to be examined and to pay a fee for the inspection.[203] The shipping company challenged the statute on the grounds that the measures imposed tonnage duties and interfered with the federal regulation of commerce.[204] The Supreme Court rejected this argument, saying that the precautions taken by the state were "part of and inherent in every system of quarantine." Despite the impact of quarantine on commerce, such matters were reserved to the states—*at least until invalidated by Congress*:

> [It] may be conceded that whenever Congress shall undertake to provide for the commercial cities of the United States a general system of quarantine, or shall confide the execution of the details of such a system to a National Board of Health, or to local boards, as may be found expedient, all State laws on this subject will be abrogated, at least so far as the two are inconsistent. But until this is done, the laws of the State on this subject are valid.[205]

No longer, then, as Marshall had articulated in 1824, did public health and quarantine lie solely within the state domain, but now the federal government could potentially act in this arena. Congress readily accepted the invitation.

Over the next five years, federal initiatives followed on nearly an annual basis.[206] A relatively important change came in 1890, when Congress gave permission to Treasury to issue regulations to prevent the interstate spread of cholera, yellow-fever, smallpox, and plague.[207] The statute carried criminal penalties: it became a misdemeanor for any U.S. officer or agent to violate federal quarantine laws.[208] Common carriers warranted stronger punishment for violations.[209]

Another important change came in 1893, when Congress repealed the 1879 legislation.[210] The statute required the supervising surgeon-general to conduct a study of all state and municipal boards of health and to help both the states and the federal government enforce the rules in force. It also gave Treasury the authority to enact further regulations where state and municipal ordinances did not exist or were inadequate. State and local officers would enforce federal regulations voluntarily; absent such cooperation, the federal government would enforce them itself.[211] Treasury could purchase warehouses to hold goods subject to quarantine under either state or federal regulations, with the secretary authorized to prolong the period of retention (at Treasury's expense), subject to state law.[212] The legislation required that all vessels entering U.S. waters from foreign ports first obtain a bill of health from U.S. officers overseas. When infected vessels arrived, Treasury could remand the vessel, at its own expense, to the nearest quarantine station.[213] To the president was given the authority to prohibit the introduction of individuals or goods from any designated region in which contagious disease was prevalent.[214] Treasury could receive any state buildings and disinfecting equipment, and pay reasonable compensation for the same, where considered necessary to defend the U.S. against disease.[215]

The judiciary continued to hold the line drawn in *Morgan's Steamship*. In 1902, Justice White explained that states had the power to enact and enforce laws to prevent, eradicate, and control the spread of contagious or infectious diseases.[216] Such authority could be preempted.

> [W]henever Congress shall undertake to provide . . . a general system of quarantine, or shall confide the execution of the details of such a system to a national board of health, or to local boards, as may be found expedient, all state laws on the subject will be abrogated, at least so far as the two are inconsistent.[217]

But until the legislature acted, "such state quarantine laws and state laws for the purpose of preventing, eradicating or controlling the spread of contagious or infectious diseases, are not repugnant to the constitution."[218] Three years later, Justice Marshall Harlan reiterated, "Upon the principle of self-defense, of paramount necessity, a community has the right to protect itself against an epidemic of disease which threatens the safety of its members."[219] Like quarantine, the compulsory smallpox vaccination at issue in *Jacobson v. Massachusetts* was a legitimate exercise of state police power to protect public health.[220]

States continued to consider public health as central to state police powers.[221] In 1913, however, another incremental shift militated in favor of federal power. The Supreme Court responded to the *Minnesota Rate Cases* by suggesting that states were free to adopt only quarantine regulations that did not conflict with federal statutory or regulatory initiatives: "In view of the need of conforming such measures to local conditions, Congress from the beginning has been content to leave the matter for the most part, notwithstanding its vast importance, to the States and has repeatedly acquiesced in the enforcement of State laws."[222] The subtle undertones of the decision suggested not that the states had the ultimate authority, but that it was only by leave of Congress that they could act in this area.

Throughout this time, federal agencies continued to assist the states and quietly accept the responsibility of running the quarantine system in what one mid-twentieth-century scholar referred to as "a process of accretion and erosion."[223] In 1921 the last state (New York) transferred its quarantine facilities.[224] The federal government at that point controlled roughly 100 stations and inspected some 2 million passengers and crew and 20,000 vessels per year.[225] Surgeon General Hugh Cumming noted:

> The transition of a quarantine system, composed of units operated by the municipal or state authorities, to a compact federal organization has been gradual, but persistent. One after another cities and states have transferred their quarantine stations to the national Government, so that, with the passing of the New York Quarantine Station from state to national control on March 1, 1921, the Public Health Service now administers every station in the United States and in the Hawaiian Islands, the Philippines, Porto Rico, and the Virgin Islands.[226]

Cumming proclaimed it the triumph of science over politics.

C. Current Federal Authorities

Within about two decades of the federal government assuming control of the ports, Congress passed measures giving the executive branch the authority to place individuals and goods in quarantine. This legislation, the 1944 Public Health Service Act,[227] is one of two pillars on which the current federal system rests. The second is the 1988 Robert T. Stafford Disaster Relief and Emergency Assistance Act.[228]

Under the former, the Secretary of Health and Human Services (HHS) has the authority to make and enforce regulations necessary "to prevent the introduction, transmission, spread of communicable diseases from foreign countries into the states or possessions, or from one State or possession into any other State or possession."[229] Quarantine can be exercised only for diseases listed in Executive Order 13295. Since 1983, cholera, diphtheria, infectious tuberculosis, plague, smallpox, yellow fever, and viral hemorrhagic fevers have been included. In April 2003 President Bush added SARS, and the following year, pandemic influenza.[230] The Secretary of HHS may apprehend and examine any individual reasonably believed to be infected with a designated disease in a qualifying stage and (1) moving or being about to move between states, or (2) a probable source of infection to individuals who may be moving between states.[231] Where infection is found, HHS can detain the individual for such a time, and in such as manner as may be reasonably necessary.[232] Current regulations prohibit infected individuals from traveling across state lines without explicit approval from a health officer of the destination region, if applicable under their law.[233] CDC maintains control over individuals arriving from foreign countries, while the surgeon general has the power to prohibit designated persons or goods from entering the United States altogether.[234]

The above regulations focus on regular authorities during peacetime. In times of war, special powers apply. The Secretary of HHS, in consultation with the surgeon general, may indefinitely detain individuals reasonably believed to be infected, and a probable source of infection to members of the armed forces of the United States or to individuals engaged in the production or transportation of supplies to the armed forces.[235] Unlike peacetime authorities, it is not necessary for an individual to be in a qualifying stage of infection. Eligible diseases continue to be limited by Executive Order 13295.

The surgeon general controls all quarantine stations and may establish whatever new stations may be considered necessary.[236] Overseas consulates are required to report on diseases overseas, consistent with rules set forth by the surgeon general.[237] Bills of health continue to be required for all vessels entering or leaving U.S. water and air space.[238] Violation of general federal quarantine provisions is punishable as a criminal misdemeanor, with the violations of specific orders subject to a fine of up to $250,000, or one year in jail, or both.[239] Federal District Courts may enjoin individuals and organizations from violating CDC regulations.[240]

The second piece of legislation marking the framework is the Robert T. Stafford Disaster Relief and Emergency Assistance Act.[241] This legislation is the legacy of the eighteenth-century measures designed to allow the federal government to respond to requests for assistance in the event of an emergency. In 2000 the Disaster Mitigation Act amended the Stafford Act to encourage state, local, and tribal areas to coordinate planning prior to actual disasters.[242]

Two types of declaration may be made under the Stafford Act: a major disaster declaration consistent with Title IV, and an emergency declaration under Title V. The former depends upon a state governor making a formal request to the president for federal assistance. Such help can apply only to natural catastrophes, or, regardless of their source, actual fires, floods, or explosions. The language, then, does not appear to include non-natural incidents, such as criminal activity, terrorist attacks, or acts of war (although it would include any fires, floods, or explosions thereby resulting). In order to qualify for assistance, states must have previously implemented a plan in coordination with the federal government. The president has the option of declining the request.[243] While the statute does not explicitly mention quarantine, it does give the executive the ability to provide health and safety measures (presumably included the detention of those suspected of carrying contagious disease).[244] There is no limit on the amount of funds that can be requested.

Under Title V, an emergency declaration may be made either pursuant to the request of a governor, or the president may simply declare an emergency in which the incident involves an area of "primary Federal responsibility." For the former, the decision to grant the request is discretionary. There are no limits on the type of emergency for which help is requested, but the total amount that can be obtained is limited to $5 million per declaration.[245] For the latter, it is not entirely clear what constitutes an area of primary responsibility. Rather, the statute provides a general category—that is, "subject area[s] for which, under the Constitution or laws of the United States, the United States exercises exclusive or preeminent responsibility and authority."[246] In practice, unilateral declarations have tended to involve federal property. In such cases, FEMA has primary responsibility (arguably bypassing the Secretary of DHS altogether).

Quarantine measures continue to be in flux. Most recently, the Centers for Disease Control have proposed new regulations that would structure quarantine along the incubation period of each disease, as well as allow for administrative review. As noted at the beginning of this chapter, these regulations are but one part of a much broader movement to address biological weapons and pandemic disease. The Department of Health and Human Services, the Centers for Disease Control, the Department of Homeland Security, and the Department of Defense, among other agencies and departments, have taken steps to engage more fully with the twin threats. Three observations about the recent measures follow: first, they tend to link biological weapons and naturally occurring disease, seeing both as a national security threat; second, they emphasize quarantine and isolation as a potential response; and third, they anticipate the use of the military to enforce social distancing provisions. As outlined in the above sections, the recent changes represent a second major shift that has occurred in the United States in the realm of public health and quarantine law. The first shift—that is, the move to a stronger national role— raises some constitutional concerns. But it is the second shift that proves most concerning.

III. Constitutional and Policy Challenges Going Forward

In the early twentieth century the move to federal control over the introduction of disease and its transfer between the states marked an uneasy detente between the powers reserved to the states through the Tenth Amendment and Commerce Clause authorities. Practical economic concerns and the Spending Clause proved critical in carving out a federal role.

The most recent shift, however, raises a number of further constitutional concerns. The placement of pandemic disease and biological weapons within a national security framework overlays public health with authorities more common to the federal government in time of war. When the country is on a war footing, wider powers, which tend to sidestep the checks that would ordinarily apply, take the place of ordinary civilian authorities. Rights alter, becoming narrower.[247] The courts become increasingly reluctant to second-guess the executive branch, and civilian agencies become less important than the militarized branch of government.[248] States, in turn, play an even more constricted role.

Scholars have considered many of the rights issues inherent in broader quarantine authorities, such as Fifth Amendment due process and the writ of habeas corpus under the Suspension Clause.[249] The courts, though, have yet to address many of the most important questions in this realm, such as how long an individual may be held in quarantine or isolation before a hearing is required, precisely what procedures may satisfy due process, or what evidence must be produced to justify restrictions on liberty. Nor have courts considered the level of direction that must be given, and the degree of noncompliance required, to justify forcible detention.[250] Challenges have also been raised on takings grounds; here, too, the record is fairly sparse.[251]

Beyond these concerns, almost no attention has been paid to the structural issues that present themselves: specifically, the articulation of public health as an Article II claim, the role of the military in executing quarantine and isolation on domestic soil, the limits of federal Commerce Clause authorities in light of Tenth Amendment state police powers, and evolution of Necessary and Proper Clause jurisprudence. Additionally, at least two important policy considerations attend: the extent to which biological weapons concerns may achieve preeminence and thus drive the subsequent public health discussion; and whether quarantine and isolation should be looked to as a first response. While it is not the intent of this chapter to conclusively explore these concerns, each deserves comment.

A. *Public Health as Article II War Powers*

The first and perhaps most important structural question that presents itself relates to the shift in collapsing pandemic disease and biological weapons into a national security framework. The most recent U.S. *National Security Strategy*, issued in May 2010, cites, inter alia, weapons of mass destruction, pandemic disease, natural disasters, and terrorism as pressing national security concerns.[252] As was discussed at the start of this chapter, extensive documents anticipate a dual response and treatment of both threats from a similar position. Coupled with movement by the Department of Defense into this area, the specter of treating public health concerns within an emergency framing presents itself. At the broadest level, this suggests an end run around the uneasy accommodation between state police powers and Commerce Clause considerations, pushing the constitutional analysis into an Article II realm.

The Constitution divides war powers between the executive and legislative branches. In Article II, it falls to the president to execute the powers of commander-in-chief.[253] Under Article I, Congress is imbued with the authority to declare war and to appropriate U.S. treasure for the same.[254] To the legislature also is given the authority to call forth the militia, suppress insurrections, and repel invasions.[255] Between these, a sort of "twilight zone" of concurrent authorities operates.[256] As Justice Jackson famously suggested in *Youngstown*, where the president acts with congressional authorization, his authority within this area of concurrent power is at its zenith.[257] Thus, where statutory measures, such as the changes to the 2007 Defense Authorization Act, explicitly award the president the authority to use the military to respond to natural disasters, pandemic disease, or terrorist attack, the president appears to be acting in full power.

But Congress did not end its treatment of the federal role in regard to quarantine with the passage of the 2007 statute. Instead, as discussed above, in response to strong opposition from state governors, the relevant provisions were subsequently withdrawn. Resultantly, in the event of pandemic disease, at least as a matter of the president's commander-in-chief authorities, a strong argument could be marshaled that the president would be acting neither in the zone of explicit congressional approval, nor absence of the same, but at the "lowest ebb": that is, where Congress has explicitly withdrawn such authority. Admittedly, withdrawing a power is not the same as affirmatively denying its existence. At a minimum, however, the explicit withdrawal of congressional consent suggests a lower threshold than that of legislative sanction.

So the framing of pandemic disease as a national security concern—particularly where the initial outbreak of disease may or may not have arisen from a biological weapons attack—gives rise to the question of where the president's defensive power ends and Congress's authority over the decision to take the nation to war begins. As a textual matter, Congress has the power to initiate a condition of war. The president does not. Conversely, the president has the power to conduct war. Congress does not. The careful selection of the word "declare," rather than "make" appears to have been designed to retain in the president the traditional authority to defend the nation against, or "repel," sudden or imminent attacks—that is, a defensive war power. It also appears to sidestep any suggestion that Congress's power to declare war also carries the authority to manage the conduct of the war. So what happens if the president responds to an outbreak of disease as an act of war, on the grounds that such events may or may not stem from biological attack? Does the president have the authority to do so?

Consider the question of mobilization—that is, the decision to employ the country's armed forces to respond to a potential pandemic (or biological weapons attack). For much of the modern period, executive practice with regard to the commitment of troops and use of the military has substantially departed from the constitutional text. The Korean War (1950–53), the Cuban missile crisis, Kosovo (1999), the recent bombing of Libya (2011), and a broad range of covert operations (such as the invasion of Grenada [1983]) have involved substantial military commitments that occurred outside explicit congressional approval or declaration of war. If an epidemic or outbreak of disease were to be classed as an act of war, in what sort of capacity could the military be used and for what duration?

The 1973 War Powers Resolution, passed in response to perceived overexpansion of unilateral presidential war-making with regard to Vietnam, is here relevant.[258] This legislation authorizes the president to use military force in three circumstances: declaration of war, specific statutory authorization, or national emergency.[259] The president must consult Congress in every possible instance. Any military action must be reported within forty-eight hours, and use of the forces must terminate within sixty days of a report to Congress, unless war is declared, a sixty-day extension is granted by Congress, or Congress is physically unable to meet. There is a sense in which this statute, coupled with a failure to terminate presidential military action, has implicitly created a sixty-day "safe harbor" for unilateral presidential action.

Successive administrations, beginning with Nixon, have questioned the constitutionality of the War Powers Resolution.[260] They have argued that it is an unconstitutional usurpation of Article II authority, undermines US foreign policy, fails to require positive congressional action, and undermines executive and legislative branch cooperation.[261] These arguments can be challenged: as a textual matter, it falls to Congress, not the president, to move the country to a state of war. If one grants the constitutionality of the resolution, then the statute may apply to situations in which the president seeks to use the military in response to a perceived pandemic or biological weapons attack. The limits, however, laid out in the statute would apply.

The debates over the War Powers Resolution, however, have been predicated largely on the president's use of the military overseas.[262] What happens when the question becomes the use of the military on domestic soil? Constitutional jurisprudence here is particularly thin. In 1862 the *Prize Cases* were argued before the Supreme Court, which considered the constitutionality of President Lincoln's blockade of Southern ports.[263] Justice Robert Grier, writing for the Court, suggested that the president, as commander-in-chief of the armed forces, had a broad range of power, including instituting a blockade.[264] Although Congress had not explicitly declared war, it had, in that instance, adopted a statute that ratified the Emancipation Proclamation. Consisting of two executive orders, the proclamation explicitly rested on the president's military power to seize and confiscate enemy resources in times of military engagement.[265] Regardless of the proclamation, however, the Court considered the president's actions constitutional.

The *Prize Cases* stand, first, for the proposition that the president's power to respond to military attacks on the United States does not depend on Congress having declared war. This is part of the executive power retained by the president, confirmed in the Commander-in-Chief Clause. Second, regardless of whether a war is formally declared, the president, as commander-in-chief, possesses the full executive power with respect to the conduct of military hostilities. Would, however, responding to a pandemic potentially stemming from a biological weapons attack qualify as military hostilities?

It may be, at the outset of a pandemic, nearly impossible to ascertain whether the spread of the disease is due to natural causes, terrorist attack, or an act of war levied by another country against the United States. Consider plague. Long a mainstay in biological weapons arsenals, the disease is also naturally occurring. A traveler from Algeria could contract the disease, return to the United States, attend community events, and eventually appear at a hospital for treatment. Initially, it may not be clear whether the individual accidentally contracted the disease or is being used as a vector by which to spread it throughout the country and to take out U.S. medical facilities. In either case, the effects on the country from the carrier's initial actions would be largely the same. And either way, significant resources may be necessary to mitigate the effects of the disease.

What authorities does the president have in such a circumstance? Can the president use the military—and to what extent? As a constitutional matter, a stronger case can be made for Article II powers in the event of known biological weapons usage and, particularly, known use of biological agents by another country. It may be, however, impossible to know at the outset if such circumstances hold. Should the executive be given power in anticipation of such a result? If not, does it make sense to leave the determination of when Article II comes into play in the hands of the executive branch—which then benefits from a significant and radical expansion in its authority? There is a certain conflict of interest in allowing the president to essentially determine the contours of executive power. If there is no overt enemy in regard to which war can be declared, then further questions arise with regard to what limits, if any, can be placed on the executive.

This leads naturally to the question of whether Congress would need to pass, for instance, an explicit authorization for the use of the military. On at least three occasions the legislature has authorized use of the armed forces short of declaring war.[266] While argument can be made that this still falls short of the constitutional provisions that require Congress to declare war—instituted precisely to set the bar high and to avoid use of the military absent legislative approval—it may be the best vehicle to ensure constitutional compliance. This analysis, however, still begs the question of the specific role of the military on U.S. soil.

B. Role of the Military

The 1807 Insurrection Act governs the president's authority to deploy troops within domestic bounds.[267] Like the Stafford Act, the statute requires that whenever an insurrection occurs, "the President may, upon the request of the legislature or of its governor if the legislature cannot be convened, call into Federal service such of the militia of the other States, in the number requested by that State, and use such of the armed forces, as he considers necessary to suppress the insurrection."[268] Absent a governor's request, in the event that the president "considers that unlawful obstructions, combinations, or assemblages, or rebellion against the authority of the United States, make it impracticable to enforce the laws of the United States . . . by the ordinary course of judicial proceedings," the militia and armed forces can be used.[269] Such measures, however, are explicitly directed to suppressing "any insurrection, domestic violence, unlawful combination, or conspiracy," where such violence interferes with execution of use laws or operation of the courts.[270]

A few observations about this language can be made. First, the mere incidence of sickness—natural pandemic or biological weapons–related in origins—is insufficient to justify military intervention. The statute explicitly requires an actual breakdown in law and order. Hypothetical risks are insufficient. Second, even if violence does result from an epidemic, the role of the military appears to be limited to suppressing the violence—not responding to the medical needs of the population by, for instance, distributing and administering vaccines, transporting ill patients, testing blood samples, treating the ill, performing quarantine and isolation on civilians, establishing triage stations, and the like. The changes made to the Insurrection Act by the 2007 Defense Authorization Act would have allowed the president to federalize the National Guard to respond to a "natural disaster, epidemic or other serious public health emergency, terrorist attack or incident," in the event that the president unilaterally determined that "authorities of the state or possession are incapable of maintaining public order." But these were precisely the changes subsequently rejected by Congress.

Even considering the role of the military in a law enforcement capacity, it is to be remembered that the Framers evinced considerable concern about standing armies.[271] Following Reconstruction, such concerns became enshrined in the Posse Comitatus Act, which significantly limited the powers of the federal government to use the armed forces to conduct law enforcement.[272] Under the Posse Comitatus Act, "Whoever, except in cases and under circumstances expressly authorized by the Constitution or Act of Congress, willfully uses any part of the Army or the Air Force as a *posse comitatus* or otherwise to execute the laws shall be fined under this title or imprisoned not more than two years, or both."[273] Congress later added proscription against use of armed forces to make arrests or conduct searches and seizures. Most recently, Congress expressed its sense reaffirming the continued importance and applicability of the Posse Comitatus Act when it established the Department of Homeland Security, leaving open the use of the armed forces for law enforcement when authorized by act of Congress or the president to fulfill constitutional obligations to respond "in time of war, insurrection, or other serious emergency."[274]

This language does constitute a statutory, not a constitutional, limit. Indeed, as a constitutional matter, it could be argued that the Posse Comitatus Act is itself an unconstitutional limit on the powers of the president. In light of the statute, however, two distinct challenges could be brought to the role of the military in establishing and enforcing quarantine and isolation measures in response to either naturally occurring pandemic or the spread of an engineered agent: (a) the type of activities in which Title 10 troops engage in the performance of quarantine; and (b) the conditions under which the government may federalize Title 32 troops, removing them from state control. The courts have yet to rule on these difficult questions.

C. Marking the Boundaries of the Commerce Clause

Setting aside for the moment the constitutional issues embedded in linking and placing pandemic disease and biological weapons within a national security framework, broader constitutional questions about the extent to which the federal government can act in public health persist. Public health law lies at the heart of state police powers. Questions remain about the extent to which Commerce Clause authorities empower the federal government to legislate in this realm. The Tenth Amendment itself remains silent on the precise scope of the powers reserved to the states—or to the people.[275] Precious little consideration of the contours of the authorities reserved to the states can be found in the papers of those present at the constitutional convention.[276] Yet what becomes clear from the historical exposition of quarantine provisions in the nineteenth century, discussed above, is that their impact on commerce was insufficient to altogether wrench them from the grasp of state power.

Chief Justice Marshall thus noted in 1824 that quarantine lay at the very heart of those authorities reserved to the states.[277] Thirty years later, Justice Grier explained that internal police powers, which included every law introduced for the preservation of public health, "are not surrendered by the states, or restrained by the Constitution of the United States, and that consequently, in relation to these, the authority of a state is complete, unqualified, and conclusive."[278] No federal regulation could "supersede or restrain their operations, on any ground of prerogative or supremacy."[279] Quarantine, whatever its impact on commerce, lay at the core of state police power:

> [Q]uarantine laws, which protect the public health, compel mere commercial regulations to submit to their control. They restrain the liberty of the passengers, they operate on the ship which is the instrument of commerce, and its officers and crew, the agents of navigation. They seize the infected cargo and cast it overboard. The soldier and the sailor, though in the service of the government, are arrested,

imprisoned, and punished for their offenses against society. ... All these things are done not from any power which the states assume to regulate commerce or to interfere with the regulations of Congress, but because police laws for the preservations of health, prevention of crime, and protection of the public welfare must of necessity have full and free operation according to the exigency which requires their interference.[280]

The exigencies of the social compact required that such state laws "be executed before and above all others."[281]

Accordingly, in 1868 Thomas Cooley explained, "Numerous ... illustrations might be given of the power in the States to make regulations affecting commerce, and which are sustainable as regulations of police. Among these," he continued, "quarantine regulations and health laws of every description will readily suggest themselves, and these are or may be sometimes carried to the extent of ordering the destruction of private property when infected with disease or otherwise dangerous."[282] Such regulations, at least with regard to Commerce Clause considerations, "generally passed unchallenged."[283] In 1886 the influential legal commentator Christopher Tiedeman further noted:

> This police power of the State extends to the protection of the lives, limbs, health, comfort and quiet of all persons, and the protection of all property within the State. According to the maxim, sic utere tuo, ut alienum non laedas, it being of universal application, it must of course be within the range of legislative action to define the mode and manner in which every one may so use his own as not to injure others. Any law which goes beyond that principle, which undertakes to abolish rights, the exercise of which does not involve an infringement of the rights of others, or to limit the exercise of rights beyond what is necessary to provide for the public welfare and the general security, cannot be included in the police power of the government.[284]

That same year, as a matter of case law, *Morgan's Steamship*, followed in 1902 by *Compagnie Francaise*, acknowledged the strong role of the states in public health—while leaving the door open to federal preemption. In 1905 *Jacobson* placed even more weight on the side of the states, reiterating Marshall's position in *Gibbons*.

As a matter of constitutional law, then, despite a significant impact on commerce, it appears that the exercise of quarantine by the states is to a great extent protected. This does not mean that the federal government has no role to play. *Morgan's Steamship* and *Compagnie Francaise*, as noted above, both left open the possibility of preemption. Encouraged by the Court's position, Congress did begin to legislate, and in 1963 the Court upheld challenge to federal quarantine.[285] At that time, the World Health Organization had declared Stockholm to be a smallpox-infected area. When a passenger from Stockholm arrived in the United States and was not able to produce documentation showing that vaccination had taken place, the Public Health Service quarantined the passenger for fourteen days. The District Court noted that the federal government had acted in good faith, that the individual had had a history of unsuccessful vaccinations, and that detention during the incubation period was required to determine whether the individual had been infected. The case, however, left unanswered the structural questions that bedevil the line between state and federal authorities. While the federal government may be able to preempt the states in some areas related to quarantine, the authority to impose the same at a state level is still firmly rooted in the powers reserved to the states.

The uneasy compromise that has been reached is that quarantine provisions related to the country's borders, such as along the coastlines or on the Canadian or Mexican border, fall firmly within the federal domain. But what happens when every airport, seaport, and bus or train station becomes a point of entry or interstate transfer? Does the federal government have the authority to quarantine and isolate *all* travelers? This is the current position of the federal government for interior quarantine—that is, coming into contact with individuals who may be about to move between states. But is this a meaningful limit on federal power? While one could devise a remote mountain scenario, where such contact would be unlikely, in an age of mass transit, such cases certainly represent the exception, not the rule. Would it allow the federal government to place a *cordon sanitaire* around a city, absent state acquiescence? At some point such authority eviscerates the power reserved to the states with regard to quarantine, in the process raising concerns well known to the founders about the concentration of authority in federal hands.

Moreover, is the test adopted by the federal government—coming into contact with interstate travelers—the correct one? For instance, what level of impact on commerce is necessary? Does it matter what the disease is? Under executive order, pandemic influenza is now included. Does that mean that every flu season the federal government could impose quarantine and isolation on citizens? What about the manner in which the disease is disseminated? Does it matter if it is criminal in nature? Would, for instance, medical measures aimed at mitigating the salmonella outbreak at salad bars in Oregon satisfy Commerce Clause considerations—or would that fall within state police powers? While the authority of Congress appeared to be expanding in this area throughout much of the twentieth century, more recent cases—namely *US v. Lopez* and *US v. Morrison*, suggest a possible contraction.

D. Limits of the Necessary and Proper Clause

A final structural question presents itself—that is, even if we have seen limits on the Commerce Clause, recent interpretations of the Necessary and Proper Clause give effect to broader congressional control of interstate commerce. That clause gives Congress the authority to "make all Laws which shall be necessary and proper for carrying into Execution the foregoing Powers, and all other Powers vested by this Constitution in the Government of the United States, or in any Department or Officer thereof."[286] *Gonzales v. Reich* proved significant in this regard, upholding federal efforts to override California's legalization of cannabis for medical purposes. Justice Scalia distinguished the case from *Lopez* and *Morrison*, writing, "Congress may regulate noneconomic intrastate activities only where the failure to do so 'could . . . undercut' its regulation of interstate commerce."

US v. Comstock extended this line of reasoning: in a 7–2 decision written by Justice Breyer, the Court upheld federal law allowing the government to indefinitely detain "sexually dangerous" federal prisoners following completion of their sentences.[287] The majority considered continued detention as "necessary and proper" to implementing congressional power to operate a penal system and act "as the custodian" of prisoners held within it.[288]

The decision, however, raises questions about how quarantine would fare in a similar context. The Court adopted a rational basis test, concluding that the clause allows any exercise of authority that "constitutes a means that is rationally related to the implementation of a constitutionally enumerated power."[289] In a separate concurrence Justice Kennedy argued against the use of this test.

> The terms "rationally related" and "rational bases" must be employed with care, particularly if either is to be used as a stand-alone test. The phrase "rational basis"

most often is employed to describe the standard for determining whether legislation that does not proscribe fundamental liberties nonetheless violates the Due Process Clause. . . . The phrase . . . should not be extended uncritically to the issue before us.[290]

While the immediate law at question in Comstock was "a discrete and narrow exercise of authority over a small class of persons already subject to the federal power," involving "little intrusion upon the ordinary processes and powers of the states,"[291] the same would not be true of a broad federal authority over state public health. Justice Alito, like Kennedy, expressed concern in his concurrence about giving Congress "carte blanche" via the Necessary and Proper Clause.[292] Justice Thomas wrote an even more scathing dissent, much of which was joined by Justice Scalia, suggesting that "Congress may act under [the Necessary and Proper clause] only when its legislation 'carr[ies] into Execution' one of the Federal Government's enumerated powers."[293]

Just as "[no] enumerated power in Article I, §8 [of the Constitution], expressly delegates to Congress the power to enact a civil-commitment regime for sexually dangerous persons . . . ,"[294] no specific enumerated constitutional power gives the federal government authority over public health. To the contrary, since the founding, this has been considered to be reserved to the states via the Tenth Amendment. Nor, under Justice Thomas's view, could quarantine provisions be upheld simply because Congress has passed other laws more directly affecting Commerce.[295] Instead, such statutes would be valid only insofar as they facilitated the use of the previous law to implement Congress's enumerated authorities.

In *Comstock*, the majority considered five factors that contributed to their decision:

We take these five considerations together. They include: (1) the breadth of the Necessary and Proper Clause, (2) the long history of federal involvement in this arena, (3) the sound reasons for the statute's enactment in light of the government's custodial interest in safeguarding the public from dangers posed by those in federal custody, (4) the statute's accommodation of state interests, and (5) the statute's narrow scope. Taken together, these considerations lead us to conclude that the statute is a "necessary and proper" means of exercising the federal authority that permits Congress to create federal criminal laws, to punish their violation, to imprison violators, to provide appropriately for those imprisoned, and to maintain the security of those who are not imprisoned but who may be affected by the federal imprisonment of others.[296]

What is less than clear, as Justice Thomas points out in his dissent, is exactly how the five-point test should be applied in the future.[297] How would this reasoning transfer over to the quarantine realm? In regard to the second consideration, for instance, there is a long history not of federal involvement in this arena but of state and local involvement. The majority's third consideration (sound reasons for enacting the statute in light of the government's responsibilities) may reflect in a strong federal interest in safeguarding the country from pandemic disease; but the fourth consideration, the extent to which state interests are accommodated, may constrict in the evolution of these provisions. The direction that the most recent quarantine measures are taking may run afoul of the factors laid out in *Comstock*. Whether the Court's jurisprudence in this area will allow greater or lesser leeway remains to be seen.

E. Risk of Distorting the Most Effective Responses to Public Health Concerns

We turn then to two policy concerns that mark the most current shifts with regard to public health. The first is whether allowing the biological weapons conversation to upstage public health—that is, set the agenda for how to respond to disease—is a good idea.

The United States spends twice as much annually on biological terrorism as on public health. But the public health threats are substantial: millions of people die from naturally occurring disease each year.[298] Communicable diseases, such as respiratory infections, HIV/AIDS, diarrheal diseases, tuberculosis, malaria, measles, tetanus, meningitis, and hepatitis B, as well as food-borne bacterial infections like salmonella and *Escherichia coli*, can be devastating. In contrast, the number of people that have died from the dissemination of biological agents is extremely small. The emphasis on biological agents risks pulling the focus away from more likely threats. Do we really want our public health structure to depend on funding and planning for biological weapons? Does it make sense to take the focus away from the more mundane, but potentially equally or even more devastating, diseases, merely because ordinary pandemics require no human intervention for their construction and dissemination? If we allow biological weapons to provide the focus, then everything from the type of disease monitored and the types of vaccines and prophylactics developed, to the nature of health surveillance may alter—even as resources become consumed that could otherwise go to better use.

The coupling of biological weapons and public health also risks shifting the relationship between the federal government and the citizens. The national security dialogue is essentially an adversarial one—in keeping with the pace of weaponization, it suggests that any one individual could pose a devastating threat to the country. It thus treats individual citizens as potential adversaries. But we currently have a public health system built on voluntary compliance. What happens when you create an adversarial relationship between citizens and the government—and then forcibly attempt to restrain their movement? What happens to voluntary reporting, general vaccination, and cooperation in the event of a public health emergency?

The recent example of CIA actions in Pakistan is here instructive. The agency, under the guise of a vaccination program, collected DNA samples from individuals living in Pakistan. Billed as a free clinic to prevent hepatitis B, the actual aim was to ascertain the presence of Bin Laden family members.[299] Health care workers are now braced for the backlash, as Pakistanis refuse to come forward for vaccination, because of suspicion that any vaccination program is being orchestrated by the United States as part of its campaign.[300] The risk of prioritizing national security is that public health, as a consequence, directly suffers.

While the vaccination campaign took place overseas, the United States has a long history of resistance to invasive federal actions. By placing public health in an adversarial framing, the risk arises of feeding into this deep-seated suspicion of coercive power and, in the process, undermining public health across the board. The movement to include military actors as a way to implement such authorities further exacerbates the problem.

Added to this are concerns about the more likely occurrence of naturally occurring disease. Biological weapons are difficult to produce and even harder to disseminate. Does it make sense to orient our public health system around the lower risk event—particularly when equally devastating consequences may follow from pandemic disease?

F. *Quarantine and Isolation under Fire*

The second and final policy consideration relates more specifically to the use of quarantine and isolation as a response. While grounded in historical precedent, it is not at all clear that quarantine—and, specifically, *cordon sanitaire*—works. Yet, even as statutes bemoaned the continued rampages of disease and the ineffectiveness of prior quarantine provisions, they introduced yet broader authorities and more stringent penalties. During the Spanish influenza epidemic, American towns otherwise cut off from the outside world found that disease nevertheless traveled into their bounds—arriving, for instance, via the post, on the outside of packages entering their space. There is serious question, in an age of such mobility and connectedness, that *cordon sanitaire* could be accomplished.[301] Indeed, the U.S. influenza plan specifically notes that quarantine may be particularly ineffective for stopping the spread of the disease. It is for this reason that, unlike the United States, the United Kingdom eschews *any* use of quarantine for pandemic influenza.[302]

The strongest argument that could be made for it is that quarantine and isolation may slow the spread of disease. This is an important consideration: time may be critical in allowing the government to amass and distribute vaccines, prophylactics, and other medications. And lives are at stake. Yet even granting that quarantine may retard the disease's advance, what unintended consequences might follow? For example, what happens to the provision of basic services—such as emergency medical care, policing, electricity, and sanitation—when population flows are severely limited? What about access to other medical services, or the economic effect of bringing business, government, and education to a standstill? In a severely weakened economy, the country's ability to respond to other threats is similarly diminished. What happens when citizens refuse to abide by the quarantine provisions? How might this undermine state control? And what happens when you add the military to a civilian mix—in light of very different rules of engagement from the ordinary law enforcement framing?

It may be, of course, that the proliferation of quarantine authorities are merely cosmetic—that the federal government does not intend to actually use the powers it is seeking—that they are, indeed, an outmoded nod to a history based on unsound science. If this is the case, however, then why even have such powers on the books? For the presence of the laws bring with them their own form of political and legal legitimacy, which may encourage their use. And the political will to use such powers may well significantly alter in a crisis.

IV. Concluding Remarks

Two major shifts have occurred with regard to the evolution of measures designed to counter pandemic disease and biological weapons: the first, which solidified in the early 20th century, carved out a role for the federal government in preventing the importation of disease into the country and in allowing for federal agencies to stem the transfer of disease between states through the use of quarantine and isolation. The second shift moved pandemic disease and biological weapons into a national security realm, linking the two in terms of institutions, identification, and approach. Quarantine and isolation appear central, and growing attention is being paid to the role of the military in executing the federal measures. As a constitutional matter, the first shift rested on an uneasy compromise between the police powers reserved to the states through the Tenth Amendment and the Commerce Clause—an agreement forged through use of the Spending Clause. The second shift, however, rests on shakier constitutional grounds. Significant questions regarding individual rights remain unanswered, even as four structural problems present themselves: the treatment of public health within war powers, the role of the military on domestic soil, the limits of Commerce Clause authority, and the extent to which the Necessary and Proper Clause empowers the federal government to act. Added to this are significant concerns about the wisdom of allowing concern about biological weapons to set the agenda for public health, and the effectiveness of quarantine and isolation as a response. These issues warrant further inquiry.

Notes

Special thanks to Georgetown Law's Laura Bedard and Todd Venie, for their extraordinary help in locating materials used in this chapter. Professors Larry Gostin, John Norton Moore, and Steven Vladeck provided particularly thoughtful remarks on the text, as did participants in the GW Foreign Relations Colloquium, the Potomac Legal History Roundtable, and the Georgetown Law Faculty Workshop.

1. See, e.g., Jullian Perry Robinson, *The Problem of Chemical and Biological Warfare: A Study of the Historical, Technical, Military, Legal and Political Aspects of CBW, and Possible Disarmament Measures,* Vol. I: *The Rise of CB Weapons* (1971); Robert Koenig, *The Fourth Horseman: The Tragedy of Anton Dilger and the Birth of Biological Terrorism* (2008) (discussing German use of anthrax and glanders to target livestock shipped to U.S. forces in World War I); Igor V. Domaradskij, *Biowarrior: Inside the Soviet/ Russian Biological War Machine* (2003) (discussing the development of the Russian biological weapons program); National Security Decision Memorandum 25, United States Policy on Chemical Warfare Program and Bacteriological/Biological Research Program, from the National Security Advisor, Henry Kissinger, to the Vice President, the Secretary of State, and the Secretary of Defense, etc. (November 25, 1969), available at http://www.gwu.edu/~nsarchiv/NSAEBB/NSAEBB58/RNCBW8.pdf; and National Security Decision Memorandum 44, United States Policy on Toxins, from the National Security Advisor, Henry Kissinger, to the Vice President, Secretary of State, Secretary of Defense, etc. (February 20, 1970), available at http://www.gwu.edu/~nsarchiv/NSAEBB/ NSAEBB58/RNCBW20.pdf (discussing the U.S. biological weapons program); S. H. Harris, *Factories of Death: Japanese Biological Warfare 1932–45 and the American Cover-up* (1994).

2. See, e.g., Protocol for the Prohibition of the Use in War of Asphyxiating, Poisonous or Other Gases, and of Bacteriological Methods of Warfare, June 17, 1925, 26 U.S.T. 571, 94 L.N.T.S. 65 ("Whereas the use in war of asphyxiating, poisonous or other gases, and of all analogous liquids, materials or devices, has been justly condemned by the general opinion of the civilized world; and Whereas the prohibition of such use has been declared in Treaties to which the majority of Powers of the world are Parties . . . [we] Declare: That the High Contracting Parties, so far as they are not already Parties to Treaties prohibiting such use, accept this prohibition, agree to extend this prohibition to the use of bacteriological methods of warfare and agree to be bound as between themselves according to the terms of this declaration) (100 states party); Convention on the Prohibition of the Development, Production and Stockpiling of Bacteriological (Biological) and Toxin Weapons and on Their Destruction, April 10, 1972, 26 U.S.T. 583, 1015 U.N.T.S. 163 (Each State Party to this Convention undertakes never in any circumstances to develop, produce, stockpile, or otherwise acquire or retain: (1) Microbial or other biological agents, or toxins whatever their origin or method of production, of types and in quantities that have no justification for prophylactic, protective or other peaceful purposes. (2) Weapons, equipment or means of delivery designed to use such agents or toxins for hostile purposes or in armed conflict.") (144 states party). But see, e.g., Jonathan B. Tucker, "Historical Trends Related to Bioterrorism: An Empirical Analysis," Emerging Infectious Diseases, Table 1, available at http://www.cdc.gov/ncidod/eid/vol5no4/tucker.htm (discussing R.I.S.E., an ecoterrorist

group that emerged in 1972 with the goal of killing off most of humanity to prevent the destruction of nature. The group began by targeting the residents of states surrounding Chicago. Members developed eight microbial pathogens with the intent to disperse them by aircraft, contaminating municipal water supplies.)

3. See, e.g., "National Security Strategy of the United States of America," September 2002, available at http://www.whitehouse.gov/nsc/nss.pdf. ("With the collapse of the Soviet Union and the end of the Cold War, our security environment has undergone profound transformation. ... [N]ew deadly challenges have emerged from rogue states and terrorists. ... [T]he nature and motivations of these new adversaries, their determination to obtain destructive powers hitherto available only to the world's strongest states, and the greater likelihood that they will use weapons of mass destruction against us, make today's security environment more complex and dangerous.")

4. Title XIV, National Defense Authorization Act for FY 1997.

5. Statement of the Hon. Richard G. Lugar, Senator (R-IN), to the House Military Research and Development Subcommittee, Hearing on the Security of Russian Nuclear Weapons, October 2, 1997, available at http://www.fas.org/spp/starwars/congress/1997_h/h971002l.htm.

6. Ibid.

7. Gillian Flaccus, "Oregon Town Never Recovered from Scare," Associated Press, the Rick A. Ross Institute for the Study of Destructive Cults (Controversial Groups and Movements Website, October 19, 2001), available at http://www.rickross.com/reference/rajneesh/rajneesh8.html.

8. Ibid.

9. Tucker, "Historical Trends Related to Bioterrorism," *supra* note 2.

10. Jessica Eve Stern, "Larry Wayne Harris," in *Toxic Terror: Assessing Terrorist Use of Chemical and Biological Weapons*, ed. Jonathan B. Tucker (1998), 227–46.

11. Tucker, "Historical Trends Related to Bioterrorism," *supra* note 2, Table 1. See also Stern, "Larry Wayne Harris," *supra* note 10.

12. J. Parker-Tursman, "FBI Briefed on District's Terror Curbs," *Pittsburgh Post-Gazette*, May 5, 1999; and Tim Weiner, "Reno Says U.S. May Stockpile Medicine for Terrorist Attacks," *New York Times*, April 23, 1998, A:12.

13. Ibid.

14. Ibid.

15. Center for Nonproliferation Studies, "WMD Terrorism Database," Monterey Institute for International Studies, password protected database available at http://cnswmd.miis.edu/wmdt//.

16. Remarks by Homeland Security secretary Michael Chertoff at the Stanford Constitutional Law Center's Germ Warfare, Contagious Disease, and the Constitution Conference, Washington, DC, April 11, 2008, available at http://www.dhs.gov/xnews/

speeches/sp_1208283625146.shtm ("We know, for example, in the late 1990s, al Qaeda became focused on developing a biological weapons program. After the invasion of Afghanistan, we determined that there was a low-tech facility in Kandahar, which was actually aimed at producing anthrax and the purpose obviously was to create a weapon.")

17. American Association for the Advancement of Science, "Science and Security in the Post-9/11 Environment: Bioterrorism," available at http://www.aaas.org/spp/post911/agents/.

18. President Bush, West Point, New York, June 1, 2002, cited in "National Security Strategy of the United States of America," *supra* note 3.

19. See, e.g., Richard A. Falkenrath, Robert D. Newman, and Bradley A. Thayer, *America's Achilles' Heel: Nuclear, Biological, and Chemical Terrorism and Covert Attack* (1998); Philip B. Heymann, *Terrorism and America: A Commonsense Strategy for a Democratic Society* (1998); Bruce Hoffman, *Inside Terrorism* (1998); Brad Roberts, ed., *Terrorism with Chemical and Biological Weapons: Calibrating Risks and Responses* (1997); Jessica Stern, *The Ultimate Terrorists* (1999).

20. The Australian mousepox case is here instructive: every four years, Australia suffers from a rodent infestation that devastates the crops and takes a considerable toll on the gross domestic product of the country. In 1998 some Australian scientists decided to try to engineer a biological disease—they did not want to kill the rodents, because this would have created a problem with disease. Instead, they chose mousepox, a highly virulent disease, and attached a secondary disease to make it impossible for the rodents to reproduce. After extensive experiments, they found, much to their surprise, that in making the disease effective even against rats with immune systems that rejected mousepox, they ended up with a disease that was 100 percent virulent—*and* fatal. Mousepox is closely linked to smallpox—one of the most devastating diseases in the history of humankind, killing 500 million people in the twentieth century alone. The researchers initially decided not to publish the information; but after the Australian military dragged its heels, they placed a paper in *Science*, an American journal. Although initially received with minimal discussion, following the anthrax mailings in autumn 2001, the incident attracted the attention of the president and members of Congress, alarmed that the experiment—with such devastating results—required just three feet of countertop and a basic knowledge of microbiology. For more discussion of this incident, see Laura K. Donohue, *The Cost of Counterterrorism: Power, Politics, and Liberty* (2008), ch. 5.

21. Highly Pathogenic avian influenza virus of type A of subtype H5N1[HPAI A(H5N1)] = causative agent of H5N1,commonly known as "avian influenza." Kristin Choo, "The Avian Flu Time Bomb: The Legal System Will Play a Key Role in Planning the Response to a Possible Onslaught of the Virus," *A.B.A. J.*, November 2005, available at http://www.cphp.pitt.edu/PDF/THE%20AVIAN%20FLU%20TIME%20BOMB.pdf.

22. Writing Committee of the World Health Organization, "Avian Influenza A (H5N1) Infection in Humans," *N. Engl. J. Med.* 354, no. 8 (2006): 884, available at http://content.nejm.org/cgi/content/full/353/13/1374; and Choo, "The Avian Flu Time Bomb," *supra* note 21.

23. There appear to be a handful of cases where the disease may have been transmitted between people (for example, mother to child, and patient to nurse). These, however, appear to be unique. Writing Committee of the World Health Organization, "Avian Influenza A (H5N1) Infection in Humans," *supra* note 22, p. 884.

24. See *supra* note 22.

25. Frederick F. Cartwright, "Pandemics Past and Future," in *Disease in Ancient Man: An International Symposium*, ed. Gerald D. Hart (Toronto, 1983), 167–80.

26. Fred R. van Hartesveldt, ed., *The 1918–19 Pandemic of Influenza: The Urban Impact in the Western World* (1992) (estimates at least 40 million); Niall Johnson, *Britain and the 1918–19 Influenza Pandemic* (New York, 2006) 103, (estimating up to 100 million).

27. As of January 30, 2008, the World Health Organization reported 224 deaths out of 357 cases of H5N1 in humans (62.74 percent). "Cumulative Number of Confirmed Human Cases of Avian Influenza A/(H5N1) as Reported to the World Health Organization," January 30, 2008, available at http://www.who.int/csr/disease/avian_influenza/country/cases_table_2008_01_30/en/index.html.

28. See, e.g., Ira M. Longini et al., "Containing Pandemic Influenza at the Source," *Science* 309, no. 5737 (2005): 1083–87; Thomas Luke, Timothy Halenkamp, and Edward Kilbane, "Naval Quarantine: Impervious to Epidemics of Virulent Disease," *U.S. Naval Inst. Proc.* 132, no. 7 (July 1, 2006): 48.

29. See Angie A. Welborn, "Federal and State Isolation and Quarantine Authority," CRS Report, January 18, 2005, 1, available at http://www.fas.org/sgp/crs/RL31333.pdf.

30. World Health Organization, "Summary of Probable SARS Cases with Onset of Illness from 1 November 2002 to 31 July 2003," available at http://www.who.int/csr/sars/country/table2004_04_21/en/index.html.

31. See, e.g., Michael T. Osterholm, *"Preparing for the Next Pandemic," Foreign Affairs* 84, no. 4 (July/August 2005); and Choo, "The Avian Flu Time Bomb," *supra* note 21.

32. Graeme T. Laurie and Kathryn G. Hunter, "Mapping, Assessing and Improving Legal Preparedness for Pandemic Flu in the United Kingdom," *Medical Law Int'l.* 10, no. 2 (2009): 101, 103.

33. See http://www.nature.com/news/specials/swineflu/index.html.

34. See, e.g., USA PATRIOT Act, §817 (expanding the biological weapons statute to make it an offense to knowingly possess any biological agent, toxin, or delivery system that is not reasonably justified for peaceful purposes; creating category of persons restricted from dealing in select agents); Homeland Security Act of 2002, Pub. L. No. 107-296, 116

Stat. 2135 (2003); Public Health Security and Bioterrorism Preparedness and Response Act of 2002, Pub. L. No. 107–88, 116 Stat. 294 (2002), codified in scattered sections of 7 U.S.C., 18 U.S.C., 21 U.S.C., 29 U.S.C., 38 U.S.C., 42 U.S.C., and 47 U.S.C. (2002) (placing controls on dangerous biological agents); CDC associated regulations (specifying over eighty biological agents considered threatening to public health and safety or animal and plant health; and creating the Select Agents Program: any facilities/individuals in possession of listed agents must register with CDC or Animal and Plant Health Inspection Service. Scientists handling must undergo security clearances, fingerprinting.); 2004 Intelligence Reform and Terrorist Prevention Act; [giving Secretary of Homeland Security authority (and money—$250 million) to obtain equipment to detect nonmetallic, chemical, biological, and radiological weapons and explosives, in all forms, on individuals and their personal property at airport screening checkpoints (§4018); requiring report from DHS on the procedures in place to address BW threats in incoming air cargo (§4053); *Subtitle I*—Weapons of Mass Destruction Prohibition Improvement Act of 2004 expands categories of restricted persons subject to prohibitions relating to select agents, enhances prosecution of WMD offenses (§6802); making it illegal to handle the variola virus outside of direct authorization by HHS (§6906)]; 2004 Intelligence Reform and Terrorist Prevention Act and Project BioShield Act of 2004, P.L. 108-276 ("To amend the Public Health Service Act to provide protections and countermeasures against . . . agents that may be used in a terrorist attack against the United States"; directing Secretary of DHS to continually monitor BW threats; directing DOJ to provide stockpile security and quarantine enforcement upon request of HHS). For regulatory changes see, e.g., 42 CFR Parts 70 and 71, under Public Health Service Act (42 U.S.C. 264-271), Proposed under 25 U.S.C. 198, 231, and 1661; 42 U.S.C. 243, 248, 249, 264–72, and 2007. *Federal Register* 70, no. 229 (November 30, 2005): 71892–948.

35. See, e.g., Homeland Security Presidential Directive 10, Biodefense for the 21st Century, April 28, 2004, available at http://www.fas.org/irp/offdocs/nspd/hspd-10.html; "National Security Strategy of the United States of America," supra note 3; National Response Plan, 2002 National Strategy to Combat Weapons of Mass Destruction; and the Pandemic Influenza Implementation Plan. More than $57 billion has been spent on these initiatives. Spencer S. Hsu, "Modest Gains against Ever-Present Bioterrorism Threat," *Washington Post*, August 3, 2008, A10, available at http://www.washingtonpost.com/wp-dyn/content/article/2008/08/02/AR2008080201624_pf.html. See also Jennifer Gaudioso and Reynolds M. Salerno, "Biosecurity and Research: Minimizing Adverse Impacts," *Science* 304 (April 30, 2004).

36. Homeland Security Act of 2002, Pub. L. No. 107-296, 116 Stat. 2135 (2003).

37. U.S. Department of Homeland Security, "Emergencies & Disasters, Planning & Prevention," National Response Plan 1, available at http://www.dhs.gov/dhspublic/interapp/editorial/editorial_0566.xml.

38. Pub. L. No. 107-188, 116 Stat. 294 (2002), codified in sections of 7 U.S.C., 18 U.S.C., 21 U.S.C., 29 U.S.C., 38 U.S.C., 42 U.S.C., and 47 U.S.C. (2002).

39. 42 CFR Parts 70 and 71, under Public Health Service Act (42 U.S.C. 264–71), Proposed under 25 U.S.C. 198, 231, and 1661; 42 U.S.C. 243, 248, 249, 264–72, and 2007. *Federal Register* 70, no. 229 (November 30, 2005): 71892–948.

40. Dr. Jeff Runge, DHS Chief Medical Officer on Pandemic Preparedness, "Press Briefing on National Strategy for Pandemic Influenza Implementation Plan: One Year Summary," July 17, 2007, available at http://www.whitehouse.gov/news/releases/2007/07/20070717-13.html. See also remarks of Dr. Venkayya, Special Assistant to the President for Biodefense, at "Press Briefing on National Strategy for Pandemic Influenza Implementation Plan: One Year Summary," July 17, 2007, available at http://www.whitehouse.gov/news/releases/2007/07/20070717-13.html.

41. Venkayya, "Press Briefing on National Strategy," *supra* note 40.

42. In concert with the initiatives described in this paper, the federal government has provided the lead to state governments in updating and strengthening their laws governing quarantine and isolation. The president's 2002 National Strategy for Homeland Security listed review of quarantine authority as a priority for state governments. Office of Homeland Security, National Strategy for Homeland Security, June 2002, available at http://www.whitehouse.gov/homeland/book/nat_strat_hls.pdf. CDC, in turn, funded the Center for Law and the Public's Health at Georgetown and Johns Hopkins universities to develop a Model State Emergency Health Powers Act. (Model Act available at http://www.publichealthlaw.net/Resources/Modellaws.htm.) The idea was for states to tailor their statutes and regulations so that they could respond to novel threats. Written in 2001, by 2006, Model Act "introduced in whole or part through 171 bills or resolutions in forty-four (44) states, the District of Columbia, and the Northern Mariannas Islands. Thirty-eight (38) states [AL, AK, AZ, CA, CT, DE, FL, GA, HI, ID, IL, IN, IA, LA, ME, MD, MN, MO, MT, NV, NH, NJ, NM, NC, OK, OR, PA, RI, SC, SD, TN, TX, UT, VT, VA, WI, and WY] and DC have passed a total of 66 bills or resolutions that include provisions from or closely related to the Act. Center for Public Health and Law, "Legislative Status Update," available at http://www.publichealthlaw. net/Resources/Modellaws.htm#TP. See also Lawrence O. Gostin et al., "The Law and the Public's Health: A Study of Infectious Disease Law in the United States," *Colum. L. Rev.* 99, no. 59 (1999): 102. Isolation is understood as "the separation of a known infected person or animal from others during the period of contagiousness in order to prevent the direct or indirect conveyance of the infectious agent." Quarantine, in contrast, relates to "the restriction of movement of a healthy person who has been exposed to a communicable disease in order to prevent contact with unexposed persons." Edward A. Fallone, "Preserving the Public Health: A Proposal to Quarantine Recalcitrant AIDS Carriers," *B.U. L. Rev.* 68, no. 24 (1988): 441.

43. Pub. L. No. 107-188, 116 Stat. 294 (2002), codified in scattered sections of 7 U.S.C., 18 U.S.C., 21 U.S.C., 29 U.S.C., 38 U.S.C., 42 U.S.C., and 47 U.S.C. (2002).

44. Modifies 42 U.S.C. 264; Act June 12, 2002.

45. Executive Order 13295: Revised List of Quarantinable Communicable Diseases, April 4, 2003.

46. Executive Order 13375, April 1, 2005.

47. 42 CFR 70.6 and 71.3.

48. 42 CFR Parts 70 and 71, under Public Health Service Act (42 U.S.C. 264–71), Proposed under 25 U.S.C. 198, 231, and 1661; 42 U.S.C. 243, 248, 249, 264–72, and 2007. *Federal Register* 70, no. 229 (November 30, 2005): 71892–948.

49. *Federal Register* 70, no. 229 (November 30, 2005): 71892.

50. See, e.g., Briefing Memo for Subcomm. on National Security, Veterans Affairs, and International Relations, http://www.house.gov/reform/ns/web_resources/briefing_memo_july_23.htm (reporting on the evolution of the TOPOFF exercise in Denver, CO, "The CDC advises that Colorado state borders be cordoned off to limit further spread of plague throughout the United States and other countries. Colorado officials express concern about their ability to get food and supplies into the state").

51. U.S. Homeland Security Council, National Strategy for Pandemic Influenza: Implementation Plan, May 2006, available at http://www.whitehouse.gov/homeland/nspi_implementation.pdf. [Hereinafter Implementation Plan] See also U.S. Homeland Security Council, National Strategy for Pandemic Influenza, available at http://www.flu.gov/planning-preparedness/federal/pandemic-influenza.pdf.

52. HSPD 10 (writing: "[T]he Department of Defense will continue to ensure that . . . our troops and our critical domestic and overseas installations are effectively protected against [biological] threats").

53. 10 U.S.C. 15, §§331–35.

54. Amending 10 U.S.C. §333.

55. Letter to the Hon. Patrick J. Leahy, U.S. Senate, and the Hon. Christopher "Kit" Bond, U.S. Senate, February 5, 2007, from Co-leads on the National Guard, Governors Michael F. Easley and Mark Sanford, available at http://www.nga.org/portal/site/nga/menuitem.cb6e7818b34088d18a278110501010a0/?vgnextoid=edd8b31eb2990110VgnVCM1000001a01010aRCRD.

56. Editorial, "Making Martial Law Easier," *New York Times*, February 19, 2007.

57. See, e.g., Bipartisan Katrina report, stating that in regard to natural disasters, "[T]he role of the National Guard is critical in the maintenance of civil order, the provision of logistical support, and the coordination of rescue and relief effort." Steve Bowman, Lawrence Kapp, and Amy Belasco, CRS, "Hurricane Katrina: DOD Disaster Response," September 19, 2005, available at http://www.fas.org/sgp/crs/natsec/RL33095.pdf; Alfred J. Sciarrino, "Part III: Epidemics, Natural Disasters and Biological Terrorism—the

Federal Response," *Mich. St. U.J. Med. & L.* 10, no. 429 (2006): 426 ("The suggestion to use the military in a national emergency is not merely academic, as in the immediate aftermath of Katrina, Americans saw the breakdown of civilian leadership, especially by the Department of Homeland Security, charged with the primary responsibility of responding to 'a terrorist attack, natural disaster or other large-scale emergency,' and by FEMA, the lead agency under the Department of Homeland Security. Only the military offered a wide range of worthwhile assistance, including proper search and rescue measures; recovering the bodies of those killed in the storm or afterward; immediately attempting to bolster and secure the levees; providing for and delivering food, shelter, and water; and restoring law and order" [internal footnotes deleted].)

58. U.S. House of Representatives, "A Failure of Initiative," Final Report of the Select Bipartisan Committee to Investigate the Preparation for and Response to Hurricane Katrina (2006), available at http://www.gpoaccess.gov/congress/index.html, p. 201.

59. See, e.g., Influenza Implementation Plan, *supra* notes 35, 40.

60. See, e.g., Act to Prevent the Coming of Sickly Vessells, &c., Abstract or Abridgment of the Laws made and past by William Penn Absolute Proprietary, and Governour in Chief of the Province of Pensilvania and Territories there unto belonging, with the Advice and Consent of the Free-men thereof in Generall-Assembly mett at New-Castle, October 14, 1700–November 27, 1700, *{{John: asterisks??}}26 ("Whereas it hath been found, by sad experience that the coming and arriving of unhealthy vessels at the ports and towns of this province and territories, and the landing of their passengers and goods, before they have lain some time to be purified, have proved very detrimental to the health of the inhabitants of this province . . ."). See also John B. Blake, "Yellow Fever in Eighteenth Century America," *Bull. N.Y. Acad. Med.* 44, no. 6 (June 1968): 674 (discussing the late seventeenth-century outbreak of yellow fever in Boston, Charleston, and Philadelphia, and the failure of containment measures there to prevent its spread to New York). For a more detailed exposition of the history of U.S. quarantine law, see Laura K. Donohue, "Biodefense and Constitutional Constraints," *National Security and Armed Conflict Law Review* (forthcoming) (comparing the evolution of quarantine law in the United States and United Kingdom).

61. See, e.g., *Records of the Governor and company of the Massachusetts Bay in New England*, ed. Nathaniel B. Shurtleff, MD, Vol. II, 1642–49 (Boston, 1853); and *Acts Relating to the Establishment of Quarantine of Massachusetts from the Settlement of the Colony of Massachusetts Bay to the Present Time* (Boston: Rockwell and Churchill, City Printers, 1881), 5 (on file with author).

62. See, e.g., An Act to prevent infectious Distempers being brought into this Colony, and to hinder the spreading thereof (1755), Act XIII, in *Laws, Statutes, Ordinances, and constitutions, Ordained, Made and Established by the Mayor, Aldermen, and Commonalty, of the City of New-York, Convened in Common Council for The good Rule and government of the Inhabitants and Residents of the said City,* November 9, 1762.

63. See, e.g., An Act to prevent sickly Vessels coming into this Government, in *The Laws of the Province of Pennsilvania Collected into One Volume, By Order of the Governour and Assembly of the said Province, 1714*, c. LXII, p. 19.

64. An Act to prevent sickly Vessels coming into this Government, in *Laws of the Government of New-Castle, Kent and Sussex, Upon Delaware, 1752*, *{{**John: ?**}}67.

65. See, e.g., An Act to oblige infected ships and other vessels coming into this province to perform quarantine, Lib. HS. Fol. 655, ch. XXV, Nov. 1766, in *The Laws of Maryland to which are Prefixed the Original Charter, with an English Translation, the Bill of Rights and Constitution, 1799*. See also Charles V. Chapin, "History of State and Municipal Control of Disease," in *A Half Century of Public Health* (1921), 143; Ralph Chester Williams, *The United States Public Health Service 1798–1950* (1951), 63.

66. See, e.g., An Act to Prevent the Spreading of Infectious Sickness, 1712, in *Acts and Laws of His Majesties Colony of Rhode-Island, and Providence-Plantations in America*, pp. 63–64 (on file with author).

67. Order regulating the quarantine of vessels from the West Indies (March) 1647–48, *{{**John: ?**}}200, reprinted in *Records of the Governor and Company of the Massachusetts Bay in New England*, Vol. II, 237. See also *Acts Relating to the Establishment of Quarantine of Massachusetts from the Settlement of the Colony of Massachusetts Bay to the Present Time*, 5–7 (referring to the "First order of General Court, regulating Quarantine of vessels passed at a session of the General Court the first month [March] 1647 or 1648" and reprinting the order).

68. *Acts Relating to the Establishment of Quarantine of Massachusetts, from the Settlement of the Colony of Massachusetts Bay to the Present Time*, 5–6 (on file with author). See also *Records of the Governor and Company of the Mass. Bay in New England*, Vol. II, 237. Brock C. Hampton, "Development of the National Maritime Quarantine System of the United States," *Public Health Reports* (1896–1970) 55, no. 28 (July 12, 1940): 1245. Hampton cites to Winthrop, *supra* note 74; and Susan Wade Peabody, "Historical Study of Legislation Regarding Public Health in the States of New York and Massachusetts," *J. Inf. Dis.*, Supp. no. 4 (February 1909). According to Hampton, the New York colony may have also implemented quarantine in the same year. For other sources citing the MA Bay Colony order, see Sidney Edelman, "International Travel and Our National Quarantine System," *Temple Law Quarterly* 37, no. 28 (1963): 29. There is discrepancy in the secondary literature about the exact date of the Massachusetts Bay order; some put it at 1647, others at 1648. Compare, e.g., Williams, *The United States Public Health Service*, 65; Lawrence O. Gostin, *Public Health Law: Power, Duty, Restraint* (2000), 205–6; Richard A. Goodman, Paul L. Kocher, Daniel J. O'Brien, and Frank S. Alexander, "The Structure of Law in Public Health Systems and Practice," in Richard A. Goodman et al., *Law in Public Health Practice* (2d ed., 2007), ch. 2, 46–51, 263; with Chapin, "History of State and Municipal Control of Disease," *supra* note 65, p. 133. The original writes, "March 1647–1648." At the time, the start of Britain's governmental

year did not line up with the Gregorian Calendar (dating from 1582), but, instead, it coincided with the Julian calendar, which began each year on March 25. By implication, this suggests that the discussion regarding quarantine and the subsequent order took place between January 1, 1648, and March 24, 1648, making 1648 the more likely date of the first quarantine order issued by the American colonies. The English government did not switch to the Gregorian calendar until 1752. See C. R. Cheney, ed., *Handbook of Dates for Students of English History* (London, 1978), 6–11. See also First Order of General Court, regulating Quarantine of vessels passed at a session of the General court the first month (March) 1647–48, *{{John: ?}}200, reprinted in *Records of the Governor and company of the Massachusetts Bay in New England*, Vol. II, 1642–1649 (Boston, 1853), 237; and *Acts Relating to the Establishment of Quarantine of Massachusetts from the Settlement of the Colony of Massachusetts Bay to the Present Time*, 5.

69. *Acts Relating to the Establishment of Quarantine of Massachusetts, from the Settlement of the Colony of Massachusetts Bay to the Present Time*, 6 (on file with author). See also *Records of the Governor and Company of the Mass. Bay in New England*, Vol. 2, 237.

70. *Acts Relating to the Establishment of Quarantine of Massachusetts, from the Settlement of the Colony of Massachusetts Bay to the Present Time*, 10.

71. *Records of the Colony of Massachusetts Bay in New England*, Vol. 2, p. 280. See also *Acts Relating to the Establishment of Quarantine of Massachusetts, from the Settlement of the Colony of Massachusetts Bay to the Present Time*, 7 (on file with author); Order that stopt [*sic*] the West Indy ships at the Castle repeld [*sic*], May 16, 1649, *{{John: ?}}235; reprinted in *Records of the Governor and Company of the Massachusetts Bay in New England*, ed. Nathanial B. Shurtleff, Vol. III, 1644–1657 (1854), 168. See also Records of the Col. Of Mass. Bay in New England, Vol. 2, *{{John: ?}}280, West India Ships, May 2, 1649, reprinted in *Acts Relating to the Establishment of Quarantine of Massachusetts from the Settlement of the Colony of Massachusetts Bay to the Present Time*, 7 ("The Courte doth thinke meete that the order concerning the stoping of West India ships at the Castle should hereby be repealed, seeing it hath pleased God to stay the sicknes there.") £100 in 1647 amounts to 114.46 times that amount in 2009; i.e., ~£11,446. Roughly translated at the current exchange rate of 0.65, this comes to $17,609. For rates of inflation and exchange see http://www.measuringworth.com/datasets/ukearncpi/result.php. In terms of earnings and purchase power, however, the number increases to some $244,000 today. Susan Wade Peabody, an early twentieth century scholar, identifies the epidemic as yellow fever. See Peabody, *Historical Study of Legislation*, *supra* note 68.

72. See, e.g., Record of the Order Establishing Quarantine, Oct. 11, 1665, reprinted in *Records of the Governor and Company of the Mass. Bay in New England*, Vol. 4, pt. 2, 1661–1674 (1854), 280 (imposing quarantine on vessels in response to a typhus outbreak in London). The order was repealed in October 1667. Order for stopping of

shipps [*sic*] at ye Castle repealed, October 9, 1667, reprinted in *Records of the Colony of the Mass. Bay in New England,* Vol. 4, pt. 2, p. 345. See also An Act for the Better Preventing of the Spreading of Infectious Sicknesses, July 18, 1699 (Massachusetts-Bay), 11 Wm. 3. Regarding the enaction of legislation in response to the outbreak of yellow fever in Philadelphia in 1699, see also "ACTS RELATING TO THE ESTABLISHMENT OF QUARANTINE OF MASSACHUSETTS FROM THE SETTLEMENT OF THE COLONY OF MASSACHUSETTS BAY TO THE PRESENT TIME (Boston, MA Board of Health, 1881)" or "An Act for the Better Preventing of the Spreading of Infectious Sicknesses, July 18, 1699 (Massachusetts-Bay), 11 Wm. 3."

73. The Massachusetts charter of 1691 expressly granted the Privy Council three years to disallow a statute. See I Poore's Charters (1877) 952. Disallowed by the Privy Council October 22, 1700. See *Acts Relating to the Establishment of Quarantine of Massachusetts from the Settlement of the Colony of Massachusetts Bay to the Present Time,* 9.

74. *Acts of the Privy Council, 1613–80,* p. 841, quoted in H. E. Egerton, "The Seventeenth and Eighteenth Century Privy Council in Its Relations with the Colonies," *J. Comp. Legis. & In'l L.* 7, 3d Ser., no. 1 (1925): 7.

75. The creation of the Lords of Trade and Plantations (more commonly referred to as the Board of Trade) in 1696 broadly coincides with the introduction of the quarantine provision and signals particular concern about trade and relations with the colonies. See Dickerson, *American Colonial Government, 1696–1765* (1912); Basye, *The Lords Commissioners of Trade and Plantations, 1748–1782* (1925); Russell, *The Review of American Colonial Legislation by the King in Council* (1915).

76. Full text or order quoted in Peabody, *Historical Study of Legislation, supra* note 68, p. 42.

77. Ibid.

78. Ibid.

79. An Act Providing in Case of Sickness, June 25, 1701, Massachusetts Bay Colony, c. 9, reprinted in *Acts Relating to the Establishment of Quarantine of Massachusetts from the Settlement of the Colony of Massachusetts Bay to the Present Time,* 11 [LB GETTING §§1–3].

80. Ibid., c. 9, §4.

81. An Act to oblige all Ships and other Vessels coming from *France,* and other parts of the World Infected with the Plague, to perform Quarentine [*sic*], reprinted in *Acts and Laws of Her Majesties Province of the Massachusetts Bay in New England, 1714,* pp. 355–56.

82. Ibid.

83. Ibid.

84. Ibid.

85. Ibid.

86. Ibid. (Emphasis in original.)

87. Ibid.

88. Ibid.

89. See Peabody, *Historical Study of Legislation, supra* note 68, p. 3.

90. Occurrence of such orders in 1702, 1714, 1716, 1725, 1738, 1742. Ibid., p. 3.

91. For details on the legal framework for the founding of the colony, see A Petition of Right to Benjamin Fletcher, Captain-General and Governor in Chief in and over the Province of Pennsylvania, and country of New-Castle, &c, reprinted in *Laws of the Commonwealth of Pennsylvania, from Oct. 14, 1700 to Mar. 20, 1810,* Vol. 1, 9–11.

92. Act to Prevent the Coming of Sickly Vessells, &c., *{{John: ?}}26 (preventing vessels without bills of health from coming within one mile of shore or landing passengers without license from the governor and council, or two justices of the peace, with a penalty of £100) (Act repealed January 22, 1774). An Act to oblige infected ships and other vessels coming into this province to perform quarantine, Lib. HS. Fol. 655, November 1766, reprinted in *The Laws of Maryland to which are prefixed the Original Charter with an English Translation the Bill of Rights and Constitution of the State as originally adopted by the convention, with several alterations by Acts of Assembly,* Vol. I, 1799, c. 25 (preventing any vessels, goods, or passengers to land before the making of an oath "that neither the small-pox, gaol fever, yellow fever, flux, or any such dangerous infectious distemper, is or hath been on board such ship or vessel on her passage, to the knowledge or belief of such captain, or other persons taking such oath respectively").

93. Ibid. See also Edelman, "International Travel and Our National Quarantine System," at 29–30. (Quoting also the preamble to the act: "Whereas it hath been found, by sad experience that the coming and arriving of unhealthy vessels at the ports and towns of this province and territories, and the landing of their passengers and goods, before they have lain some time to be purified, have proved very detrimental to the health of the inhabitants of this province . . .") See also Hampton, "Development of the National Maritime Quarantine System of the United States," *supra* note 68, p. 1246.

94. Edelman, "International Travel and Our National Quarantine System." See also Hampton, "Development of the National Maritime Quarantine System of the United States," *supra* note 68, p. 1246.

95. An ACT, to Prevent the Spreading of Infectious Sickness, February 27, 1711, *{{John: ?}}65–66, reprinted in *The Earliest Acts and Laws of the colony of Rhode Island and Providence Plantations 1647–1719* (1977), pp. 201–2. This act appears verbatim in 1719, again, without a terminal date. See *Acts and Laws of His Majesties Colony of Rhode-Island, and Providence-Plantations in America, 1719,* *{{John: ?}}65–66.

96. Ibid., *{{John: ?}}65, p. 201.

97. Ibid.

98. An Act to prevent the Small Pox being brought into this Colony from the Town of Boston, &c., August, 10, 1721, *{{John: ?}}120. The Charter Granted by His Majesty King Charles the Second, to the Colony of Rhode Island, and Providence-Plantations, in America. Newport, Rhode-Island. Printed by James Franklin, and sold at his shop near the town School-House, 1730. [2], 12, [12], [2], 210, p. 29 cm (fol.); Early American Imprints, Series 1, no. 3346 (filmed).

99. Ibid.

100. Ibid., *{{John: ?}}121–22.

101. An ACT to prevent the Spreading of the Small Pox and other contagious Sickness in this Colony, 1743, *{{John: ?}}274. The Charter Granted by His Majesty King Charles II, Newport, 1744, 15, [18], 308. (The charter was printed to accompany the 1745 ed. of the Acts and Laws, with which it is here reproduced.)

102. Ibid., *{{John: ? And see 103-110}}274–75.

103. Ibid., *275.

104. Ibid., *276.

105. Ibid., *277.

106. Ibid., *278.

107. Ibid., *279.

108. Ibid.

109. Ibid., *279–80.

110. Ibid., *280.

111. Ibid.

112. Ibid. (Emphasis in original.)

113. Elizabeth Anne Fenn, *Pox Americana: The Great Smallpox Epidemic of 1775–82* (2001), 273. In autumn 1777, Valley Forge became the site for general inoculation. Francis Randolph Packard, *The History of Medicine in the United States* (1901), 264, 283, 315.

114. Fenn, *Pox Americana, supra* note 113, p. 131.

115. Quoted in ibid., 131.

116. Discussed by Fenn, ibid.; see also Benjamin Franklin, "The Retort Courteous," in *The Writings of Benjamin Franklin,* Vol. 10, ed. Albert Henry Smyth (1907), 111.

117. *Pox Americana*, 132. Robert Donkin, for instance, a British officer in New York, explicitly directed the use of smallpox as a weapon, writing, "Dip arrows in matter of smallpox and twang them at the American rebels, in order to inoculate them; This would sooner disband thee stubborn, ignorant, enthusiastic savages, than any other compulsive measures. Such is their dread and fear of that disorder!" Later in the war, General Alexander Leslie sent a letter to Lord Cornwallis, indicating his plan to distribute sick soldiers throughout the "Rebell Plantations." Ibid.

118. Ibid.

119. 1776–77, c. 7.

120. See, e.g., An Act permitting Inoculation for the Small-Pox to be practiced in this Colony, Colony of Rhode-Island &c. in General Assembly, June Session, 1776.

121. The original act, An Act to oblige infected ships and other vessels coming into this province to perform quarantine, Lib. HS. Fol. 655, ch. XXV, November 1766, was to continue in force for three years. Ibid., §8. It was renewed by 1769, c. 4; continued again in June 1773, c. 2; continued for seven years by February 1777, c. 17; continued until the end of the next session by 1784, c. 83, continued for seven years by 1785 c. 77, and again continued to October 30, 1799 by 1792, c. 77. An Act to oblige infected ships and other vessels coming into this province to perform quarantine, Lib. HS. Fol. 655, ch. XXV, November 1766, in *The Laws of Maryland to which are Prefixed the Original Charter, with an English Translation, the Bill of Rights and Constitution, 1799*, p. §8.

122. The Constitution of Maryland, Art. 33, reprinted in *The Laws of Maryland to which are prefixed the Original Charter with an English Translation the Bill of Rights and Constitution of the State as originally adopted by the convention, with several alterations by Acts of Assembly*, Vol. I, 1799.

123. See Ibid.

124. An ACT to define and ascertain the powers of the governor on the subject therein mentioned. Lib. JG. No. 2 fol. 30, reprinted in *Laws of Maryland to which are prefixed the original charter with an English translation, the bill of rights, and the constitution of the state*, Vol. II (1800).

125. An ACT to appoint a health officer for the port of Baltimore-town in Baltimore county. Lib. JG. No. 2 fol. 70., reprinted in *Laws of Maryland to which are prefixed the original charter with an English translation, the bill of rights, and the constitution of the state*, Vol. II (1800).

126. See, e.g., An Ordinance to preserve the health of the city, and to prevent the introduction of pestilential and other infectious diseases into the same, Apr. 7, 1797 (repealed by an Ordinance passed February 27, 1799); A Supplement to the ordinance, entitled "An ordinance to preserve the health of the city, and to prevent the introduction of the pestilential and other infectious diseases, into the same," July 17, 1797 (repealed by an Ordinance passed February 27, 1799); A Further Supplement to the ordinance entitled "An ordinance to preserve the health of the city and to prevent the introduction of the pestilential and other infectious diseases into the same," September 4, 1797 (repealed by an Ordinance passed February 27, 1799); A Further additional Supplement to the ordinance, entitled "An ordinance to preserve the health of the city and to prevent the introduction of the pestilential and other infectious diseases into the same," February 28, 2798 (repealed by an Ordinance passed February 27, 1799); A Supplement to the ordinance entitled "An ordinance to preserve the health of the city and to prevent the introduction of the pestilential and other infectious diseases into the same," July 15, 1800 (repealed by an Ordinance passed March 20, 1801), reprinted in *Ordinances of the*

Corporation of the City of Baltimore, with the Act of Incorporation and Supplement thereto prefixed, 1801, 300–317.

127. See, e.g., An Act to prevent the bringing in and spreading of infectious Distempers in this State, Passed May 4, 1784, Laws of the State of New-York, Seventh Session, 1784, ch. LVII, pp. 82–83. See also *Greenleaf's Laws of New York* 1, no. 117; An Act to prevent the spreading of contagious Sickness, June 22, 1797, reprinted in *The Laws of the commonwealth of Massachusetts from Nov. 28, 1790 to Feb. 28, 1807, with the Constitutions of the United States of America and of the commonwealth,* Vol. II, June 1807, p. 788; An ACT to prevent infectious diseases being brought into this state, and for other purposes, Jan. 24, 1797, reprinted in *Laws of the State of Delaware, from the fourteenth Day of October, 1700 to the Eighteenth Day of August, 1797,* Vol. II, 1354–58; A Supplement to the act, entitled, An act to prevent infectious diseases being brought into this State, and for other purposes, 1799, reprinted in *Laws of the State of Delaware, from Jan. 2, 1798 to Jan. 25, 1805,* Vol. III, 1816, 47–52; An Act Providing in Case of Sickness, 1794, Acts and Laws of the State of Connecticut in America, p. 227–31; See, e.g., An ACT to prevent infectious diseases being brought into this state, and for other purposes, Jan. 24, 1797, reprinted in *Laws of the State of Delaware, from the fourteenth Day of October, 1700 to the Eighteenth Day of August, 1797,* Vol. II, 1354–58; A Supplement to the act, entitled, An act to prevent infectious diseases being brought into this State, and for other purposes, 1799, reprinted in *Laws of the State of Delaware, from Jan. 2, 1798 to Jan. 25, 1805,* Vol. III, 1816, 47–52; Acts and Resolutions of the General Assembly of the State of South-Carolina, passed in April, 1794, Resolution in the House of Representatives, April 30, 1794, *{{**John: ?**}}20; An Act reducing into one, the several Acts to oblige Vessels, coming from foreign Parts, to perform Quarantine, December 26, 1792, reprinted in *A Collection of all such Acts of the General Assembly of Virginia, of a public and permanent Nature, as are now in Force* (1794), 254–56.

128. An Act to prevent the spreading of contagious Sickness, June 22, 1797, reprinted in *The Laws of the Commonwealth of Massachusetts from Nov. 28, 1790 to Feb. 28, 1807, with the Constitutions of the United States of America and of the commonwealth,* Vol. II, June 1807, p. 788.

129. Ibid.

130. Ibid., 789.

131. Ibid.

132. Ibid.

133. Ibid., 789–90.

134. An ACT to empower the Town of Boston to choose a Board of Health, and for removing and preventing Nuisances, June 20, 1799, reprinted in *The Perpetual Laws of the Commonwealth of Massachusetts, from the Establishment of its of its Constitution in the year 1780, to the end of the year 1800,* Vol. III, containing the Laws from January 1799 to November 1800, March 1801, pp. 41–50.

135.	Ibid. (Emphasis in original.)

136.	Ibid., §8.

137.	An Act Providing in Case of Sickness, 1794, Acts and Laws of the State of Connecticut in America, pp. 227–31.

138.	Ibid., 228.

139.	Ibid., 229.

140.	Ibid.

141.	Ibid., 230.

142.	Ibid., 231. ("[W]henever any Person shall be brought to Trial for Breach of this Act, in communicating or receiving the Small-Pox, aiding or assisting therein, such Person shall be deemed and adjudged guilty thereof, although the complainant shall not be able to produce any other Proof than to render it probable.") The statute allowed, however, for the accused to counter the accusation by swearing to the court that he or she did not voluntarily, directly, or indirectly give or receive the infection. Ibid.

143.	See, e.g., A Supplement to the act, entitled, An act to prevent infectious diseases being brought into this State, and for other purposes, 1799, reprinted in *Laws of the State of Delaware, from Jan. 2, 1798 to Jan. 25, 1805*, Vol. III, 1816, pp. 47–52 (granting the local authorities "with full power and authority, to suspend altogether the intercourse by land, between any cities, towns or places in the United States, or elsewhere, during the existence or prevalence of any infectious or contagious disorder, and the said borough, town, or other part or district in this State . . .").

144.	1 Stat. 353 (1794), 2 U.S.C. §27 (1958).

145.	An Act Relative to Quarantine, May 27, 1796, ch. 31, 1 Stat. 474 (repealed 1799) 1789–1799. See also 6 *Annals of Congress*, 2916 1796–1797 ("Be it enacted, &c., That the President of the United States be and he is hereby authorized to direct the revenue officers and the officers commanding forts and revenue cutters, to aid in the execution of quarantine, and also in the execution of the health laws of the States respectively, in such manner as may to him appear necessary"). For discussion of the yellow fever epidemic raging at the time, see J. H. Powell, *Bring out Your Dead: The Great Plague of Yellow Fever in Philadelphia in 1793* (1949).

146.	Act of May 27, 1796, ch. 31, 1 Stat. 474 (repealed 1799). See also 43 Am. L. Rev 382 at 384.

147.	See *Annals of Congress*, 4th Cong., 1st Session, col. 87, May, 13, 1796 (committing "An act relative to quarantine" to Mssrs. Rutherfurd, Bingham, and Langdon, to consider and report to the Senate); The Debates and Proceedings of the Congress of the United States; with an Appendix containing Important State Papers and Public Documents, Fourth Congress—First Session, Dec. 7, 1795–June 1, 1796 (1855), 1347–1360. See also Goodman et al., Law in Public Health Practice, *supra* note 68 (noting the tenor of the debates).

148.	Statement of Mr. Milledge, The Debates and Proceedings of the Congress of the United States; with an Appendix containing Important State Papers and Public Documents, Fourth Congress—First Session, December 7, 1795–June 1, 1796 (1855), May 12, 1796, 1350–51 ("spoke . . . of the power of regulating quarantine being in the State Governments").

149. See, e.g., Statement of Mr. W. Lyman, ibid., 1352 (who "thought the individual States had the sole control over the regulations of quarantine. It was by no means a commercial regulation, but a regulation which respected the health of our fellow-citizens"); Statement of Mr. Lyman, ibid., May 12, 1796, 1354 ("Quarantine was not a commercial regulation, it was a regulation for the preservation of health. If commerce was incidentally affected, it ought so to be, when the object was the preservation of health and life. The United States, it was true, could prevent the importation of any goods, whether infected or not, but it did not thence follow that they could permit the landing of infectious goods contrary to the laws of any State. The several States possessed the sole power over this subject. They were the best judges of the due exercise of it"); Statement of Mr. Page, ibid., May 12, 1796, 1357 ("the right of the people to preserve their health . . . was one of the first rights of Nature"). See also Statement of Mr. Gallatin, ibid., May 12, 1796, 1353 ("[T]he regulation of quarantine had nothing to do with commerce. It was a regulation of internal police. It was to preserve the health of a certain place, by preventing the introduction of pestilential diseases, by preventing persons coming from countries where they were prevalent. Whether such persons came by land or by water, whether for commerce or for pleasure, was of no importance. They were all matters of police"). See also Statement of Mr. Lyman, ibid., May 12, 1796, 1354 ("The right to preserve health and life was inalienable. The bill was not only unnecessary and improper, but it was an injudicious interference with the internal police of the States"); Statement of Mr. Holland, ibid., May 12, 1796, 1358 (noting "The Constitution being silent with respect to health laws, he supposed the passing of them was left to the States themselves"); Statement of Mr. Brent, ibid., May 12, 1796, 1358 (suggesting that "the Constitution did not authorize" such federal interference with state police powers).

150. Statement of Mr. Milledge, ibid., May 12, 1796, 1351.

151. Ibid.

152. Statement of Mr. Giles, ibid., May 11, 1796, 1348.

153. Statement of Mr. Swanwick, ibid., May 12, 1796, 1350. ("the time during which quarantine should be performed, and at what particular place, which would certainly be best determined by the State Governments. . . . Indeed, most of them having already fixed on places for the purpose, and erected suitable buildings for the sick, for purifying goods, &c. It was said, the right of regulating quarantine did not reside in the State Governments; he believed it did, and that the individual States had conceived so, was evident from the expense which some of them had been at in erecting buildings, &c., for the purpose").

154. See, e.g., Statement of Mr. S. Smith, ibid., May 11, 1796, 1348. ("the performing

of quarantine was in the direction of the General Government: it was a commercial regulation"); Statement of Mr. Bourne, ibid., May 12, 1796, 1350; Statement of Mr. Sitgreaves, ibid., May 12, 1796, 1350 ("[T]he strongest and best reason for a law, such as the one proposed, is, that it is a matter of very serious doubt whether, upon this subject, the States had any authority at all, and whether all such power is not vested by the Constitution in the congress, under their general authority to regulate commerce and navigation"); Mr. Hillhouse, ibid., (1855), May 12, 1796, 1352–1353 ("Gentlemen might as well say that the individual States had the power of prohibiting commerce as of regulating quarantine: because, if they had the power to stop a vessel for one month, they might stop it for twelve months. This might interfere with regulations respecting our trade, and break our Treaties").

155.   See, e.g., Statement of Mr. Smith, ibid., May 11, 1796, 1348 ("[States] could not command the officer of a fort to use force to prevent a vessel from entering their port. The authority over him was in the General Government"); Statement of Mr. Smith, ibid., May 11, 1796, 1348 ("[T]he Constitution did not give to the State Governments the power of stopping vessels from coming into their ports"); Statement of Mr. Sitgreaves, ibid., May 12, 1796, 1350 ("It was true, the State of Pennsylvania had made some regulations on the subject of quarantine; but, without the aid of the United States, they could not carry them into effect. They may direct, by their Governor and board of Health, quarantines to be performed, but they could not force any vessels to observe their directions, without the aid of the General Government").

156.   Elizabeth Fee, "Public Health and the State: The United States," in *The History of Public Health and the Modern State*, ed. Dorothy Porter (1994), 224, 233.

157.   An Act Respecting Quarantines and Health Laws, Fifth Congress, Sess. III, ch. 12, 1799, February 25, 1799, 619–21, §1. See also 1 Stat. 619 (1799), 42 U.S.C. §97 (1958). For discussion of this statute, see Maxey, "Federal Quarantine Law," *Pol. Sci. Q.* 23, no. 4 (December 1908): 617–18.

158.   An Act Respecting Quarantine and Health Laws, 1 Stat. 619 (1799), 42 U.S.C. §97 (1958), §2.

159.   See Debates and Proceedings of the Congress of the United States, Fifth Congress, May 15, 1797–March 3, 1799 (1851), 2792–95.

160.   Act of February 25, 1799, ch. 12, I Stat. 619.

161.   Act of February 25, 1799, ch. 12, I stat. 620, §3.

162.   Hugh S. Cumming, "The United States Quarantine System during the Past Fifty Years," in *A Half Century of Public Health* (1921), 120–21.

163.   *Gibbons v. Ogden*, 22 U.S. 1, 205–6 (9 Wheat) (1824).

164.   Opinions of the Attorneys-General of the United States, 1829, 2, 263–66.

165.   See, e.g., *Mitchell v. City of Rockland*, 45 Me. 496 (1858).

166.   By 1873, more than thirty boards of health had formed. Chapin, "History of

State and Municipal Control of Disease," *supra* note 65, pp. 137–38. For further discussion see Donohue, "Biodefense and Constitutional Constraints," *supra* note 60.

167.　See, e.g., American State Papers, Documents, Legislative and Executive, of the Congress of the United States, March 3, 1789–March 3, 1815, Vol. VII (1832), 532 ("The recent accounts of the severe quarantine of 120 days, imposed upon American vessels, in some of the principal ports of Spain, must fill every friend of our commerce with regret. It amounts to an almost total prohibition of our trade with those cities; and is viewed by your committee, as arising from the false alarms and unfounded suggestions among our own citizens. In order to prevent these alarming evils, it is necessary to form our health laws upon more scientific principles, and to regulate our commercial intercourse upon maxims more accordant with domestic neatness and economy"); and various Privy Council Orders specifically targeting vessels from the United States. See also discussion in Donohue, "Biodefense and Constitutional Constraints," *supra* note 60.

168.　See, again, orders of the Privy Council specifically targeting vessels arriving vessels from the United States.

169.　Maxey, "Federal Quarantine Law," 617–18.

170.　American State Papers, Documents, Legislative and Executive, of the Congress of the United States, March 3, 1789–March 3, 1815, Vol. VII (1832), 532.

171.　Ibid., 532.

172.　Ibid.

173.　Michael Les Benedict, "Contagion and the Constitution: Quarantine Agitatio from 1869 to 1866," *J. of the History of Medicine (and Allied Sciences)* 25, no. 3 (April 1970): 178.

174.　Ibid.

175.　National Quarantine and Sanitary Convention, Proceedings and debates of the fourth national quarantine and sanitary convention, June 14, 15, and 16, 1860 (Boston, 1860), 170.

176.　See, e.g., National Quarantine and Sanitary Convention, Proceedings and debates of the second national quarantine and sanitary convention, held in the city of Baltimore, May 3, 1858, available at http://query.nytimes.com/mem/archive-free/pdf?r es=F30D1EFA3E581B7493C1A9178ED85F4C8584F9; National Quarantine and Sanitary Convention, Proceedings and debates of the third national quarantine and sanitary convention, held in the city of New York, April 27, 28, 29, and 30, 1839 (New York, 1859); National Quarantine and Sanitary Convention, Proceedings and debates of the Fourth National Quarantine and Sanitary convention, June 14, 15, and 16, 1860 (Boston, 1860).

177.　Jeffery K. Smart, "Chemical and Biological Warfare Research and Development during the Civil War," U.S. Army Soldier and Biological Chemical Command, p. 5, available at http://www.wood.army.mil/ccmuseum/ccmuseum/Library/Civil_War_ CBW.pdf .

178.   See, e.g., Ibid.; Albert Clarke, "The Youngest Officer in the War," in *Stories of Our Soldiers* (1893), 229; J. D. Haines, "Did a Confederate Doctor Engage in a Primitive Form of Biological Warfare? The Northern Press Thought So," *America's Civil War* 12, no. 4 (September 1999): 12, 16, and 20; Andrew G. Robertson and Laura J. Robertson, "From Asps to Allegations: Biological Warfare in History," *Military Medicine* 160, no. 8 (August 1995): 369–70.

179.   War Department General Orders No. 100.

180.   Les Benedict, *supra* note 173, p. 181.

181.   *Cong. Globe,* 39 C., 1 S., p. 1201.

182.   Ibid., 2444–45.

183.   Ibid., 2445.

184.   Les Benedict, *supra* note 173, p. 188.

185.   Ibid., 189.

186.   *Cong. Globe,* 39 C., 1 S., p. 2521.

187.   In 1879 marine hospitals were folded into a national Marine Hospital Service. Sciarrino, "Part III: Epidemics," *supra* note 57, pp. 432–33; and Cumming, "The United States Quarantine System," *supra* note 162, p. 120. The surgeon general began calling for a uniform federal system. Comments by Surgeon General Woodworth at the International Medical Congress in Philadelphia, 1876, discussed in Cumming, "The United States Quarantine System," *supra* note 162, p. 121. Discoveries by Louis Pasteur, Ferdinand Cohn, and Robert Koch led to the field of microbiology, entrenching the germ theory of disease. *Colum. L. Rev.* 93 (1833, 1865). The germ theory of disease took hold. Frederick P. Gorham, "The History of Bacteriology and Its Contribution to Public Health Work," in *A Half Century of Public Health* (1920), 69. For other influences of the germ theory of contagion on calls for quarantine law, see "Report of the committee of the college of Physicians of Philadelphia: Appointed to Investigate the Efficiency of Our Quarantine Arrangements for the Exclusion of Cholera and Other Epidemic Diseases, October 28, 1887," p. 1 (writing, "The acceptance of the germ theory of infectious and contagious diseases, or the probability at least of its truth, places in a new light the management of quarantine for detention and disinfection of vessels and their passengers"). See also Cumming, "The United States Quarantine System," *supra* note 162, p. 120.

188.   An Act to prevent the introduction of contagious or infectious diseases into the United States, April 29, 1878, ch. 66, 20 Stat 37.

189.   Ibid.

190.   Ibid.

191.   Ibid., §2.

192.   Cumming, "The United States Quarantine System," *supra* note 162, p. 121. The following year, Congress repealed the sections of the statute empowering the Marine Hospital Service to make rules and regulations independent of state boards. An act to

prevent the introduction of infectious or contagious diseases into the United States, and to establish a national board of health, March 3, 1879, ch. 202, 20 Stat 484, §10. See also Act of July 1, 1879, ch. 61, 21 Stat. L. 47 (amending the 1879 act and designating a disbursing agent). In a twist of sunset standards, the repeal (not the act) was set to expire after four years, at which time the original legislation went back into force. An act to prevent the introduction of infectious or contagious diseases into the United States, and to establish a national board of health, March 3, 1879, ch. 202, 20 Stat 484, §10; "Government Officers Anxious: The Power of the Federal Authorities in Quarantine Matters," *New York Times*, September 1, 1989, available at http://query.nytimes.com/ mem/archive-free/pdf?res=F60C1EF83C5F1B738DDDA80894D1405B8285F0D3.

193.　An act to prevent the introduction of infectious or contagious diseases into the United States, and to establish a national board of health, March 3, 1879, ch. 202, 20 Stat 484.

194.　"Government Officers Anxious: The Power of the Federal Authorities in Quarantine Matters," *New York Times*, September 1, 1892.

195.　See, e.g., Cumming, "The United States Quarantine System," *supra* note 162, p. 122 (highlighting the role of the MHS in stemming an 1882 yellow fever epidemic in Texas).

196.　See J. C. Wilson, E. O. Shakespeare, and R. A. Cleemann, "Report of the Committee of the College of Physicians of Philadelphia: Appointed to Investigate the Efficiency of Our Quarantine Arrangements for the Exclusion of Cholera and Other Epidemic Diseases," *Transactions of the College of Physicians of Philadelphia* 1044, 3rd series (October 28, 1887): 23–45.

197.　Ibid., 16 (writing, "The ability of the National Government, by an existing act of Congress, to come to the aid of local quarantine authorities in answer to the appeal of the Executive of any State in time of grave danger, implies a function of very narrow scope and uncertain application. Appeals of this kind are apt to be deferred until the emergency is extreme, and the aid obtained from the Government is, therefore, likely to be rendered too late to accomplish its most important purpose, namely, the prevention of an invasion").

198.　Ibid., 3. See also p. 19, writing, "Municipalities are selfish, and knowing that with the trader quarantine is not a favorite institution, and that it is his tendency to sail into that port where the quarantine is most lax, they are assailed with a sore temptation to wink at the neglect of proper precautions, if, by so doing, they may circumvent a possible commercial rival."

199.　See, e.g., ibid., 13 (discussing the failure of the exterior ports to act with dispatch to prevent the 1873 cholera epidemic, which ended up hurting Ohio, Minnesota, and the Dakotas the most); ibid., 18 (discussing failure of Florida port to prevent the 1887 yellow fever outbreak).

200. Ibid., 5–6.

201. Ibid., 20.

202. See, e.g., "Report of the committee of the college of Physicians of Philadelphia: Appointed to Investigate the Efficiency of Our Quarantine Arrangements for the Exclusion of Cholera and Other Epidemic Diseases, October 28, 1887," p. 44 (writing, "We know that there are legislative difficulties in the way; that quarantine partaking of the nature of police regulation, its exercise, it may be claimed, belongs to the local authorities. Yet, even if it be conceded to be a police regulation, its scope is not local, but extends over the whole country, and it would seem, in justice, that it should be exercised and paid for by the whole country"); Col. J. C. Clark, Vice-President Mobile & Ohio Railroad, "Quarantine Regulations," in Proceedings of the Quarantine Conference Held in Montgomery, Alabama, March 5–7, 1889, Appendix III, pp. 69–70 (writing, "The national government should take charge of and maintain a rigid maritime quarantine, and locate such quarantine stations at such points on the sea-coast and on navigable rivers, at proper points, so as to prevent the introduction of yellow fever or any other contagious or infectious disease into any state or territory of the United States, leaving to the state authorities, the power to deal with these matters in the states, outside of maritime quarantine"); "Resolutions offered by Mr. B. R. Foreman, of New Orleans," in Proceedings of the Quarantine Conference Held in Montgomery, Alabama, March 5–7, 1889, Appendix V, p. 86.

203. Act 69 of the Legislature of Louisiana of 1882, §1.

204. *Morgan's Steamship Company v. Louisiana Board of Health,* 118 U.S. 455 (1886). U.S. Const., Art I, §10(2) states, "No State shall, without the Consent of the Congress, lay any Imposts or Duties on Imports or Exports, except what may be absolutely necessary for executing its inspection Laws: and the net Produce of all Duties and Imposts, laid by any State on Imports or Exports, shall be for the Use of the Treasury of the United States; and all such Laws shall be subject to the Revision and control of the Congress." Art. I §10(3) states, "No State shall, without the Consent of the Congress, lay any duty of Tonnage." Article I, §8(3) gives congress power to regulate commerce ([The Congress shall have Power] To regulate Commerce with foreign Nations, and among the several States, and with the Indian Tribes." Art. I, §9(6) declares, "No Preference shall be given by any Regulation of Commerce or Revenue to the Ports of one State over those of another; nor shall Vessels bound to, or from, one State, be obliged to enter, clear, or pay Duties in another."

205. *Morgan's Steamship Company v. Louisiana Board of Health,* p. 464.

206. An Act to Perfect the Quarantine Service of the United States, August 1, 1888, ch. 727, 25 Stat. L. 355; An act to Prevent the Introduction of Contagious Diseases from one state to another and for the punishment of certain offenses, [also known as the "Epidemic Diseases Act"], March 27, 1890, ch. 51, 26 Stat. L. 31; Immigration Act of March

13, 1891; An Act Granting Additional quarantine Powers and Imposing Additional Duties upon the Marine-Hospital Service, February 15, 1893, ch. 114, 27 Stat. L. 449, *repealing* An act to prevent the introduction of infectious or contagious diseases into the United States, and to establish a national board of health, March 3, 1879.

207. An act to Prevent the Introduction of Contagious Diseases from one state to another and for the punishment of certain offenses, March 27, 1890, ch. 51, 26 Stat. L. 31, §1.

208. Ibid.

209. Ibid.

210. An Act Granting Additional quarantine Powers and Imposing Additional Duties upon the Marine-Hospital Service, February 15, 1893, ch. 114, 27 Stat. L. 449, *repealing* An act to prevent the introduction of infectious or contagious diseases into the United States, and to establish a national board of health, March 3, 1879.

211. Ibid., at §3.

212. Ibid., at §4794.

213. Ibid., at §6.

214. Ibid., at §7. It is not clear how often this power was used. By 1921, however, the authority was considered to be based on unsound science. See Cumming, "The United States Quarantine System," *supra* note 162, p. 122 ("In light of modern knowledge of the spread of disease, this radical measure is no longer deemed necessary, since the application of rational preventive measures provides adequate safeguards without material interference with commerce or travel").

215. An Act Granting Additional quarantine Powers and Imposing Additional Duties upon the Marine-Hospital Service, February 15, 1893, §8.

216. *Compagnie Francaise de Navigation a Vapeur v. Louisiana State Bd. of Health,* 186 U.S. 380 (1902).

217. Ibid., 388.

218. Ibid., 387. See also *Asbell v. Kansas,* 209 U.S. 251 (1908).

219. *Jacobson v. Massachusetts,* 197 U.S. 11, 27 (1905).

220. Wendy E. Parmet et al., "Individual Rights versus the Public's Health—100 years after Jacobson v. Massachusetts," *New England J. Med.* 352, no. 652 (2005).

221. See, e.g., *Wong Chow v. Transatlantic Fire Ins. Co.,* 13 Haw. 160, 161 (1900) (upholding quarantine in Honolulu). *Crayton v. Larabee,* 110 N. Rep. 355, 220 N.Y. 493 (N.Y. Ct. of App. 1917) (writing in relation to the quarantine of a woman suspected of having been exposed to smallpox, "The police power defines precise definition and rigid delimitation. We hold here that the ordinance was authorized, was legally adopted, was a reasonable and valid health regulation under the police power of the state, vesting in the health officer a stated discretionary power, which, if lawfully exercised, protected those exercising it against the consequent damages to person or property").

222. *The Minnesota Rate Cases,* 230 U.S. 352, 406 (1913).

223. Edelman, "International Travel and Our National Quarantine System," 35.

224. *Colum. L. Rev.* 93 (1833, 1865).

225. Chapin, "History of State and Municipal Control of Disease," *supra* note 65, p. 132; Cumming, "The United States Quarantine System," *supra* note 162, p. 131.

226. Cumming, *supra* note 162, pp. 123–24.

227. Codified as amended at 42 U.S.C. §§264–72.

228. Robert T. Stafford Disaster Relief and Emergency Assistance Act (PL 100-707), amending the Disaster Relief Act of 1974, PL 93-288. Current codified provisions, as further amended, at 42 U.S.C. §5121–5207 (2007).

229. 42 U.S.C. §264(a); and 42 C.F.R. §§70–71. See also 21 CFR §1240.3 et seq. In 1953 the Eisenhower administration launched the Department of Health, Education and Welfare (HEW) under the executive's then-existing authority to form new bureaucratic entities absent legislative veto. President Dwight D. Eisenhower, Reorganization Plan No. 1 of 1953, Transmitted to Congress March 12, 1953, available at http://www.presidency. ucsb.edu. In 1980 HEW became the Department of Health and Human Services. 20 U.S.C. 3508 (Redesignation of Department of Health, Education, and Welfare).

230. SARS (April 4, 2003), and pandemic influenza (April 2005).

231. 42 U.S.C. §264(d). "Qualifying stage" means disease is in communicable stage, or is in a precommunicable state, if the disease would likely cause a public health emergency if transmitted to other individuals. 42 U.S.C. §264(d)(2).

232. 1944 Public Health Services Act, 58 Stat. 682, §361; codified at 42 U.S.C. §264(d). In 2000 federal regulations delegated this authority to the director of the CDC, with the actual determination made by the CDC's Division of Global Migration and Quarantine. 65 FR 49906; and 42 C.F.R. 70.2. See also 21 CFR §5.10 et seq.

233. 42 C.F.R. 70.3.

234. See 42 C.F.R. §71; 42 U.S.C. §265 (stating, "Whenever the Surgeon General determines that by reason of the existence of any communicable disease in a foreign country there is serious danger of the introduction of such disease into the United States, and that this danger is so increased by the introduction of persons or property from such country that a suspension of the right to introduce such persons and property is required in the interest of the public health, the Surgeon General, in accordance with regulations approved by the President, shall have the power to prohibit, in whole or in part, the introduction of persons and property from such countries or places as he shall designate in order to avert such danger, and for such period of time as he may deem necessary for such purpose").

235. July 1, 1944, c. 373, Title III, §363, 58 Stat. 704; June 12, 2002, Pub.L. 107–88, Title I, §142(a)(3), (b)(2), 116 Stat. 626, 627.) 42 U.S.C. §266. Special Quarantine Powers in Times of War (stating, "To protect the military and naval forces and war workers of the

United States, in time of war, against any communicable disease specified in Executive orders as provided in subsection (b) of section 264 of this title, the Secretary, in consultation with the Surgeon General, is authorized to provide by regulations for the apprehension and examination, in time of war, of any individual reasonably believed (1) to be infected with such disease and (2) to be a probable source of infection to members of the armed forces of the United States or to individuals engaged in the production or transportation of arms, munitions, ships, food, clothing, or other supplies for the armed forces. Such regulations may provide that if upon examination any such individual is found to be so infected, he may be detained for such time and in such manner as may be reasonably necessary").

236. 42 U.S.C. §267 (stating "[T]he Surgeon General shall control, direct, and manage all United States quarantine stations, grounds, and anchorages, designate their boundaries, and designate the quarantine officers to be in charge thereof. With the approval of the President he shall from time to time select suitable sites for and establish such additional stations, grounds, and anchorages in the States and possessions of the United States as in his judgment are necessary to prevent the introduction of communicable diseases into the States and possessions of the United States").

237. 42 U.S.C. §268(a) (stating, "Any consular or medical officer of the United States, designated for such purpose by the Secretary, shall make reports to the Surgeon General, on such forms and at such intervals as the Surgeon General may prescribe, of the health conditions at the port or place at which such officer is stationed").

238. 42 U.S.C. §§269–70.

239. 42 U.S.C. §271.

240. 28 U.S.C.A. §1331.

241. Robert T. Stafford Disaster Relief and Emergency Assistance Act, 42 U.S.C. §5121–5206 (2000). The Stafford Act (Pub. L. 100-707) is a 1988 amended version of the Disaster Relief Act of 1974 (Pub. L. 93-288).

242. Disaster Mitigation Act of 2000, 42 U.S.C. §68 (Pub. L. 106-390) (2000) (also called DMA2K); "Disaster Relief—The Public Health and Welfare."

243. {402} 42 U.S.C. 5170a. Specifically, the statute empowers the president to (1) direct any federal agency, with or without reimbursement, to utilize its authorities and the resources granted to it under federal law (including personnel, equipment, supplies, facilities, and managerial, technical, and advisory services) in support of state and local assistance efforts; (2) coordinate all disaster relief assistance (including voluntary assistance) provided by federal agencies, private organizations, and state and local governments; (3) provide technical and advisory assistance to affected state and local governments for—(A) the performance of essential community services; (B) issuance of warnings of risks and hazards; (C) public health and safety information, including dissemination of such information; (D) provision of health and safety measures; and

(E) management, control, and reduction of immediate threats to public health and safety; and (4) assist state and local governments in the distribution of medicine, food, and other consumable supplies, and emergency assistance.

244. 42 U.S.C. §5170(a)(3)(D). According to FEMA Regulations, when an "incident occurs or threatens to occur in a State" that would not qualify as a major disaster, a governor may request that the President declare an 'emergency," defined as "any occasion or instance, for which, in the determination of the President, [f]ederal assistance is needed to supplement State and local efforts and capabilities to save lives and to protect property and public health and safety. . . ." CFR §206.2. Once these conditions are met, the FEMA associate or regional director "may provide assistance," including directing "any federal agency, with or without reimbursement, to utilize its authorities and the resources granted to it under federal law (including personnel, equipment, supplies, facilities, and managerial, technical and advisory services) in support of state and local emergency assistance efforts to save lives, protect property and public health and safety." CFR §206.6. See also Jason W. Sapsin, Center for Law and the Public's Health at Georgetown and Johns Hopkins University, "Overview of Federal and State Quarantine Authority," p. 4 (2002), available at http://www.publichealthlaw.net/Resources/REsourcesPDFs/2proprietary.pdf.

245. See 42 U.S.C. §§5191–93. See also Alan Cohn, *Disaster Preparedness,* available at http://www.cap-press.com/pdf/2318.pdf.

246. 42 U.S.C. §5191(b).

247. See., e.g., Donohue, *The Cost of Counterterrorism* (discussing the constriction of rights).

248. See, e.g., refusal of the Supreme Court to adjudicate on the constitutionality of "police action" in Korea; three times refusing to adjudicate on the war in Vietnam; Korematsu, decision upholding Lincoln's blockade of Southern ports, ex parte quirin (1942). David J. Barron and Martin S. Lederman, "The Commander in Chief at the Lowest Ebb—a Constitutional History," *Harv. L. Rev.* 121, no. 4. (February 2008): 1106, 1107 (writing, e.g., "The fact that many interbranch disputes over war powers will not be resolved in court does not mean they will be uninfluenced by constitutional understandings.")

249. U.S. Const., 5th Amend; and Art. I(9)(2). For a discussion of the impact of quarantine law on these provisions see, e.g., Gostin, *Public Health Law,* 205–6 (2000); Paula Mindes, "Tuberculosis Quarantine: A Review of Legal Issues in Ohio and Other States," *J. of L. and Health* 10, no. 403 (1995–96); Wendy E. Parmet, "Legal Power and Legal Rights—Isolation and Quarantine in the Case of Drug-Resistant Tuberculosis," *N. Engl. J. Med.* 357, no. 5 (2007): 357.

250. The question here turns on what would be considered the least restrictive alternative. See discussion in Parmet, "Legal Power and Legal Rights." But see *In re Washington,* 716 N. W.2d 176, 292 Wis.2d 258, 2006 WI App 99 (Wis. App. 2006)

(upholding the forcible detention of woman living in a homeless shelter, found to have pulmonary tuberculosis).

251. See, e.g., *Miller v. Campbell Cty.*, 722 F. Supp. 687 (D.Who. 1989) (holding that a temporary forced evacuation from someone's home does not count as a taking for purposes of 42 U.S.C. §1983).

252. "National Security Strategy of the United States of America," supra note 3, pp. 8, 18.

253. U.S. Const. Art. II(2)(1).

254. U.S. Const., Art. I(8)(11), (12).

255. U.S. Const., Art. I(8)(15).

256. *Youngstown Sheet & Tube Co. v. Sawyer,* 343 U.S. 579 (1952).

257. Ibid.

258. 50 U.S.C. 1541–48.

259. Ibid.

260. See Nixon veto, November 7, 1973. See also Phil Bobbitt, "War Powers: An Essay on John Hart Ely's War and Responsibility: Constitutional Lessons of Vietnam and Its Aftermath," *Michigan Law Quarterly* 92, no. 6 (May 1994).

261. But note that the Obama administration has not challenged the War Powers Resolution specifically on these grounds.

262. See, e.g., *Dellums v. Bush.*

263. *Prize Cases* (1863), 67 U.S. 635.

264. Ibid.

265. Emancipation Proclamation, January 1, 1863; U.S. Navy General Order no. 4, January 14, 1863.

266. Authorization for Use of Military Force against Iraq Resolution of 1991, H.R.J. Res. 77; Authorization for Use of Military Force against Terrorists, Pub. L. No. 107-40; Authorization for Use of Military Force against Iraq Resolution of 2002, Pub. L. No. 107-243.

267. 10 U.S.C. §331–§335.

268. 10 U.S.C. §331.

269. 10 U.S.C. §332.

270. 10 U.S.C. §333.

271. See, e.g., Alexander Hamilton, *Federalist* no. 26 (addressing the question generally and noting that from the English experience, "[T]he people of America may be said to have derived an hereditary impression of danger to liberty, from standing armies in time of peace"); Brutus, *Anti-Federalist Papers*, no. 10, January 24, 1788 ("[T] he liberties of a people are in danger from a large standing army, not only because the rulers may employ them for the purposes of supporting themselves in any usurpations of power, which they may see proper to exercise, but there is great hazard, that an army will subvert the forms of the government, under whose authority, they are raised . . .");

James Madison, *Federalist* no. 46, January 29, 1788 (discussing limits on the size of a standing army).

272. 18 U.S.C. §1385.

273. Ibid.

274. 2002 Homeland Security Act, §780.

275. For a discussion of the distinction between the authorities reserved to the states and to the people, see Randy E. Barnett, "The Proper Scope of the Police Power," *Notre Dame L. Rev.* 79, no. 429 (2004).

276. But see Notes of the Secret Debates of the Federal Convention of 1787, Taken by the Late Hon Robert Yates, Chief Justice of the State of New York, and One of the Delegates from That State to the Said Convention, June 7, 1787, available at http://avalon. law.yale.edu/18th_century/yates.asp. (Mr. Wilson: "The State governments ought to be preserved—the freedom of the people and their internal good police depends on their existence in full vigor—but such a government can only answer local purposes—That it is not possible a general government, as despotic as even that of the Roman emperors, could be adequate to the government of the whole without this distinction. He hoped that the national government would be independent of State governments, in order to make it vigorous, and therefore moved that the above resolution be postponed, and that the convention in its room adopt the following resolve: That the second branch of the national legislature be chosen by districts, to be formed for that purpose"; Mr. Martin: "A general government may operate on individuals in cases of general concern, and still be federal. This distinction is with the States, as States, represented by the people of those States. States will take care of their internal police and local concerns. The general government has no interest but the protection of the whole.") See also Barnett, "The Proper Scope of the Police Power," *supra* note 275.

277. *Gibbons v. Ogden,* 22 U.S. 1, 205–6 (9 Wheat) (1824).

278. Grier, J., 46 U.S. 631 (1847).

279. Grier, J., 46 U.S. 632 (1847).

280. Ibid.

281. Ibid.

282. Thomas Cooley, *A Treatise on the Constitutional Limitations Which Rest Upon The Legislative Power of the United States of the American Union* (Boston: Little, Brown, and Company, 1868), 584. See also remarks of Grier, J. in *License Cases,* 5 How. 632; *Meeker v. Van Rensselaer,* 15 Wend. 397.

283. Ibid.

284. Christopher G. Tiedeman, *A Treatise on the Limitations of the Police Power in the United States* (1886), 4–5, citing *Thorpe v. Rutland R.R.,* 27 Vt. 140, 149–50 (1854).

285. *U.S. v. Shinnick,* 219 F. Supp. 789 (E.D.N.Y. 1963).

286. U.S. Const. art. I, §8, cl. 18.

287. The court had previously determined that the Due Process Clause does not prevent the indefinite detention of mentally ill individuals considered likely to commit "predatory acts of sexual violence." *Kansas v. Hendricks*, 521 US 346, 352 (1997).

288. *Comstock*, 130 S.Ct. at 1958–64.

289. Ibid., 1956.

290. Ibid., 1966 (Kennedy, J., concurring).

291. Ibid., 1968 (Kennedy, J., concurring).

292. Ibid., 1970 (Alito, J., concurring).

293. Ibid., 1974 (Thomas, J., dissenting) (quoting U.S. Const. art I, §8, cl. 18).

294. Ibid., 1973 (Thomas, J., dissenting).

295. Ibid., 1976 (Thomas, J., dissenting).

296. Ibid., 1965.

297. Ibid., 1975 (Thomas, J., dissenting).

298. See, e.g., http://www.cdc.gov/flu/weekly/regions2007-2008/datafinal/senregallregion07-08.htm.

299. Saeed Shah, "CIA Organised Fake Vaccination Drive to Get Osama bin Laden's family DNA," July 11, 2011, Guardian, UK, available at http://www.guardian.co.uk/world/2011/jul/11/cia-fake-vaccinations-osama-bin-ladens-dna; CNN World Report, "CIA Organized Vaccination Drive for DNA from bin Laden Home," July 12, 2001, available at http://articles.cnn.com/2011-07-12/world/pakistan.bin.laden.dna_1_bin-laden-family-members-laden-dna-vaccination?_s=PM:WORLD; Grace Wyler, "Pakistan Arrests Doctor for Running CIA Vaccination Drive to Get Bin Laden's DNA," *Business Insider*, July 11, 2001, available at http://www.businessinsider.com/pakistan-arrests-doctor-for-running-cia-vaccination-drive-to-get-bin-ladens-dna-2011-7; Nick Allen, "CIA Set up Fake Vaccination Programme to Capture Osama bin Laden's DNA," *Telegraph*, August 29, 2011, available at http://www.telegraph.co.uk/news/worldnews/al-qaeda/8631420/CIA-set-up-fake-vaccination-programme-to-capture-Osama-bin-Ladens-DNA.html; Mark Mazzetti, "Vaccination Ruse Used in Pursuit of Bin Laden," *New York Times*, July 11, 2011, available at http://www.nytimes.com/2011/07/12/world/asia/12dna.html.

300. S. Reardon, "Decrying CIA Vaccination Sham, Health Workers Brace for Backlash," *Science* 333, no. 6041 (July 22, 2011): 395, available at http://www.sciencemag.org/content/333/6041/395.citation.

301. See, e.g., Richard E. Hoffman and Jane E. Norton, "Lessons Learned from a Full-Scale Bioterrorism Exercise," *Emerging Infectious Diseases* 6, no. 652 (2000).

302. See discussion in Donohue, "Biodefense and Constitutional Constraints," *supra* note 60.

From Antiwar Politics to Antitorture Politics

SAMUEL MOYN

Introduction: Abu Ghraib and My Lai

At the end of April 2004, CBS News broadcast the first Abu Ghraib torture photos in the leadup to the *New Yorker* publication of Seymour M. Hersh's bombshell article on the site. The photos depicted horrendous acts from a makeshift prison the U.S. military had set up after its invasion of Iraq in 2003 by recycling one of Saddam Hussein's detention facilities: the mementos of American troops inflicting sickening cruelty on captives.

But there are other pictures in American history. As terrible as they were, the Abu Ghraib images were far less horrendous than the images that Americans viewed in late 1969, when the Cleveland *Plain Dealer* and then *Life* magazine published photographs of the horrifying scenes of the aftermath of the My Lai massacre leaked by former army photographer Ron Haeberle. That notorious war crime had occurred when a platoon of "Charlie Company" slaughtered hundreds of civilians, including women and children, in a Vietnamese village. As a result of the lurid photos of bodies by the side of the road, Charlie Company's leader, Lt. William Calley, eventually stood trial for murder.

After the photos at Abu Ghraib, public debate about the war was profoundly and lastingly transformed. "It seems gloomily possible that in years to come, when people in the Middle East recall the invasion of Iraq," the *New York Times* predicted the month after the revelations, "they will speak not of lost American lives or the toppling of a brutal dictator. The most enduring image of the occupation may be those pictures of grinning American soldiers torturing Iraqi prisoners."[1] In a later stage, the erection of the Guantanamo Bay site for indefinite detention of suspected terrorists occupied the public imagination as a symbol of American excesses. Both Abu Ghraib and Guantanamo became prominent because of their centrality to a mode of attention and dissent that targeted not *the war* itself but *the illegal means of fighting it*. Both focused on behavior that tested the boundaries—and arguments that doubted the very applicability—of international law norms governing conduct of the war. And academic commentary has since tracked public opinion in this regard, concentrating intensively on matters of detainee classification, treatment, and trial.

At first glance American inhumanity and dissent in response to it might seem very similar in Vietnam and Iraq—and the very same reporter, Seymour Hersh, broke the single most scandalous and high-profile story about crimes in both wars. Yet remembering Vietnam is crucial in order to put post-9/11 inhumanity and dissent in a new light: to show how different we now are. What commitment there is to the restraint of war in American law is very largely the result of the moment of horror in the early 1970s when larger numbers of people than before or since were prepared to see government officials and America's citizens themselves as potential and actual evildoers. But that crystalline moment of insight, in which concerns about how America fought were explicitly linked to what justification it had to fight at all (and what role it ought to play in the world) has since passed. The torture debate after 9/11 reflected primarily its truncation, not its fulfillment.

To show this, this essay surveys the central American invocations of international law in the Vietnam era. And at the threshold, it is important to acknowledge that in an era of massive political movements, the law of war simply had much less salience in Vietnam-era national debate. What legal arguments were made, it is true, take on great interest now as a point of comparison for the recent attempt to legalize warfare, and especially in contrast to the high profile international law assumed in post-9/11 debates. But it will be obvious to anyone who has studied or lived through the period that none of the legal monuments in an American landscape roiled by the Vietnam war were terribly prominent in the scheme of things. "It is a humbling realization of no small moment," the leading figure, Richard Falk, observed bitterly in 1973, "to acknowledge that only international lawyers have been paying attention to the international law arguments on the war."[2]

More important, to the minor extent that legalization of the Vietnam conflict took place, it was never separate from explicit concern about the politics of the war itself. Opposition to the war, or moral outrage about its conduct, came in the first instance not from lawyers or in terms of law but in ethical frameworks and not infrequently linked to visions of domestic and international transformation. As for lawyers, in the disappearing shadow of the actual Nuremberg trials that had made aggression, not war crimes, foremost among charges and concerns, most attempts to legalize the war in the Vietnam era were focused on its *jus ad bellum* justification in international law rather than the *jus in bello* validity of its means and methods. In the beginning, indeed, the war's lawyerly opponents turned to international law constraining military intervention in the first place as their primary recourse, and lawyers inside and outside government were forced to reply.

Rules governing the military conflict once it has begun were indeed almost entirely peripheral even to the peripheral legal debate, in the starkest of contrast to now. Almost no one made much of their routine violation for a long time—and no John Yoo emerged to exempt America from them. It was for some reason too early for the laws regarding humanitarian conduct of hostilities to pose much threat to waging the war; and in spite of extraordinary excesses, rules about means of warfare and detention of prisoners were entirely ignored even by the war's critics. Finally, though there certainly were late-breaking efforts, in a spike after My Lai, to target illegal conduct, those efforts were allied to a powerful social movement to end the war, indeed were essentially an attempt to pursue that movement with new means.

It would be wrong either to forget entirely what little attention there was to war crimes in their own right during Vietnam or the small antiwar movement that arose as the American invasion of Iraq loomed in 2003. And it is also fair to say that outrage about Abu Ghraib and Guantanamo ultimately counted as a moral issue, in spite of their unprecedented public legalization. Yet on balance, the differences between past and present are more striking. In particular, neither the priority of the debate over the legality of the war itself nor the inextricable alliance of the legal attack on the war with a broad-based social movement has obtained in domestic post-9/11 contention about constraints on the global struggle against violent extremism.

In this sense, it seems justifiable to observe a relative but palpable shift from a legal concern with aggression to one with atrocity. While constitutional and policy debate over the initiation of war surely remains today, the prospects of imposing international legal controls on American warfare do not receive comparable attention. In exchange, the focus on international standards for the conduct of war is much more intense. In the Vietnam years the former came first and remained the framework within which the latter emerged. By contrast, in the crucial months and years after the invasion of Iraq, when there were few antiwar voices and almost no movement, it was the scandalous news of atrocity—and the administration attempts to skirt international law—that became the initial and most single-minded focus. Today, the law of war frequently remains politics by other means. But the political struggle takes place less often on the explicitly politicized terrain of rationales for war and America's global role, making argument in the supposedly more neutral space of the modalities of conflict much more passionate and heated. Even when, under Barack Obama's presidency, targeted killings and signature strikes by drones in extended battlespaces elicited legal argument about the available geography of military engagement, opposition to government policies often took the form of allegations that their collateral damage in civilian death outweighed military advantage.[3]

In what follows, I do not try to explain this profound divergence, which evidently flows from a long list of critical differences in the nature of the conflicts as well as in the contexts in which they have been fought militarily and debated publicly. (Of course, there are similarities too, beginning with the pretexts for war, which in the cases of Vietnam and Iraq alike were substantially undermined after the fact.) The goal is simply to provide a contrast of before and after, so as to promote distance on and reflection about the contemporary obsession with legalizing means and methods of warfare as an end in itself in the so far brief current era of "human rights." Like the culture of human rights as a whole, the post-9/11 focus, which organized moral sentiments and intellectual dissent around the laws of war in general and international law governing the conduct of war in particular, is not a cultural or legal necessity, but a choice made in the face of perceived constraints. Of these, perhaps the most obvious is the disappearance of social mobilization—or its migration from left to right.

American War Crimes in Liberal and Conservative Memory

Vietnam has been surprisingly absent from post-9/11 debate about American military conduct in an era of renewed global engagement, especially against asymmetrical enemies and in the heat of counterinsurgent warfare. It has entered, interestingly, mainly in the form of worries about "quagmire," including in presidential deliberations, rather than through public meditation on the moral risks of global military engagement.[4] Forgetfulness might explain this absence but for the fact that both liberals and conservatives routinely invoke earlier memories—and for the fact that recollecting Vietnam poses such a stark challenge to the historical narratives both sides have cultivated.

Consider Jane Mayer's high-profile series of *New Yorker* articles, which were extraordinarily influential in constructing the liberal narrative of the war that underlay the intellectual worldviews and legal activism of many others. Mayer claimed that the nation's commitment to the law of war was ancient and strong in order to cast George W. Bush and his servants as abhorrent outliers to pristine national traditions. "There was nothing new about torture," Mayer acknowledged in collecting her articles in book form. But "its authorization by Bush administration lawyers represented a dramatic break with the past." Indeed, she explained, "America had done more than any nation on earth to abolish torture and other violations of human rights." But now, the United States "became the first nation ever to authorize violations of the Geneva Conventions." Even the worst episodes of the Cold War, she added in an extraordinary assertion, did not elicit the terrible conduct to which the United States now stooped: "This country has in the past faced other mortal enemies, equally if not more threatening, without endangering its moral authority." Celebrating a few "good conservatives" like Jack Goldsmith and Alberto Mora for refusing to compromise their integrity and morality when asked to do so by all the president's men, Mayer singled out another administration official, Matthew Waxman, for acting courageously in hopes of "restoring" the "country's values"—as if the latter had been a transhistorical constant until Bush intervened. Reviewing Mayer's book in the cover story of the *New York Times Book Review*, liberal historian Alan Brinkley agreed that it would be "difficult" to find "any precedent in American history" for "the scale, brutality and illegality" of Bush-era conduct.[5]

Well, not that difficult. Even when it came to detainees and torture, let alone wartime operations on the ground and from the air, the most basic facts about the Vietnam conflict make it rather implausible that Mayer could simply omit them from a story of American exceptionalism instrumentally told for the sake of stigmatizing current political enemies. But it is not as if conservatives did much better in acknowledging how Vietnam interferes with the picture of America and the law of war they wanted to achieve. In fact, one of Mayer's protagonists, Jack Goldsmith, provides useful evidence of this corresponding perspective. Unlike Mayer, Goldsmith—former Office of Legal Counsel head, later Harvard Law School professor—registers in his provocative book *The Terror Presidency* a seismic shift that created new legal conditions for the prosecution of the "global war on terror." Where Mayer saw the law of war as strong until recently, Goldsmith contended that it had come out of nowhere and now risked becoming too strong. But because he also omits Vietnam, it would be rather hasty to credit his alternative scenario.[6]

The debates that swirled around Bush, his law, and his lawyers were due, Goldsmith thinks, to two factors. One was simply Bush's failure to seek consent by reaching out to the legislative branch and otherwise "packaging" the necessities to which wartime exigency led. But Goldsmith also worries about a new culture of legality around warfare, which made Bush's penchant for self-aggrandizement so controversial.[7] If the liberal narrative correctly singles out the fact that after 9/11 the U.S. government consciously shirked the applicable requirements of international law in ways that were indeed unprecedented, it downplays or omits the more interesting truths—patently obvious to conservatives like Goldsmith who have dedicated their academic careers to resisting "global legalism" in the name of sovereign prerogatives— that the framework of normative expectations has changed much more than the deployment of violence has, even in the short space of a few decades.

Yet Goldsmith describes this very transformation better than he explains it. Goldsmith frequently repeats that the war itself had become newly legalized. "[W]ar itself," Goldsmith reports, "was encumbered with legal restrictions as never before. . . . Many people think the Bush administration has been indifferent to wartime legal constraints. But the opposite is true: the administration has been strangled by law."[8] All the same, the Geneva Conventions of 1949 in particular, so much in play in the last few years, were hardly new. As a result, this argument by itself leaves it rather unclear why those restrictions were now perceived as relevant. Then Goldsmith occasionally suggests that whatever the changes in the legal relevance of law to war, the really important transformation was what he repeatedly calls a "legalistic" attitude toward law. As if it went without saying, Goldsmith never spells out what is new about the new "legalism," which supplemented old and recent law alike with an unprecedented and stringent approach to it. "After 9/11, the Bush administration feared for the nation's safety as much as Franklin Roosevelt had," Goldsmith notes in an illustrative passage. "But Roosevelt's political conception of legal constraints had largely vanished, and by 2001 had been replaced by a fiercely legalistic conception of unprecedented wartime constraints on the presidency."[9] Not only is it unclear in this account what exactly it means to interpret law "politically" (unless it is a synonym for consensually ignoring it when enemies threaten); it leaves completely unexplained why people came to approach the law "legalistically."[10]

If Goldsmith leaves out why legalism in general rose, or legalism appealing to international standards in particular, the main reason is his omission of the Vietnam crisis. Returning to the politics of law in that crisis does not so much gratify nostalgic longing for an executive facing no constraint with respect to war's conduct as offer an invigorating memory of one who faced political contestation with respect to the war itself. Goldsmith says that the point of his book is "historical perspective," and he provides a considerable amount of it. But the comparisons he routinely invokes for Bush's dilemmas are so-called good wars, such as the Civil War and World War II—not Vietnam or other Cold War engagements.[11] His points of comparison for George W. Bush are always Abraham Lincoln and Franklin Roosevelt, never Lyndon Johnson or Richard Nixon. If Vietnam, then, so usefully reveals the glaring omissions of liberal memory, it is also a war that conservatives seemingly would prefer to forget. Its history reveals an era of political contest over war—and the political crucible in which the constraint of the executive and the culture of legalism were forged. Today's dominant concern with humanity in warfare was born in its heat too, but no longer maintains its original relationship with the concern about aggression and American power that contributed so powerfully to the circumstances of its production.

In Search of Lost Crime

Many investigations of the deep past of the law of war systematically overstate its humanitarian intent, which began to affect the conduct of hostilities seriously only in recent times. What historians agree was the pinnacle of contained war—though not achieved for directly humanitarian reasons—was increasingly superseded by new assumptions forged in Napoleon Bonaparte's total war against "barbaric insurgents," and then most of all in colonial warfare in which no limits were respected.[12] From that time to this day, "small wars" on the periphery have repeatedly promoted outrageous conduct either openly tolerated by metropolitan norms or treated as necessary exceptions given the supposed barbarity of the insurgent opposition. As the United States flirted with colonialism, and fought counterinsurgent warfare in places like the Philippines at the turn of the twentieth century, before assuming its post–World War II global hegemony, the conduct of its armies abroad was not seriously constrained by international law, including the international law of war. If American counterinsurgency of the Philippines at the turn of the twentieth century raised the troubling specter of torture, criticism concerned the abhorrence of the practice and the moral propriety of empire and did not engage legal rules—so much so that to view it as "the first torture debate" is to miss what made the real one so unprecedented.[13]

America's formal acceptance of constraints on means and methods of warfare associated with the Hague Regulations of the turn of the twentieth century had played little role when push came to shove in World War II, especially in East Asia. The earlier Geneva Conventions on prisoner of war treatment were given more respect; but if the new Geneva Conventions of 1949 were forged and adopted uncontroversially by colonial powers—as well as by the United States in an era when conservatives opposed and scuttled human rights treaties—it was in part because they were compatible with counterinsurgency viewed as necessary in a new era of restive natives.[14] The Korean conflict, and especially the scorched earth campaign in the winter of 1950, showed how brutally Americans were willing to fight on the Cold War periphery, without public dissent and even as the nation prepared to accede to the new Geneva requirements (the United States signed the conventions immediately, the Senate ratified them in 1955, and the military incorporated them in its regulations in 1956).[15] American assistance in the suppression of the Huk rebellion in the Philippines—if Korea is the forgotten war, this simultaneous counterinsurgency remains even in its shadow—was another sign of things to come.

It might have seemed dangerous that, unlike colonial powers, the United States wasn't waging counterinsurgent warfare in places it could treat as part of its domestic space and thus outside the ambit of international law—except that for a long time the United States avoided any trouble in doing so, and especially domestic trouble.[16] With the Vietnam escalation in 1965, the State Department advised the International Committee of the Red Cross that it accepted the full sway of the Geneva Conventions as applicable to what it took to be an international conflict. Amazingly, academic commentators wondered if counterinsurgency in the south, even when aided by external intervention, could fall under the weaker regime of the now famous Common Article 3, originally designed for civil war, but the U.S. government forced Saigon to comply with its interpretation, though it meant more full-spectrum formal obligations for both patron and client. The United States "has always abided by the humanitarian principles enunciated in the Geneva conventions and will continue to do so," Secretary of State Dean Rusk noted in a public statement.[17] But, as it turned out, this generosity was feasible because levels of patriotic engagement were high enough at the time, and traditions of debate around the laws of war weak enough, that current contestation over means and methods of conflict was simply unimaginable. Accordingly, combined with the conduct that followed, such affirmations suggest not that American allegiance to powerful humanitarian norms was high, but instead that no one—including the war's critics—regarded the international law of war as a threatening constraint. And so, it was all too frequently broken, eventually massively, due to converging forces: cavalier attitudes, cultural preconceptions, counterinsurgent realities, and strategic policy.

The results were devastating. Much remained impossible to know, and therefore contest, in the era, yet a surprising amount of information was available. In an age-old story, few stared the facts of their country's activities in the face. To begin with current obsessions, it is clear that mistreatment of POWs was rampant. Far harsher treatment than would now be acceptable was not yet seen to push the envelope in the Vietnam era, but it was pushed anyway.

A bit euphemistically, but unquestionably correctly, Goldsmith reports: "Today the military and the CIA are barred from using techniques that were thought to be consistent with the Geneva Conventions and available to the President as recently as the 1960s."[18] More interestingly, for a long time the military, the Central Intelligence Agency, and the president went far beyond what was consistent with the laws of war with no adverse consequences.

In the early years of the conflict, American forces handed over all captured enemies to its extremely brutal South Vietnamese client state, to the point that eventually the United States supplemented this basic policy by building some of its own holding facilities in recognition that its ally—which also held a huge number of "political" prisoners frequently captured in battle spaces—engaged in routine violations of the law of war.[19] Even so, no one wanted American forces to fully take over detention, even after a congressional delegation visited South Vietnam and, the summer after the My Lai story broke, word of the "tiger cages" of Con Son island (for the regime's political prisoners) hit the news accompanied by their own lurid images in *Life* magazine. As for the American military itself, as the war passed more and more evidence surfaced about nonchalant attitudes toward the requirement to treat captured prisoners humanely, or even leave them alive; evidence accumulated of incidents of simply shooting prisoners, especially once the command emphasis fell on enemy body count quotas. And sometimes the military was directly involved in torture. A version of Abu Ghraib happened, to take one example, at the hands of the 173rd Airborne Brigade, between twenty and thirty members of which acted as "interrogation specialists" committing heinous acts, according to Lt. Col. Anthony Herbert's once notorious allegations.[20]

Torture occurred not simply as part of everyday processes, but most glaringly, beginning in 1967, as part of the CIA's infamous Phoenix program, in which it advised and participated in the South Vietnamese detention and interrogation of suspected subversives—what came to be known after 9/11 as extraordinary rendition before its time and on a far vaster scale.[21] Targeting National Liberation Front (Viet Cong) leaders for torture, other forms of harsh treatment, and summary execution, and apparently exceeding fifty thousand in the number of victims it claimed, the program became known in stages after 1969. Yet even once war crimes became an issue, there was no torture debate in the Vietnam years, at first because the practice was tolerated and then because it was folded into an exploding dissent rather than singled out as a uniquely heinous transgression.[22]

These offenses were small beer, however, compared with two other classes of war crime. One was simply the everyday excesses of a counterinsurgent war in which the requirement of discrimination between combatant and noncombatant became exceptionally difficult if not impossible to sustain. In part, the cause was rules of engagement not adequately designed for the realities of the war; in part, the horror followed from NLF's insurgent maxim to be in the midst of the people in the same way a fish swims in water—when it did not fully convert its "civilian" host into a liberation force. Troops in South Vietnam were ordered into situations that were recipes for systematic violations of existing rules, notably when it came to civilians. "Search and destroy" missions throughout the late 1960s commonly involved shooting at targets on the barest suspicion of NLF involvement. Larger techniques, like the destruction of "hooches" and villages, frequently on slim grounds, or extraordinary population displacement in the name of clearing the water to find the fish, were also well known. Worst of all were free-fire and free-strike zones created after "fair warning" and population displacement, an approach apparently pioneered by the British in the successful Malayan counterinsurgency, in which soldiers and pilots often shot at anything that moved.[23] In village-level combat, close air support from helicopters and airplanes—including the C-52, a.k.a. "Puff the Magic Dragon"—assisted ground operations but not in careful and judicious ways that avoided grievous civilian harm. Many observers felt that incontestable war crimes, such as My Lai, or the gang rape and murder case reported by Daniel Lang just before news of My Lai broke, were expectable outcomes of the lack of interest in distinguishing soldiers from noncombatants that infected rules of engagement and their interpretation, as well as pervasive quotidian attitudes about acceptable conduct rooted in cultural assumptions about the value of Vietnamese lives.[24]

In testimony to the House Armed Services Committee in 1970, General William Westmoreland (who commanded U.S. ground forces in the era of the My Lai massacre) insisted on the importance of one-hour classes on the law of war as part of basic training, and all soldiers were supposed to carry a pocket card that called on them to behave humanely. But in one investigation of My Lai, Charlie Company member Herbert Carter remarked under direct examination that the way this instruction occurred ended up communicating that soldiers could "do what you want to do."[25] My Lai led to a recognition within the military that education in the laws of war for troops and commanders had been woefully insufficient; all evidence suggests that, despite an often functioning system of military justice, the military culture of the day excused callous and deadly treatment of civilians and frowned on allegations of wrongdoing. One reason no one will ever know how far the criminality went is that the Department of Defense began systematically collecting information about alleged violations, notably through the Vietnam War Crimes Working Group, only after the My Lai cover-up failed and the topic finally became central to the antiwar movement.[26]

In addition, American use of napalm and phosphorus in everyday counterinsurgency became particularly controversial for a growing domestic activism, notably in West Coast demonstrations around Dow Chemicals, whose products "burned babies." This focus on means of warfare is exceptional on the list, for it started unusually early after 1965, especially after photographs of victims began to circulate, long before the climactic publication in 1972 of the terrible image of Kim Phúc fleeing burning death. It is true that almost no one thought that these weapons—or the defoliants that some tried to cast as "ecocide" later—were illegal per se, though many felt that the Hague Regulations ban on excessively cruel means of warfare had to mean something. But even tolerant observers found recourse to these weapons excessive, in contradiction of American rules constraining their deployment, and clearly their uses were frequently instances of flagrant violation of the key principles of discrimination and proportionality.[27]

The other major domain of criminality was the air war, not in Air Force assistance to army and marine activities in the south, but in bombing there and throughout the north, which began in 1965 as the "Rolling Thunder" campaign and soon expanded to Cambodia and Laos (eventually massively). At first, in spite of the living memory of the incendiary bombing and atomic destruction of Japanese cities, the assumption was that military targets only were being chosen in fierce air activity in North Vietnam. But *New York Times* correspondent Harrison Salisbury's reporting, upon invitation from Hanoi to visit and tour in late 1966, made this belief hard to sustain, since the devastation of the countryside he described could not plausibly be ascribed to honest mistakes.[28] Yet though startling to some, this news did not have domestic effects in the same league as My Lai (or Abu Ghraib), and indeed did not seriously transform aerial practices. Nevertheless, a few began to document the effects of the air war on the North Vietnamese landscape, and distressing evidence accumulated, though to this day no one could estimate how many tens of thousands of civilians died needlessly as a result of failures of discrimination and proportionality.[29] As with the napalm used in the south, there was no specific law prohibiting aerial bombardment with B-52s raining destruction from on high, and there still is not. But it is nevertheless self-evident that the informal norms and legal supervision of targeting at the time were nothing compared with current practices—with horrendous consequences for all concerned.

In the eyes of those few who came to grips with the overall scene, the extent of the violations could make law seem not a necessary tool but a laughable irrelevance. (According to fictional Captain Benjamin Willard, Martin Sheen's character in *Apocalypse Now*, "Charging a man with murder in this place was like handing out speeding tickets in the Indy 500.")[30] At home, in spite of mounting evidence of exceptional brutality, few spoke out before My Lai brought many over a critical threshold. The most creditable reason for this was that it was easy to believe (and to some extent correct to believe) that allegations were communist propaganda designed to undermine the American cause. The fact that the far left was the almost exclusive source of the charge of war crimes also made dismissal easy until it was impossible.

Towering above all other sources was Bertrand Russell's famous international war crimes tribunal, which, thanks to Jean-Paul Sartre's personal intervention, went so far as to charge American genocide. Yet like most of those who would eventually raise the specter of American war crimes, for Russell and his fellow "judges" American aggression loomed largest, with war crimes not a separate or distinct matter but the expectable consequence of a larger violation America had once done so much to criminalize, from the days of the Kellogg-Briand pact through the Nuremberg trials of the Nazis as aggressive warmongers. The Russell tribunal, however, was broadly scorned at the time, especially in the United States, as the sad result of a great thinker gone senile, assuming it was not a "communist" show trial. In fact it is still given short shrift in the history of consciousness of war crimes, the movement for legal accountability in the

Nuremberg tradition, and especially the international idea of genocide, in all of which it played a fateful but unacknowledged role.[31]

The Russell tribunal had its domestic followers, but the American "movement" against the Vietnam war was highly pluralistic. Those liberals who joined it early considered the war a strategic blunder and sometimes cited Vietnamese self-determination as a moral rationale before that idea became fundamental to a leftist framing for the conflict's meaning. Students, often given excessive centrality in histories of the movement, had their own evolution and a complex relation to the larger antiwar coalition, integrating the leftist critique of American "imperialism" intermittently but eventually strongly—though their central target, especially from 1966 to 1968, remained the draft. Like leftists, pacifists opposed the war on principle. Religious pacifists like the Clergy and Laymen Concerned about Vietnam (CALCAV) were to be especially prominent in making its brutality an early cause for concern, but essentially in a moral rather than legal register. CALCAV's interdenominational clergy banded together in 1967 simply to document, based on mainstream press coverage, what seemed to be massive and intentional violations. Their numbers included Daniel Berrigan, Robert McAfee Brown, William Sloan Coffin, Abraham Joshua Heschel, and Martin Luther King, Jr., and they released their book-length compilation and argument a month before the My Lai slayings. But even though harder to dismiss than leftist agitation because of its provenance, before My Lai came to light the clergy's attempt to air the moral issues in the daily paper made no serious impact.[32] In part for this very reason, it seems fair to say that, especially before My Lai, it was the leftist camp that most emphasized international law as a source of constraint on American war—and it did so in a way that differs starkly from its uses today.[33]

Not being lawyers, most of those who made up the antiwar movement spoke in a moral rather than a legal register—including when they targeted brutality either for its own sake or as part of a larger critique of the conflict. Further, they most frequently combined their moral criticisms of a government at war with commitment to visions for widespread social change; it suffices to recall that the antiwar movement overlapped with the civil rights and other movements in complex but important ways. While the following analysis of more strictly legal activism does not emphasize this critical feature of the Vietnam past, it is perhaps the most important one for understanding the gulf that separates then and now.

But what is even more interesting than the delay of the focus on war crimes was that, even when it came, almost no one denounced American presidents for stepping over legal boundaries in the conduct of war; once the stir started—including among lawyers—a few and then millions of people denounced American presidents for waging an evil or even criminal war. My Lai changed this, but not in favor of our politics; instead, it resulted in an intensification of the attack on the war. Decades later, in a time lacking both mass conscription and generational unrest, more activist and "political" modes of dissent had lost their luster and prominence. Legalism has since become a conceivable response because, for the first time, it could be: law regulating the conduct of war now mattered. But it has also been a plausible response because of an absence of other political tools.

The Lawyers Committee

The Lawyers Committee Concerning American Policy in Vietnam was organized in 1965 after the Tonkin Gulf resolution and the escalation of American military involvement which, from a baseline of some 15,000 troops, eventually topped 500,000. The two central figures were both New York lawyers in private practice: William Standard, an expert on the law of the sea who served as chairman; and Joseph Crown, a tax specialist who as secretary and treasurer stood at its center.[34] Carey McWilliams, editor of *The Nation*, served as honorary vice chairman, and soon after its founding the committee formed a consultative council of law professors that eventually took on the main legal analysis.

As a group of elites founded prior to the crystallization of a massive antiwar movement a couple of years later, the Lawyers Committee would also differ from Russell tribunal affiliates (as well as from Richard Falk, the committee's own main supporter in legal academia) in persisting in a fully elite model of agitation. Its main audience was policy-makers, from the president to friendly congressmen, notably senators Wayne Morse (D-Oregon) and Ernest Gruening (D-Alaska), who alone had voted against the intervention, and Senator J. William Fulbright (D-Arkansas) once he became the most prominent congressional critic of the war.[35] Its main weapon was the letter to the editor, though it certainly attempted, by reducing its legal memoranda to pamphlet form and widespread newspaper advertisement, to make its views known to as wide a circle of Americans as possible.[36]

Crown and Standard drafted an initial memo disputing the grounds of intervention, and alleging violation of the UN charter, the Geneva Accords of 1954, and the Southeast Asian Treaty Organization treaty. Turning the tables on widespread rhetoric of communist aggression, including Dean Rusk's public justification for the war, Crown and Standard used the memo to argue that, judged by its treaty obligations beginning with the UN charter, it was America that was the aggressor.[37] Quite strikingly, where the administration claimed that Vietnam was clearly an international conflict (in spite of the far greater burden in terms of the law of war that theory imposed), the Lawyers Committee insisted it was a civil war in which outside parties were not welcome (though this would have left the conflict under the sway of Geneva Conventions Common Article 3 alone).

Morse read this memo into the *Congressional Record* in September 1965; but in these very early days, it attracted only 700 signatures of the 178,000 lawyers and 3,750 law professors to whom Crown and Standard sent their work.[38] In January 1966 the committee re-sent it to the president, with some amendments and news of the response it had received so far.[39] The White House Counsel's office initially asked academic allies, notably Yale Law School professor Myres McDougal, to respond; when Attorney General Nicholas Katzenbach decided it was unworthy of official reply, the White House then prompted McDougal to organize an even fuller response.[40] (The White House was also involved in a unanimous American Bar Association resolution affirming the legality of the war, to which the Lawyers Committee reacted angrily.)[41] Intellectually, the committee's antagonist in these years was Leonard C. Meeker, who served as the State Department's Legal Adviser, and who made public the government's legal rationale for war only after the committee argued that there was none.[42] After law professors came to the administration's defense, and Meeker offered his main memo, the Lawyers Committee turned to its own affiliates in legal academia.[43] John H. E. Fried of its Consultative Council, a body chaired by Falk, drafted what became a book-length memo. The committee then arranged to publish it (with the same marginal New Jersey publisher that initially tried to circulate the Russell tribunal proceedings). In spite of their low visibility, Meeker did reply publicly to these arguments in a speech.[44]

In all this agitation, international law appeared as a constraint on American's intervention, not on how the military conducted it. Before atrocity, to put it differently, there was aggression, as the exclusive target of what legalist opprobrium there was. In all this, as befits its primary attention to the legality of the intervention, the committee's basic goal was the political one, and it freely and openly announced its goal of encouraging a settlement that would include the southern rebels. Where was attention to the law governing the conduct of warfare in these activities? Nowhere. The same was true as the war unfolded further; having failed to influence administration policy, the Lawyers Committee took its case global, with its leaders attending European conferences of activists and lawyers in 1966–67, and urged the International Court of Justice to pronounce on America's international law violations.[45] Having furnished the principal arguments about the illegality of the war, the committee and its members also became active in Selective Service cases, in hopes of having an American court declare the illegality of the war (which never occurred); it also organized the publication of academic work on the subject and participated in related invocations of the arguments as rationales for acts of civil disobedience.[46] Later, in 1969, the committee offered a Five-Point peace program.[47]

But despite these efforts, the committee's moment of prominence and relevance had already passed, as elite debate about the war, which the committee failed to swing, was overtaken by the rise of a mass antiwar movement. After Morse was punished for his antiwar views with a loss in his 1968 Senate race to Bob Packwood, he became the committee's honorary chairman, and when he spoke to the group in New York in October 1969, a month before the news of My Lai broke, Crown expressed his hope that the attendance of more than five hundred lawyers reflected "the turn of the tide."[48] But campus and public activism proved the true agent of transformation. The committee considered proposing Johnson's impeachment and, two years later, did urge Nixon's impeachment, and Crown and Standard also attempted to put the issues on the agenda of the Supreme Court confirmation hearings of William Rehnquist in 1971—wondering why the fact that Rehnquist had written legal justifications of the Cambodian incursion as a matter of presidential prerogative was not even being queried.[49] In spring 1971, members of the committee testified at congressional hearings in which what became the War Powers Resolution was first debated.

As for war crimes, targeting them was hardly the committee's priority at any point. After My Lai, the committee certainly paid attention to the issue, along with many other Americans. It circulated Falk's work on the scope of responsibility for the massacres. When Crown, Falk, and others attended a major international conference of lawyers in Toronto in 1970, much more emphasis fell on war crimes than before, but still as a rationale for a politics of ending the war.[50] The committee remained in touch with nonlegal bodies much more focused on the matter, such as the Education/Action Conference on U.S. Crimes of War, headed by Temple University English professor Mark Sacharoff, and its delegates attended sessions of the International Commission of Enquiry into U.S. Crimes in Indochina in 1971–73, a follow-up to Russell's tribunal chaired after his death by Gunnar Myrdal.[51] But even when Crown visited Hanoi for a week in October 1971, movingly testifying to the ravaged landscape and the massive death of civilians resulting from aerial bombardment, the Lawyers Committee remained focused on seeking an end to the conflict.[52]

The Passion of Richard Falk

Born in 1930, Richard Falk was a young Princeton University professor teaching international law in the era to policy and political science students.[53] Trained at Yale Law School, and massively prolific, he was, methodologically, McDougal's follower.[54] Though politically closer to McDougal, a staunch Cold Warrior, at the beginning of his career, Falk slowly moved away, even as he continued to hew to his teacher's "policy-oriented" approach, acknowledging the power of exporting legal realism into international law often and fulsomely. Falk's first book, *Law, War, and Morality in the Contemporary World* (1963), concurred in the necessity of America's Cold War interventions, much along McDougal's lines.[55] But Falk's alliance with Saul Mendlovitz, a Rutgers University law professor, in an effort to devise models within McDougal's "world order" approach that might end war rather than court nuclear armageddon and tolerate if not exacerbate third-world conflict, showed his evolution.[56] Even as he remained an admirer of McDougal's theory, Falk attempted to replace

McDougal's Cold War sympathies with other values, notably an interest in the aspirations of new nations beyond the era's bipolar confrontation.[57]

Yet nothing in Falk's writings, including early ones on the international law of war, really anticipated his extraordinary activism in the late 1960s and beyond, which ultimately gave him what one observer plausibly called "unchallengeable preeminence" among those trying to legalize debate around the Vietnam conflict.[58] When the Lawyers Committee wrote him in 1965, in a large mailing to solicit his agreement with its initial memorandum, Falk signed on with alacrity.[59] Soon after, he set to writing a classic *Yale Law Journal* article on the Vietnam war as illegal under international law and especially the prohibition of aggression—a piece that sparked a contentious academic debate.[60] (Given that University of Virginia law professor John Norton Moore, principal academic defender of the war's legality and Falk's sparring partner, was also a declared disciple of McDougal, the debate in the late 1960s had something of a fratricidal character.)[61] In the same period, as noted above, Falk helped prepare a book-length memorandum as chair of the Lawyers Committee Consultative Council that expanded the legal case against the war. At around the same time, he initiated through the Civil War Section of the American Society of International Law a compilation of articles on *The Vietnam War and International Law*, whose first volume (of what ended up as four) appeared in 1968. None of these initiatives dealt with war crimes.[62]

It should be remembered that by and large Falk's attempt at academic activism, like that of the Lawyers Committee, at first attracted very few. In a once visible fracas, Harvard Law School professor Richard Baxter tasked Falk in the pages of the *Times* of London for his wild arguments and insisted that readers know how unrepresentative Falk's views were. They were, Baxter wrote, "*not* the view of the matter entertained by the great majority of American international lawyers." As if to suggest the centers of opinion that mattered, he added (correctly) that Falk's Consultative Council did "not include a single member of the law faculties of Harvard, Yale, Columbia, Michigan, Chicago, California, or Pennsylvania."[63] Another Harvard law professor, Louis Sohn, responded to the Lawyers Committee with a bitter memorandum justifying American engagement in the conflict; like several others central to the formation of international human rights in the next decade, Sohn did not believe in a turn to international law as a tool to restrain American conduct abroad.[64] And of course, the support of some for the war, perhaps most notably former Yale Law School dean Eugene Rostow (brother of one of its principal architects), was not to be shaken by any events.[65] For other international lawyers, by and large Cold War liberals of various hues at the beginning of the era, only erosion of domestic support for the war would change the equation.

Falk's itinerary was completely different. His own reasons for his legal engagement as the most prominent international lawyer in the antiwar movement were consciously political and proudly so. While he surely championed international law, it was in recognition of its possible use as one political tool among others—a view that harmonized with his more realist bent. When Nicholas Katzenbach, once a teacher of Falk's at Yale Law School, moved from the attorney general's office to become undersecretary of state in late 1966, Falk wrote him as a "dissenter" in hopes of opening a dialogue. "Needless to say," Falk explained, "I regard the legal interpretation of United States policy to be of secondary importance in this setting, confirmatory or not of a policy that satisfies more general considerations bearing on the welfare of the country and on the prospects for global stability and justice."[66] His overridingly political aims could, on dark days, lead him to conclude that the law had little role in the movement and had shown its limits as a tool. As the strategy he and the Lawyers Committee adopted of legalizing the conflict seemed to make no discernible difference, he confessed to a colleague the next year that "at this stage in the conflict an appeal to legal reason does not have much relevance either to the policy-forming process or to the shaping of public attitudes. It remains important not to create a legal vacuum to be filled by official positions, but legally oriented arguments aimed at the public assume a legalistic quality by virtue of their irrelevance."[67] Around the same time, Falk reflected academically on such facts, and on how to forge a role for the lawyer in the conduct of foreign affairs, given the power of the realist view that legal arguments were no more than rationalizations of policy decisions—and "less a fig-leaf than a see-through garment."[68]

Of course, Falk never gave up on legal argument, but even as he decried the subordination of law to politics in the justification of war, his own governing politics became more and more radical.[69] Falk visited Hanoi and then, with Crown, attended the Conférence mondiale des juristes pour le Vietnam, held in Grenoble, France, in July 1968.[70] Falk agreed with the dominant tone, which focused on American aggression and illegal intervention, and with North Vietnamese representatives in the room championing the right of self-determination as the basis of struggle.[71] Reporting on the effects of his trip as a "representative of international juridical conscience," Falk described his "general shift in orientation" from a negative resistance against the American government in a local context to a positive affiliation with Vietnamese desires for liberation as part of a global struggle against empire. This coincided, he reported, with "a very sharp shift in priorities with respect to the legal issues." But this was not in the direction from *jus ad bellum* to *jus in bello*. Merely resisting the justification for intervention, Falk argued, "misses the primary issue, in my judgment, that the war is at its deepest level a war fought for the fulfillment and expression of Vietnamese national self-determination; this war is a continuation of the colonial struggle in a phase of neo-colonialism; this imperialist quality is disguised in its character as a consequence of legal fictions that have played a very destructive role in understanding what the issues at stake really are." In his speech, Falk did mention that his trip to the north impressed upon him the brutality of war; the bombing of the north amounted to "cumulative forms of genocide," while in the south "the most illegal and brutal military tactics ever known" had been and were still being unleashed. But this was a passing complaint mainly showing how thoroughly Falk had moved in the direction of frank affiliation with national liberation in a few short years.[72] He never wrote this explicitly for American audiences, though he did go so far as to excuse NLF "terrorism" as a weapon of the weak to which guerrillas naturally had recourse as a matter of military necessity.[73] If his domestic framing of the war evolved, it was from a critical perspective on the American rationale for intervention to a settlement proposal in view of legitimate Vietnamese claims.[74]

Yet even as he ended up occupying the political position of the Russell tribunal on the far left, Falk did not give comparable attention to wartime brutality. He did give far more than any other lawyer in the United States prior to the My Lai revelations, but provided little basis on which to predict how much more he would focus on them afterward.[75] In his preface to CALCAV's compilation on war crimes, he took horrific reports seriously, though he knew that they were easily contradicted, and that no serious mechanism existed in the American landscape at that time for creating a culture of legalism around military conduct. He closed by reminding readers of the overriding importance of the debate he had helped initiate about the legal propriety of the war itself, and he reflected that the laws of war the clergy wanted to bring to the public were intended "not to encourage legal debate as much as to provide benchmarks for a searching moral reappraisal."[76]

After My Lai, it is fair to say, Falk along with many others invoked international standards on the conduct of war much more, initiating precisely the legal debate about crimes he had once hoped to spark around the intervention itself.[77] As time passed, the political circumstances changed rapidly. With the Tet offensive and Lyndon Johnson's decision not to seek reelection in 1968, the nature of the war shifted profoundly. It did so even more as Richard Nixon and Henry Kissinger famously sought through extraordinary measures optimal circumstances for an "honorable" settlement. The "Vietnamization" of the war meant the departure of American boots on the ground, coupled with the escalation of fierce bombardment everywhere in the country, not forgetting the massive expansion of bombing in Cambodia and Laos and the 1970 Cambodian ground incursion.[78] And under the combination of the My Lai exposure and public disappointment that the promised "withdrawal" seemed to make the conflict more brutal, Falk reoriented his activism around war crimes. The Nuremberg precedent now mattered not simply for the charge of aggression but for its principle of command responsibility—and its imperative to trace how high up accountability went. As Falk wrote soon after the revelations in a classic article in *The Nation*, "The Circle of Responsibility": "It would . . . be misleading to isolate [My Lai] from the overall conduct of the war."[79] At the moment when Falk's attention was most focused on brutality, however, it was never for its own sake. Falk now followed the Russell tribunal in insisting that such attention was not isolable from legalization of the war itself. "The Nuremberg principles suggest a broader human responsibility to oppose an *illegal war* and *illegal methods of combat*."[80] It was not a matter of dropping a focus on the one in favor of a new agenda. It was a new tool with which to pursue the old agenda.

Of course, in many ways, just as with the Lawyers Committee, Falk's specifically legal expertise did not determine the overall mass consciousness of war crimes after My Lai. Public reaction to these infractions was convulsive in its moral opprobrium, notably in the winter of 1970–71, and connected inseparably to outrage that Nixon was expanding a conflict he had promised to end. The Russell tribunal proceedings, once ignored, were republished by a trade press, and the *New York Times Book Review* took the radical step of sending Sacharoff's entire bibliography for extended review to Neil Sheehan, in a catalytic intervention for highbrow readers.[81] On the ground, it was probably the Vietnam Veterans against the War that staged the most visible appeal to rules governing means and methods of conflict, in a mock trial in Detroit in which they described their acts in a once well-known Winter Soldier Investigation.[82] All of these also included direct considerations of the propriety of America's war itself.

Indeed, Falk had his greatest role with respect to war crimes in joining with nonlawyers around the issue and taking it up as a moral and political one never unrelated to the project of ending the war. He had ties to the American Friends Service Committee, which organized a congressional conference on individual responsibility for war crimes in early 1970, that intersected with the creation of a Citizens Commission of Inquiry into U.S. War Crimes in Vietnam (begun by American affiliates of the Russell tribunal, it took on a life of its own after the My Lai news).[83] Falk participated in a grand inquest to brand America's leaders as "war criminals."[84] Above all, Falk joined with leftist historian Gabriel Kolko and celebrated psychologist Robert Jay Lifton to edit a mass-circulating compilation, *Crimes of War*, to spur the debate.[85]

These figures hoped to take advantage of My Lai as a moment of breakthrough, in which Americans would come to grips with the evil of the war from its beginning and in its totality. As Kolko contended at the congressional conference, My Lai "is merely the foot soldier's direct expression of the axiom of fire and terror that his superiors in Washington devise and command from behind desks."[86] In their compilation, Falk's interpretation of the clarity and scope of the international law of war pushed the envelope not in the direction of exoneration but instead of the generalized culpability of American soldiers, generals, statesman, and the people as a whole. In the preface to *Crimes of War*, the editors agreed "with Jean-Paul Sartre and others in conceiving of the entire war—or any massive counterinsurgency campaign by outside forces relying upon modern weaponry—as one all-embracing war crime."[87] Though a massive counterinsurgency campaign by outside forces relying upon modern weaponry, Iraq inspired no one to make that claim.

Telford Taylor and the Liberal Conscience

Concern about war crimes largely absent among elites or the general public through the most vicious periods of the Vietnam war, first stressed by the international far left, then after My Lai by a huge number of movement actors, came to be framed with full doctrinal rigor and with extraordinary impact by Telford Taylor in his bestselling and widely reviewed *Nuremberg and Vietnam: An American Tragedy*, which appeared in late 1970.[88] A retired brigadier general famous as lead prosecutor at the Nuremberg "successor" trials, Taylor (1908–98) mattered first of all because he was so morally serious—but also because he made allegations of war crimes "respectable" by moving them from the far left to the liberal center and offering a judicious discussion of why Americans had indeed violated international standards. His significance may also have been to suggest the reenactment of the original separation of concerns around modalities of conflict within the ethics of warfare—a classic separation between *jus ad bellum* and *jus in bello* that the antiwar movement had blurred. More generally, Taylor's contribution was to sever legal claims from the political movement that had first inspired them. For part of Taylor's role depended on the fact that he formulated his decisive allegations much more independently of the antiwar movement than any had done before.

A former supporter of the intervention, Taylor could draw on his reputation as a moral voice above politics to make the impact he did.[89] As Falk himself was to put it, Taylor might have been "the only person alive who was in a position to change the public climate sufficiently to make the issue of war crimes [one] which would be taken seriously."[90] Before My Lai broke, Taylor had participated in the defense of the "Boston Five," a group of prominent protestors arrested for picketing a Selective Service center in 1968; and he attended the congressional conference on the subject in the months after the massacre was revealed. But it mainly mattered that unlike Falk, who was in fact the main target of criticism in *Nuremberg and Vietnam*, Taylor stigmatized the irresponsible left and excused a great deal of conduct on the way to his extremely sobering conclusions about what had gone wrong. The same work was done, it is worth noting, by Neil Sheehan's highly public meditation on American war guilt. Not two months before his grave and wide-ranging *New York Times Book Review* essay—in fact in the same issue in which Falk's review of Taylor's book appeared—Sheehan had attacked the propensity of the antiwar left to fabricate atrocity stories. In such moments, it matters as much who accedes to inconvenient truths as what those truths are. It is illustrative that Falk frequently dedicated his books to Vietnamese victims, whereas Taylor dedicated *Nuremberg and Vietnam* "to the flag, and the liberty and justice for which it stands."[91]

Apparently, Taylor was first moved to intervene not by minor percolations of the Nuremberg precedent—including at the Russell tribunal or in Falk's passing arguments—but by disturbing post–My Lai parallels constructed by journalists immediately after the revelations. He then wrote his book quickly in the summer of 1970.[92] Taylor's first move in *Nuremberg and Vietnam*, after historical preliminaries, was very striking in relation to prior American agitation: he cast doubt on the whole idea of aggressive warfare. The malleability of "aggression" did not mean it could never have legal clarity, Taylor allowed, but unlike at Nuremberg where it was obvious who had started World War II, the Vietnam era showed that one man's aggressor was another man's victim (and vice versa). In particular, Taylor continued, Falk was wrong that domestic courts could and therefore should responsibly adjudicate whether the United States was guilty of aggression. Rejecting Falk's arguments for an extremely expansive circle of potential liability, Taylor observed that Nuremberg never conferred a right—let alone a responsibility—to avoid military service on the grounds of personal opinion about a war's illegality.[93] As for courts adjudicating that claim, in the course of the war (and without the captured archives on which Nuremberg relied) it made no sense to hope that the finding of a criminally aggressive war might lead very far, since Nuremberg judges who acquitted generals and industrialists had been willing to hold only the highest leaders to account. So much for pre–My Lai legal agitation; Taylor simply put it to one side.

Instead, Taylor's attention, like that of so many others, now fell squarely on the conduct of war, of which he provided a damning account even as he decoupled it from the legality of the war itself. What may be most impressive about his analysis—in view of the maximalist inclusion of all possible misdeeds and even the entire conflict as one grand crime by Falk and others—was Taylor's isolation of the American actions he felt were unquestionably criminal.[94] Beyond My Lai, Taylor indicted routine and massive civilian reprisals, which were obviously not justified when there was no suspicion of enemy presence, and not justified even if any evidence suggested some. Shocked by *New Yorker* journalist Jonathan Schell's heartrending depictions of counterinsurgent practices, Taylor was also concerned about the use of air power in South Vietnam, notably free strike zones; and he expressed considerable doubt about the legality of displacing civilians with no intention of bringing them back.[95] Taylor also deplored the cavalier attitude toward prisoners of war, as revealed in the trial of Lieutenant James Duffy in the spring of 1970, where embarrassing testimony surfaced that the imperative to achieve high body counts sometimes overrode the rules of war, including even the rule against the denial of quarter. But, focusing on the highest directives of General Westmoreland, Taylor deemed the army's rules of engagement "impeccable," ignoring how their ambiguities licensed rather different interpretations. He did not care to mention the Phoenix program, even once much more was known about it.[96] Finally, he was surprisingly dismissive of worries that aerial bombardment of North Vietnam was criminal. In his closing report at Nuremberg, Taylor had viewed strategic bombing as clearly in accordance with customary law, since all sides in World War II had conducted it.[97] A quarter-century later, Taylor hoped the norm against bombing civilians had strengthened, but it still did not seem to him that American aerial practices involved wanton cruelty against civilians sufficient to qualify as criminal, either because they failed to distinguish civilian from military targets or because they caused civilian suffering out of proportion to military advantage. Even if one conceded, as Taylor now did, that the bombings of Dresden and Nagasaki had probably been illegal because supererogatory, it did not follow that Americans had now broken the law. After all, he noted, in Vietnam "there have been no urban holocausts."[98]

Taylor changed his mind on this critical point when, with folk singer Joan Baez, he traveled to Hanoi in winter 1972–73 in order to deliver holiday mail to POWs and happened to be present during the tremendous wrath of the Linebacker II bombing of Hanoi and Haiphong, which Nixon and Kissinger fondly hoped would coerce favorable settlement.[99] When he emerged from the bomb shelter near his hotel, reporters asked Taylor whether his viewing of a destroyed hospital and devastated residential areas occurred because he had been deliberately led there rather than elsewhere. He responded: "We might not have seen some things that we would have liked to have seen, but nonetheless we did see the things we saw."[100] Instead of saying that such aerial fury was tragic but legal, as he had two years before, Taylor merely commented that no court was ever likely to bring a great power to justice for such enormities as the Christmas bombings. (So far, he is right.) Indeed, he concluded, much more generously than before, that while no treaty yet outlawed aerial bombardment, American conduct—though no comparison to the World War II destruction of cities—incontestably ran afoul of the basic norms of discrimination and proportionality.[101] It is not clear how much credit he deserves for grasping a truth that applied all along, and not just in cities, as many had seen before his accidental personal experience led him to it.[102]

Yet Taylor's intervention in *Nuremberg and Vietnam* was extraordinarily consequential not least because, as Falk noted in his laudatory review, "despite Taylor's conservative stance he reaches radical conclusions." His legal caution and his liberal patriotism, Falk recorded, meant that even though Taylor avoided indicting America except in cases of absolutely clear wrongdoing, the remarkable thing was that he had gone so far: the book was "a *minimalist indictment* in the sense of being the minimum conclusion that an honest, conservative, and well-informed man can make about the criminal status of American war policies."[103] In particular, Falk celebrated Taylor's conclusions that the inquest over My Lai—even if Charlie Company's murders were exceptional—should reach as high as evidence could lead. The *Yamashita* case of World War II, Taylor had written, implied that military accountability should go all the way to the top, and perhaps into civilian corridors of power too. Soon after Falk's review, Taylor stated clearly on the Dick Cavett Show that Westmoreland was liable for war crimes and that, while he reserved judgment on this tricky question, Johnson might be too (this appearance caused a large stir).[104] While he surely disagreed with elements of the legal analysis of Taylor's book, the only point about which Falk chose to bridle was—very revealingly— in response to Taylor's belittlement of the antiwar movement. Where Taylor chided popular demonstrations as counterproductive, Falk wrote, in a remarkable form of direct rhetorical address: "But what, General Taylor, is 'productive' given the circumstances of a continuing criminal war that is being carried on by individuals you yourself characterized as seeming criminals?" (Falk and Taylor, after this review, barnstormed around American universities for several personal debates, and struck up a friendship playing squash.)[105]

Due to Taylor's marginalization of aggression in favor of attention to the conduct of the war, the early 1970s, when liberals like Taylor moved to legalize the conflict, were arguably a fateful moment in the contemporary reimagination of the Nuremberg precedent.[106] From having been primarily concerned in real history with crimes of aggression in the initiation of war, in belated memory today Nuremberg is widely and mistakenly understood to have been primarily about the conduct of war. Still, it would be an error to take this line of argument too far, for at the end of *Nuremberg and Vietnam* Taylor made clear that if law could play no role in ending the war, he hoped politics would, and he considered his own post–My Lai reflection inseparable from political activism against a war he now viewed as ill-conceived if not immoral. Taylor noted: "To say judges should not answer the question [of whether Americans were aggressors] is not to deny the reality and significance of the question itself." Without gainsaying the idealism with which American policy had been framed, Taylor concluded, the course of the war suggested that the rationales for war had now been shown to be comprehensively ideological: "Whatever peace-keeping and protective intentions may have governed our initial involvement in Vietnam have by now been so completely submerged under the avalanche of death and destruction that they no longer are credible descriptions of the operation as a whole." To this extent, the Nuremberg charge of aggression, though unviable as a legal claim, still did matter as a political instrument to undermine the war itself.[107] Even as his official legal hope for judicial accountability for war crimes went unrealized, and as he steered clear of popular mobilization against war, Taylor's intended and explicit contribution to the political deployment of law was self-evident.[108] In this sense, Taylor was still living in a different world than ours.

Conclusion: Vietnam and Post-9/11 Legal Thought

In the United States, human rights spiked in and as part of the Vietnam aftermath. Historian Barbara Keys has shown that the stimulus to the first human rights legislation the country enacted—conditioning foreign assistance on conduct—followed directly after the peace agreement both out of a novel perception of dirty hands and a will to wash them clean.[109] Over the longer term, one dimension of the post-Vietnam international human rights movement was further work on the laws of war and, indeed, the attempted doctrinal merger of that traditional subject with newly ascendant human rights ideas—something almost no one countenanced until Vietnam sparked the possibility.[110] After the Cold War, significant changes to American law, notably the federal torture statute and the federal war crimes act, went far beyond where American field manuals applicable during the Vietnam era had left the matter; along with a remarkable parallel military evolution in the direction of legal control, the creation of these laws and a new culture of legalism changed the environment for American warfare beyond recognition.[111]

We are heirs of the Vietnam war's moral aftermath thanks to such innovations—but wayward heirs. Most obviously, the strong focus on America's global role lost its priority, as the imaginative move from aggression to atrocity as the prime object of stigmatization and criminalization went very far.[112] To be sure, policy debate remained about the initiation of war, but even as Vietnam afforded new statutory tools, international law receded. Congress was occasionally prodded, without great success, to assert the constitutional role in war it was supposed to have shouldered after the Vietnamese disaster. Even if a slowly roused Congress and academia responded to the recent Libyan incursion, making minor noises over violations of War Powers Resolution, the restraints on war in international as opposed to domestic law that seemed so worth arguing in the days of the Lawyers Committee remain apparently irretrievable in American debate—in part because America learned to certify its actions through UN approval, even at the height of "unilateralism" in George W. Bush's presidency.[113] Much more constantly and floridly in public controversy, academic jousting, and legal work since the invasion of Iraq, the international dictates of detainee treatment and the law governing means and methods of war are taken very seriously—if first of all because their requirements were so brazenly denied. It is rarely noted, however, that the intense focus on the conduct of war in the feud of liberals and conservatives occurs in the relative absence of interest in rationales for hostilities and America's global role. With these priorities liberals risk humanizing war even as conservative defenses against encroaching law have simply not had to contend with invocations of international legal constraints on going to war in the first place.[114]

Yet even when it comes to a historically novel regulation of the conduct of war, the Vietnam-era social movements that led to various achievements are missing, and so the achievements themselves frequently prove brittle. Before the ghosts of counterinsurgency and global warfare were reanimated in the post-9/11 world, legal theorists had spent a generation recovering from a hollow hope in the value of legal constraints without political backing. Then, after 9/11, given where "the people themselves" in a moment of patriotism and fear wanted to take the country, judges—or proxies like actual or possible legal advisers within the executive branch—quickly returned to favor in the legal imagination. It was forgotten that the very goal on which so many fell back, of restraining the executive through law in a time of war, one laudable in itself, owed its origins and embedding to the very movement power that those in favor of restraint now clearly lacked more than ever. But instead of reckoning with the inevitably political setting of legal reasoning, liberals have preferred to stigmatize conservative arguments about the law of war as "beyond the pale" (or celebrate conservatives who take principled stands against going there); while conservatives have developed a culture ruefully accepting the legalization of conflict and complaining publicly and privately of lawfare.

The comparison with Vietnam suggests that, for better or for worse, after 9/11 America had a debate about American torture and related violations instead of having a debate about American war. Both could have occurred— as in Vietnam after My Lai—but didn't. Although it may be a catastrophe politically, what matters for these purposes are the theoretical implications of this shift. To say that post-Vietnam legal constraints find their origins in political movements is, of course, not to say that "political opinion" is all there is to them.[115] If this were true, liberals would not rally today around the law in the absence of other political options, and conservatives would not contradict themselves in an obsession with the very legal constraints on executive authority whose authority they claim does not exist. (How can the liberal project of global legalism be perilous if it is delusional?)[116] But it is to say that the legal constraints are not likely to be robustly defended without alliance with a political movement. To put it a somewhat different way, after 9/11 a movement around war arose, but it was restricted in its aims, and conceded or supported America's global role as a condition of insisting the country subject its military to some legal rules governing the conduct of the fight.[117]

After the Vietnam war, a morally introspective America first turned to human rights; after the Cold War finally ended, it went even further in defining itself in terms of the humanitarian values of international law, including the law of war. It is worth celebrating those moves, but not as uncomplicated goods to which there are no possible alternatives besides a world in which the executive can fight—or torture—without constraint. In the Vietnam past, much worse crimes occurred without significant consciousness of or bulwarks against atrocity, and surely it is preferable now to count on the array of new controls created by hard work and nearly from scratch. We have what they lacked— yet the converse is also true. There was a massive popular movement that helped end the war and, in its congressional sequels, led to the most significant constraints on executive power ever put on paper in American history. But then, such social movements were not easy to recall in a later era.

Notes

I am grateful to the Amherst College Law and War series audience for helpful comments that prompted me to rewrite my rough draft from scratch, to Gabriella Blum, Lawrence Douglas, Matthew Waxman, and James Q. Whitman for informed guidance, and to Sanford Diehl and Kristen Loveland for exceptional assistance in finalizing the text.

1. "The Torture Photos," *New York Times*, May 5, 2004.

2. Richard A. Falk, "Review" (of Frances FitzGerald, *Fire in the Lake: The Vietnamese and the Americans in Vietnam* [New York: Little, Brown, 1972]), *Texas Law Review* 51, no. 3 (March 1973): 618.

3. See, in particular, "Living under the Drones," a much noted report generated by human rights clinics at two major American law schools: http://livingunderdrones.org/report/ (last consulted November 7, 2012).

4. See Marvin Kalb, "The Other War Still Haunting Obama," *New York Times*, October 8, 2011; Marvin and Deborah Kalb, *Haunting Legacy: Vietnam and the American Presidency from Ford to Obama* (Washington, 2011).

5. Jane Mayer, *The Dark Side: The Inside Story of How the War on Terror Turned into a War on American Ideals* (New York: Doubleday, 2008), 8–9, 325; Alan Brinkley, "Black Sites," *New York Times Book Review*, August 3, 2008.

6. Jack L. Goldsmith, *The Terror Presidency: Law and Judgment inside the Bush Administration*, rev. ed. (New York: W. W. Norton, 2007, 2009).

7. After Barack Obama's election, Goldsmith rather plausibly concluded that it is mainly rhetoric that meaningfully separates the current prosecution of the war on terror from the years of division around presidential excesses; and rhetoric matters. But Obama, having learned Bush's error on the easy front of selling the war, still faces the novel situation of legality that Bush did—a fact that his more consensual prosecution of the war on terror makes only somewhat less flagrant. Jack Goldsmith, "The Cheney

Fallacy," *New Republic*, May 18, 2009; and Goldsmith, *Power and Constraint: The Accountable Presidency after 9/11* (New York: W. W. Norton, 2012), which appeared too late to consider here.

8. Goldsmith, *The Terror Presidency*, 130, 69.

9. Ibid., 90.

10. His analytical perspective also seriously downplays the enabling role of the law of war, which does not simply limit room for maneuver by wise statesmen and commanders but also provides authority for the deployment of violence—as, for example, in deterritorialized drone wars today. Compare David Kennedy, *Of Law and War* (Princeton: Princeton University Press, 2006).

11. Goldsmith, *The Terror Presidency*, 12. To the extent Goldsmith has a theory of what prompted executive restraint, he mentions Watergate but not war (ibid., 68, 65–66, 81, 86, 183).

12. Compare James Q. Whitman, *The Verdict of Battle: The Law of Victory and the Making of Modern War* (Cambridge, MA: Harvard University Press, 2012).

13. Paul Kramer, "The First Torture Debate," *New Yorker*, February 25, 2008; see also John Fabian Witt, *Lincoln's Code: The Laws of War in American History* (New York: Free Press, 2012), which emphasizes continuity in America's paradoxical engagement with the laws of war but does not explain the fate of its commitments in the twentieth century. Compare Jennifer Schuessler, "Trying to Set Legal Rules for Brutal War," *New York Times*, October 10, 2012.

14. Pieter Lagrou, "1945–1955: The Age of Total War," in *Histories of the Aftermath: The Legacies of the Second World War in Europe,* ed. Frank Biess and Robert G. Moeller (New York: Berghahn Books, 2010). For the specific exclusion of human rights from humanitarian law in the 1940s, see William I. Hitchcock, "Human Rights and the Law of War: The Geneva Conventions of 1949," in *The Human Rights Revolution: An International History,* ed. Akira Iriye et al. (New York: Oxford University Press, 2011).

15. U.S. Department of the Army, *Field Manual No. 27-10: The Law of Land Warfare* (Washington, DC: Government Printing Office, 1956); compare Josef L. Kunz, "The U.S. Field Manual on the Law of Land Warfare," *American Journal of International Law* 51, no. 2 (April 1957): 388–405.

16. For the law of war in the major postwar counterinsurgencies by Britain and France, see Fabian Klose, "The Colonial Testing Ground: The International Committee of the Red Cross and the Violent End of Empire," *Humanity* 2, no. 1 (Spring 2011): 107–26; and David French, *The British Way in Counter-Insurgency, 1945–1967* (New York: Oxford University Press, 2011), ch. 2 and 229–32.

17. [Dean Rusk,] "U.S. Continues to Abide by Geneva Conventions of 1949 in Viet-Nam," *Department of State Bulletin,* September 13, 1965. There was some dispute in the literature about whether South Vietnamese civilians counted as "protected persons"

when they were in U.S. hands for the purposes of the relevant Geneva Convention, given that "nationals of a co-belligerent State" (IV, Art. 4) are excluded from coverage on the grounds that their state will see to them through diplomatic arrangements. But so far as I know, the U.S. government never invoked this exclusion.

18.   Goldsmith, *The Terror Presidency*, 222, citing William Ranny Levi, "Interrogation's Law," *Yale Law Journal* 118, no. 7 (May 2009): 1434–83.

19.   The Geneva Conventions (III, Art. 12) allow such transfers only if the capturing power ensures that the detaining power follows the treaty's requirements; but it is clear that the South Vietnamese shortcomings in this regard were rather serious.

20.   Anthony B. Herbert, *Soldier* (New York: Holt, Rinehart, and Winston, 1973).

21.   The small library on this point includes Jennifer Harbury, *Truth, Torture, and the American Way: The History and Consequences of U.S. Involvement in Torture* (Boston: Beacon Press, 2005); Alfred McCoy, *A Question of Torture: CIA Interrogation from the Cold War to the War on Terror* (New York: Metropolitan Books, 2006); and Michael Otterman, *American Torture: From the Cold War to Abu Ghraib and Beyond* (New York: Pluto Press, 2007). More generally, see Darius Rejali, *Torture and Democracy* (Princeton: Princeton University Press, 2007), ch. 8 and passim.

22.   As Tobias Kelly has argued more generally, torture became a privileged concern in international law only after the human rights revolution, largely because colonial rule no longer required harsh measures and America left behind direct Cold War engagement. Before that occurred the incidence of torture raised no hackles among the very sorts of people who were to find it so alarmingly beyond the pale a generation later. Kelly, "What We Talk about When We Talk about Torture," *Humanity* 2, no. 2 (Fall 2011): 327–43; and Kelly, *This Side of Silence: Torture, Human Rights, and the Recognition of Cruelty* (Philadelphia: University of Pennsylvania Press, 2012), ch. 1, "Talking about Torture after the Human Rights Revolution."

23.   See French, *The British Way in Counter-Insurgency*.

24.   The best study is now Bernd Greiner, *War without Fronts: The U.S.A. in Vietnam*, trans. Anne Wyburd and Victoria Fern (New Haven: Yale University Press, 2009), including 95–103 on rules of engagement; compare Michael Walzer, *Just and Unjust Wars: A Moral Argument with Historical Illustrations*, 2nd ed. (New York: Basic Books, 1992), 186–96. Daniel Lang, "Casualties of War," *New Yorker*, October 18, 1969; Lang, *Casualties of War* (New York: McGraw Hill, 1969).

25.   James S. Olson and Randy Roberts, *My Lai: A Brief History with Documents* (New York: Bedford–St. Martin's, 1998), 42.

26.   Greiner, *War without Fronts*; based on similar sources, but including perpetrator recollections, see Deborah Nelson, *The War Behind Me: Vietnam Veterans Confront the Truth about U.S War Crimes* (New York: Basic Books, 2008). Compare Guenter Lewy, *America in Vietnam: Myth, Illusion, and Reality* (New York: Oxford University Press,

1980), chs. 7–10. On the JAG corps and military justice, see George S. Prugh, *Law at War: Vietnam, 1964–1973* (Washington, DC: Government Printing Office, 1975); and William Thomas Allison, *Military Justice in Vietnam: The Rule of Law in an American War* (Lawrence: University of Kansas Press, 2007).

27.   William F. Pepper, "The Children of Vietnam," *Ramparts* 5, no. 7 (January 1967): 59; Denise Chong, *The Girl in the Picture: The Story of Kim Phuc, the Photograph, and the Vietnam War* (New York: Viking, 2000); Robert M. Neer, Jr., *Napalm: An American Biography* (Cambridge, MA: Harvard University Press, 2012).

28. These *New York Times* pieces were immediately gathered as Harrison E. Salisbury, *Behind the Lines: Hanoi, December 23, 1966–January 7, 1967* (New York: Harper and Row, 1967).

29.   The major sources were Frank Harvey, *Air War—Vietnam* (New York: Bantam, 1967); John Gerassi, *North Vietnam: A Documentary* (Indianapolis: Bobbs-Merrill, 1968); and Cornell Air War Study Group, *The Air War in Indochina* (Boston: Beacon, 1972). The best reflection on the legality of the air war at the time, given such revelations, was a student paper, Lawrence C. Petrowski, "Law and the Conduct of the Vietnam War," in Falk, ed., *The Vietnam War and International Law*, 4 vols. (Princeton: Princeton University Press, 1968–76), 2: 439–515, esp. 487–500. Later consider W. Hays Parks, "Rolling Thunder and the Law of War," *Air University Review* 33, 2 (January-February 1982): 2–23.

30.   *Apocalypse Now*, dir. Francis Ford Coppola (United Artists, 1979).

31.   See Bertrand Russell, *War Crimes in Vietnam* (London: Allen and Unwin, 1967); John Duffett, ed., *Against the Crime of Silence: Proceedings of the Russell International War Crimes Tribunal* (New York: Bertrand Russell Peace Foundation, 1968); Jean-Paul Sartre, *On Genocide* (Boston: Beacon Press, 1968).

32.   See, pioneeringly, Eric Norden, "American Atrocities in Vietnam," *Liberation* 10, no. 11 (February 1966): 14–27, reprinted as a pamphlet, then Clergy and Laymen Concerned about Vietnam, *In the Name of America* (self-published, 1968). Like the Russell tribunal allegations and the Lawyers Committee experts brief discussed below, it was published marginally and ignored for a long time. Compare Edward B. Fiske, "Clerics Accuse U.S. of War Crimes," *New York Times*, February 4, 1968; and Mitchell K. Hall, *Because of Their Faith: CALCAV and Religious Opposition to the Vietnam War* (New York: Columbia University Press, 1990).

33.   For these claims, see Charles DeBenedetti and Charles Chatfield. *An American Ordeal: The Antiwar Movement of the Vietnam Era* (Syracuse, NY: Syracuse University Press, 1990); Adam M. Garfinkle, *Telltale Hearts: The Origins and Impact of the Vietnam Antiwar Movement* (New York: St. Martin's Press, 1995); Hall, *Because of Their Faith*; Rhodri Jeffrys-Jones, *Peace Now!: American Society and the Ending of the Vietnam War* (New Haven: Yale University Press, 1999); Melvin Small et al., *Give Peace a Chance:*

Exploring the Vietnam Antiwar Movement (Syracuse, NY: Syracuse University Press, 1992); and N. L. Zaroulis and Gerald Sullivan, *Who Spoke Up?: American Protest against the War in Vietnam, 1963–1975* (Garden City, NY: Doubleday, 1984).

34. See "William L. Standard, 78, A Lawyer for Seafarers and Writer on War, Dies," *New York Times*, May 7, 1978; "Joseph Crown; Questioned Vietnam Policy," *New York Times*, October 22, 2002.

35. On these figures, see Randall B. Woods, ed., *Vietnam and the American Political Tradition* (Cambridge: Cambridge University Press, 2003).

36. I have followed these activities based on a bequest of papers Joseph Crown left Columbia University, which are available as Lawyers Committee on American Policy towards Vietnam Records, 1962–1979, Rare Books and Manuscript Library, Columbia University (hereinafter Lawyers Committee papers).

37. Dean Rusk, "The Control of Force in International Relations" (address at American Society of International Law, April 23, 1965), *Department of State Bulletin*, May 10, 1965. Summing up the terms of rebuttal in a title, Standard eventually published *Aggression: Our Asian Disaster*, with preface by Morse (New York: Random House, 1971).

38. "American Policy vis-à-vis Vietnam," *Cong. Rec.*, 89th Cong., 1st Sess. (September 23, 1965), 111: 24903–10; "700 Lawyers Submit Anti-Viet War Brief," *New York World-Telegram and Sun*, November 12, 1965.

39. "America Policy vis-à-vis Vietnam," *Cong. Rec.*, 89th Cong., 2nd Sess. (February 9, 1966), 112: 2665–73, which Gruening introduced; see later 89th Cong., 2nd Sess. (February 26, 1966), 112: 4166–73, which Morse introduced.

40. The first result was a short letter from McDougal and others, which appears in *Cong. Rec.*, 89th Cong., 2nd Sess. (February 23, 1966): 112: 3843; the second result was John Norton Moore and James L. Underwood with McDougal, "The Lawfulness of United States Assistance to the Republic of Viet Nam," May 1966, distributed by the American Bar Association to all congressmen, the full text of which is in *Cong. Rec.*, 89th Cong., 2nd Sess. (July 13, 1966), 112: 15519–67; a shorter version is Moore, "The Lawfulness of Military Assistance to the Republic of Viet-Nam," *American Journal of International Law* 61, no. 1 (January 1967): 1–34. Compare William Conrad Gibbons, *The U.S. Government and the Vietnam War: Executive and Legislative Roles and Relationships*, 4 vols. (Princeton: Princeton University Press, 1986–92), 4: 246n.

41. Austin A. Wehrwein, "Bar Group Finds U.S. Policy Legal Under U.N.," *New York Times*, February 22, 1966; "A.B.A. under Attack for Vietnam Stand," *New York Times*, March 15, 1966; letter of Standard and Crown to Edward W. Kuhn, ABA president, March 15, 1966, Lawyers Committee papers, Box 10. Compare Eberhard P. Deutsch, "The Legality of the United States Position in Vietnam," *ABA Journal*, May 1966; and Standard, "United States Intervention in Vietnam Is Not Legal," *ABA Journal*, July 1966.

42. Meeker had previously treated this as sufficiently unimportant as to pass on a

memo prepared by a subordinate, "Legal Basis for United States Actions against North Vietnam," March 1965, which a congressional staffer who saw it called "the sloppiest piece of legal work I have ever seen." Cited in Gibbons, *The U.S. Government and the Vietnam War*, 3: 79n.

43. [Leonard C. Meeker,] "The Legality of United States Participation in the Defense of Viet Nam" (March 4, 1966), *Department of State Bulletin*, March 28, 1966, reprinted widely in the years thereafter.

44. A draft, "The Military Involvement of the United States in Vietnam: A Legal Analysis, October 1, 1966," can be found in Lawyers Committee papers, Box 11. The book is Lawyers Committee, *The Vietnam War and International Law* (Flanders, NJ: O'Hare, 1967). Fried, a fascinating German Jewish emigre lawyer who adjuncted at the City University of New York, deserves more attention than I can give him here. Meeker, "Viet-Nam and the International Law of Self-Defense," *Department of State Bulletin*, January 9, 1967; Hedrick Smith, "U.S. Aide Says Law Justifies Vietnam Bombing," *New York Times*, December 14, 1966.

45. "Lawyers' Group Urges Ruling by World Court on Vietnam," *New York Times*, December 9, 1966.

46. See esp. Consultative Council member Lawrence R. Velvel's "The War in Vietnam: Unconstitutional, Justiciable, and Jurisdictionally Attackable," *Kansas Law Review* 16, no. 4 (1968): 449–503, and *Undeclared War and Civil Disobedience: The American System in Crisis*, with preface by Falk (New York: Dunellen, 1970). For various cases, see Anthony A. D'Amato and Robert M. O'Neil, *The Judiciary and Vietnam* (New York: St. Martin's Press, 1972); and John F. and Rosemary S. Bannan, *Law, Morality, and Vietnam: The Peace Militants and the Courts* (Bloomington: Indiana University Press, 1974).

47. "Lawyers Group Asks Congress to End 'Disastrous' Vietnam Policy," *New York Times*, April 1, 1969.

48. Letter of Crown to Morse, October 23, 1969, Lawyers Committee papers, Box 11.

49. "Lawyers' Anti-Viet Group Weighs Presidential Bill of Impeachment," *New York Law Journal*, January 19, 1968; for Nixon, see Lawyers Committee, Boxes 20–21, and Falk, "Why Impeachment?" *New Republic*, May 1, 1971; Standard and Crown, "Rehnquist's Achilles Heel" (letter to the editor), *New York Times*, November 14, 1971.

50. "Toronto Declaration on Vietnam, Laos, and Cambodia: A Realistic Program to End the War," jointly issued by Canadian Lawyers Committee on Vietnam and Lawyers Committee on American Policy towards Vietnam, Lawyers Committee papers, Box 7; Ross H. Munro, "Lawyers Call for Unconditional Withdrawal of All U.S. Forces from Indo-China Theatre," *Globe and Mail*, May 25, 1970.

51. Frank Browning and Dorothy Forman, eds., *The Wasted Nations: Report of the International Commission of Enquiry into United States Crimes in Indochina, June 20–25, 1971*, with preface by Falk (New York: Harper and Row, 1972).

52. "Report of Delegation to Hanoi, October 14–21 [1971] of Lawyers Committee on American Policy towards Vietnam," Lawyers Committee papers, Box 3. In one of its last acts, the committee sent a letter to congressmen in protest of the Christmas bombings, January 16, 1973, Box 22. "[Nixon's] employment of B-52 carpet bombing against densely populated civilian cities such as Hanoi and Haiphong—unprecedented in military history—to force North Vietnam to capitulate to his terms constitutes a war crime under the Nuremberg principles," it noted.

53. For a prominent portrait from the era, see "Professor Whose Cause Is Peace: Richard Anderson Falk (Man in the News)," *New York Times*, August 15, 1968.

54. He taught at Ohio State Law School beginning in 1955, and moved to Princeton in 1962, and was given an S.J.D. by Harvard Law School on the basis of his published writings the same year. Two collections gather his early writings: *Legal Order in a Violent World* (Princeton: Princeton University Press, 1968) and *The Status of Law in International Society* (Princeton: Princeton University Press, 1970), including Appendix C, "Some Thoughts on the Jurisprudence of Myres S. McDougal." For a much later barometric reading, see Falk, "Casting the Spell: The New Haven School of International Law," *Yale Law Journal* 104, no. 7 (May 1995): 1991–2008.

55. As he put it to a correspondent in fall 1967, "I have grown doubtful myself about the book's affirmation of an American role to thwart Communist-led aggression." Richard A. Falk Papers, Syracuse University Library (hereinafter Falk papers), Letter to Eugene Maier, Box 7, Corres. M II.

56. Falk and Saul H. Mendlovitz, "Towards a Warless World: One Legal Formula to Achieve Transition," *Yale Law Journal* 73, no. 3 (January 1964): 399–424; Falk and Mendlovitz, eds., *The Strategy of World Order*, 4 vols. (New York: World Law Fund, 1966). Continuing earlier international law proposals for "structural change" epitomized by Grenville Clark's and Louis Sohn's famous scheme, Falk and Mendlovitz, first supported by the World Law Fund, eventually worked closely with the Institute for World Order.

57. See, usefully, Rosalyn Higgins, "Policy and Impartiality: The Uneasy Relationship in International Law," *International Organization* 23, no. 4 (Autumn 1969): 914–31. Writing to McDougal, who had made this demand in response to his introduction to the collection of Vietnam-related scholarship Falk edited, Falk responded: "I do take seriously your challenge 'to come up with a comprehensive and homogeneous framework.' It requires a kind of intellectual maturity that I have not yet felt able to command. Besides, it is not easy to contemplate undertaking a task of such a scale beneath the shadow of your own example, both because of the magnitude of your enterprise and the extraordinarily high quality of its achievement." Letter to McDougal, September 1, 1967, Falk papers, Box 19, Folder *The Vietnam War and International Law*.

58. Leonard B. Boudin, "War Crimes and Vietnam: The Mote in Whose Eye?" *Harvard Law Review* 84, no. 8 (June 1971): 1940. For Falk's early writings on the law of

war, "Janus Tormented: The International Law of Internal War," in *International Aspects of Civil Strife*, ed. J. N. Rosenau (Princeton: Princeton University Press, 1964), 185–248; and esp. Falk, "The Claimants of Hiroshima," *Nation*, February 15, 1965, posing the illegality of the World War II nuclear bombing, a topic pursued in Falk, "The Shimoda Case: A Legal Appraisal of the Atomic Attacks upon Hiroshima and Nagasaki," *American Journal of International Law* 59, no. 4 (October 1965): 759–93.

59. Letter of Falk to Standard, November 1, 1965, Lawyers Committee files, Box 9.

60. Falk, "International Law and the United States Role in the Viet Nam War," *Yale Law Journal* 75, no. 7 (June 1966): 1122–60; in the immediate aftermath, see John Norton Moore, "International Law and the United States Role in Viet Nam: A Reply," *Yale Law Journal* 76, no. 6 (May 1967): 1051–94; and Falk, "International Law and the United States Role in Viet Nam: A Response to Professor Moore," *Yale Law Journal* 76, no. 6 (May 1967): 1095–1158. See later Falk, "Alchemy and Analysis: The Two Faces of John Norton Moore," *Virginia Journal of International Law* 13, no. 1 (Fall 1972): 120–31.

61. Moore, *Law and the Indo-China War* (Princeton: Princeton University Press, 1972), with preface by McDougal, with its "Prolegomenon to the Jurisprudence of Myres McDougal and Harold Lasswell." See also Roger H. Hull and John Novogrod, *Law and Vietnam*, with preface by McDougal (Dobbs Ferry: Oceana, 1968).

62. Falk, ed., *The Vietnam War and International Law*. A short section on the laws of war appeared in the second volume (1969). Leaving aside a piece on POWs by Howard Levie, it consisted of three student notes on the applicability of the Geneva Conventions and a translation of an essay by a French law professor. In the third volume (1972) the coverage of war crimes became central.

63. R. R. Baxter, "Legality of the American Action: The War in Vietnam," *The Times*, September 5, 1967; see Falk's reply, *The Times*, October 9, 1967. Baxter did acknowledge the presence of Hans Morgenthau, primarily in political science at Chicago, and Quincy Wright, a major legal figure who had since departed the same university. (After Wright's 1970 death, the Lawyers Committee organized a Quincy Wright prize, which Falk bestowed on Daniel Ellsberg at a ceremony on February 6, 1972.) Though not on the Consultative Council, significant figures like Thomas Emerson and Wolfgang Friedmann, who taught at places Baxter named, did affiliate with the Lawyers Committee in other ways. The same was true of Harvard political science professor Stanley Hoffmann, who participated on the Consultative Council from the beginning.

64. See letter of Louis B. Sohn to Standard, November 2, 1965, Lawyers Committee papers, Box 9, enclosing memo disputing the lawyers' brief and invoking the right of self-defense as rationale for American intervention.

65. See, e.g., William Whitworth, "Some Questions about the War" (interview with Eugene Rostow), *New Yorker*, July 4, 1970; Eugene Rostow, "Indochina as Arena of First Principles," *New York Times*, May 29, 1973.

66. Letter of Falk to Nicholas deB. Katzenbach, September 22, 1966, Falk papers, Box 7, Folder Corres. K.

67. Letter of Falk to Burns Weston, July 13, 1967, Falk papers, Box 7, Folder Corres. Lawyers Committee on American Policy towards Vietnam.

68. Falk, "Law, Lawyers, and the Conduct of Foreign Affairs," *Yale Law Journal* 78, no. 6 (May 1969): 922.

69. See, esp., Falk, *The Six Legal Dimensions of the Vietnam War* (Princeton: Center of International Studies, 1968).

70. "Two U.S. Law Professors Meet with Hanoi Premier," *New York Times*, July 3, 1968.

71. Although the main declaration of the Grenoble conference shows that these jurists primarily indicted American aggression (and championed the Vietnamese right of self-determination), they also issued a Résolution de la 3ème Commission, "Derniers aspects des moyens et méthodes de guerre appliqués par les forces d'agression en violation du droit international," Lawyers Committee papers, Box 2.

72. "Address of Richard Falk, Delegate of the United States, World Congress of Lawyers for Vietnam," Lawyers Committee papers, Box 2.

73. Falk, *The Six Legal Dimensions of the Vietnam War*, 30.

74. Falk, *A Vietnam Settlement: The View from Hanoi* (Princeton: Center of International Studies, 1968); "A Political Solution for Vietnam?" *Dissent* 16, no. 3 (May–June 1969): 196–98; "Saigon Notwithstanding," *Nation*, June 2, 1969. He also befriended the roving anticolonial intellectual Eqbal Ahmad and testified as an expert in his trial as part of the so-called Harrisburg Seven; Falk also participated in many Selective Service cases.

75. See, esp., Falk, *The Six Legal Dimensions of the Vietnam War*, 29–32, 42–48.

76. Falk, "International Law and the Conduct of the Vietnam War," in Clergy and Laymen Concerned about Vietnam, *In the Name of America*, 27.

77. Noam Chomsky, for example, wrote about war crimes only after My Lai, beginning in Chomsky, "After Pinkville," *New York Review of Books*, January 1, 1970, reprinted in *At War with Asia* (New York: Pantheon, 1970). See also, e.g., Edward Herman, *Atrocities in Vietnam: Myths and Realities* (Philadelphia: Pilgrim Press, 1970).

78. Much of Falk, *The Vietnam War and International Law*, vol. 3, is devoted to the legality of the Cambodian ground incursion.

79. Falk, "The Circle of Responsibility," *Nation*, January 26, 1970.

80. Ibid.; compare Falk, "Songmy: War Crimes and Individual Responsibility," *TRANS-action* 7, no. 3 (January 1970): 33–40. See later Falk, "The Nuremberg Tradition," *Intercom* 13, no. 1 (January/February 1971): 29–32; "War Crimes and Individual Responsibility," *Church and Society* 61, no. 5 (May–June 1971): 23–32 and 61–62; and Falk, "Son My: War Crimes and Individual Responsibility," *Toledo Law Review* 3, no. 1

(Fall–Winter 1971): 21–41. And see later Falk, "Keeping Nuremberg Alive," in *Marxismo, democrazia, e diritto dei popoli: Scritti in onore di Lelio Basso*, ed. Giuliano Amato (Milan: Franco Agneli, 1979).

81. Neil Sheehan, "Should We Have War Crimes Trials?" *New York Times*, March 28, 1971; compare the letters in response praising the paper for the bold step of commissioning the review at all, *New York Times*, April 25, 1971. See also Mark Sacharoff, "War Crimes: Made in the U.S.A.," *Nation*, January 25, 1971.

82. Vietnam Veterans against the War, *The Winter Soldier Investigation: An Inquiry into American War Crimes* (Boston: Beacon Press, 1971). See also Andrew E. Hunt, *The Turning: A History of Vietnam Veterans against the War* (New York: New York University Press, 1999); and Elliott Meyrowitz and Kenneth Campbell, "Vietnam Veterans and War Crimes Hearings," in *Give Peace a Chance*, 129–40. Among academics, the Committee of Concerned Asian Scholars mobilized prominently; see *The Indochina Story: A Fully Documented Account* (New York: Pantheon, 1970), much of which deals with war crimes.

83. See Falk papers, Box 15, Folder AFSC-War Crimes. The congressional conference, sponsored by several Democrats, involved Falk and Telford Taylor as well as Hannah Arendt, Daniel Ellsberg, Hans Morgenthau, Jonathan Schell, and others. See Erwin Knoll and Judith Nies McFadden, eds., *War Crimes and the American Conscience* (New York: Holt, Rinehart, and Winston, 1970). The Citizens Commission held events around the country and in April 1971 collaborated with Rep. Ron Dellums to hold war crimes hearings; see Citizens Commission of Inquiry, *The Dellums Committee Hearings on War Crimes in Vietnam* (New York: Vintage, 1972).

84. Falk, "In Defense of the Movement," *New York Times*, November 28, 1971.

85. Falk, Gabriel Kolko, and Robert Jay Lifton, eds., *Crimes of War* (New York: Vintage, 1971). For a high-profile reception, see Anthony Lewis, "Law and War," *New York Times*, April 26, 1971. Falk reunited with old collaborators to produce a similar volume on Iraq, which received considerably less attention. Falk, Irene Gendzier, and Lifton, eds., *Crimes of War: Iraq* (New York: NationBooks, 2004).

86. Gabriel Kolko, "War Crimes and the Nature of the Vietnam War," Congressional Conference on War and Individual Responsibility, February 20–21, 1970, in Falk papers, Box 19, Folder "War and National Responsibility."

87. Falk et al., eds., *Crimes of War*, xi. Herbert Wechsler remarked acidly that "Professor Falk makes up a lot of law that I don't think exists and then expects the judicial system to apply it." "War Crimes, Just and Unjust Wars, and Comparisons between Nuremberg and Vietnam," *Columbia Journal of Law and Social Problems* 8, no. 1 (Fall 1971): 129.

88. He first commented in Telford Taylor, "Judgment on Mylai," *New York Times*, January 10, 1970, then wrote *Nuremberg and Vietnam: An American Tragedy* (Chicago:

Quadrangle, 1970; New York: Bantam, 1971), excerpted as "Nuremberg in Son My," *New York Times*, November 20, 1970.

89. See Jonathan Bush, "Soldiers Find Wars: A Life of Telford Taylor," *Columbia Journal of Transnational Law* 37, no. 3 (1999): 675–92.

90. Falk comments in a Columbia University symposium, "War Crimes, Just and Unjust Wars," 113–14. Falk also participated with Noam Chomsky in the *Yale Law Journal* symposium on the book: Falk, "Nuremberg: Past, Present, and Future," *Yale Law Journal* 80, no. 7 (June 1971): 1501–28.

91. Sheehan, "Conversations with Americans," *New York Times*, December 27, 1970; compare the letters of Edward Herman and Ralph Schoenman, and Sheehan's response to them, *New York Times*, January 24, 1971. When Taylor's book went into paperback and the publisher designed a cover with a swastika imposed on an American flag, Taylor protested and had the cover changed. See letter of Taylor to Jean Highland, April 23, 1971, Telford Taylor Papers, Arthur W. Diamond Law Library, Columbia University Law School (hereinafter Taylor papers), Series 8, Subseries 2, Box 16, Folder 152.

92. Geoffrey Cowan and Judith Coburn, "The War Criminals Hedge Their Bets," *Village Voice*, December 4, 1969, to which former undersecretary of the Air Force Townsend Hoopes, then famous for his anatomy of escalation, replied. See Townsend Hoopes, "The Nuremberg Suggestion," *Washington Monthly*, January 1970, with replies by the journalists in the February issue. In 1967, Taylor had attended a conference organized by Columbia law students on the possible relevance of Nuremberg to Vietnam; see Taylor papers, Series 9, Subseries 1, Box 1, Folder 11.

93. Taylor, *Nuremberg and Vietnam*, 118–21; on this point, see Nuremberg prosecutor Benjamin Ferencz's "War Crimes Law and the Vietnam War," *American University Law Review* 17, no. 3 (June 1968): 403–23.

94. For instance, Taylor deemed the gang rape and murder reported by Daniel Lang "apparently" not a war crime because he was not sure South Vietnamese civilians were protected persons under the Geneva Conventions and because the victim seemed to have been taken from "friendly" territory. Taylor, *Nuremberg and Vietnam*, 134.

95. Jonathan Schell, "The Village of Ben Suc," *New Yorker*, July 15, 1967; *The Village of Ben Suc* (New York: A. A. Knopf, 1967); "Quang Ngai and Quang Tin 1 and 2," *New Yorker*, March 9 and 16, 1968; *The Military Half: An Account of Destruction in Quang Nai and Quang Tin* (New York: A. A. Knopf, 1968).

96. See Taylor, Tom Farer, Brig. And Gen. Robert G. Gard, "Vietnam and the Nuremberg Principles: A Colloquy on War Crimes," *Rutgers-Camden Law Journal* 5, no. 1 (Fall 1973): 7 for the "impeccable" comment.

97. Taylor, *Final Report to the Secretary of the Army on the Nuremberg War Crimes Trials under Control Council Law No. 10* (Washington, DC: U.S. Government Printing Office, 1949), 65.

98. Taylor, *Nuremberg and Vietnam*, 144.

99. In her memoir, Baez wrote that on the trip, before the bombing began, "legally, I was of no use, especially because of my deep-seated opinion that war itself is a crime; that the killing of one child, the burning of one village, the dropping of one bomb sinks us into such depths of depravity that there's no use bickering over the particulars. But Telford was a terribly conscientious man and was carrying out his duties to the last detail with endless questions about logistics, dates and so forth. [I was] fascinated with the way his mind worked." Joan Baez, *And a Voice to Sing With* (New York: Simon and Schuster, 1987), 199. In a similar spirit, see her undated note, in Taylor papers, Series 8, Subseries 1, Box 4, Folder 93.

100. Deirdre Carmody, "4 Who Visited Hanoi Tell of Destruction," *New York Times*, January 2, 1973; Taylor, "Hanoi under the Bombing: Sirens, Shelters, Rubble, and Death," *New York Times*, January 7, 1973. See also Taylor, "North Vietnam," *Atlantic*, May 1973.

101. Taylor, "Defining War Crimes," *New York Times*, January 11, 1973. After reading Drew Middleton, "Hanoi Films Show No 'Carpet Bombing,'" *New York Times*, May 2, 1973, Taylor sent an angry letter acknowledging that the city (unlike Dresden and Nagasaki) survived but insisting on the fact that indiscriminate bombing had indeed taken place. Taylor papers, Series 8, Subseries 1, Box 4, Folder 93.

102. Progressive lawyer Leonard Boudin, also involved with the Boston Five defense (and later Daniel Ellsberg's lawyer), wrote in his hard-hitting review, "It is hardly a tribute to objectivity in legal circles that few other than Taylor could have had such an effect today, and that not even he would have had the same audience, much less taken the same position, five years ago." Boudin, "War Crimes and Vietnam," 1940.

103. Falk, "Nuremberg and Vietnam," *New York Times*, December 27, 1970. See similar reviews by John Fried, calling the work one of a "tormented conservative," *American Political Science Review* 65, 4 (December 1971): 1257–58; and by Richard Wasserstrom, "Criminal Behavior," *New York Review of Books*, June 3, 1971.

104. *In re Yamashita*, 327 U.S. 1 (1946). Sheehan, "Taylor Says by Yamashita Ruling Westmoreland May Be Guilty," *New York Times*, January 9, 1971. In his memoirs, Westmoreland dismissed Taylor's remark as an "emotional outburst," and it is true that the moment of its traction was fleeting. William Westmoreland, *A Soldier Reports* (Garden City, NJ: Doubleday, 1976), 379. See, generally, Allan A. Ryan, *Yamashita's Ghost: War Crimes, MacArthur's Justice, and Command Accountability* (Lawrence: University of Kansas Press, 2012), ch. 18.

105. See Falk's memorial essay, "Telford Taylor and the Legacy of Nuremberg," *Columbia Journal of Transnational Law* 37, no. 3 (1999): 693–723, esp. 698–99.

106. Such a move could also serve to minimize culpability, as in the case of Richard Baxter's post–My Lai criticisms of Falk. When he attacked Falk's charge of aggression early in the war, Vietnam was for Baxter an international conflict; later it turned out

to be a civil war, with, alas, few laws governing its conduct. See Baxter, "Comments," in Peter D. Trooboff, ed., *Law and Responsibility in Warfare: The Vietnam Experience* (Chapel Hill: University of North Carolina Press, 1975), a book that includes post hoc commentary from leading international lawyers, as well as some policy thinkers such as Robert W. Komer (who ran the Phoenix program), on most of the domains of possible illegality in the war.

107. Taylor, *Nuremberg and Vietnam*, 184, 188. Similarly, see his letter to the editor with Wolfgang Friedmann and Walter Gellhorn on Laos, which considered the relevant incursion "not so much [a matter] of international law as of moral and political responsibility." "What Is to Be Done in Indochina?" *New York Times*, February 21, 1971.

108. Taylor, "Judging Calley Is Not Enough," *Life*, April 9, 1971; Taylor, "The Course of Military Justice," *New York Times*, February 2, 1972; Taylor, "Foreword," in *The Law of War: A Documentary History*, ed. Leon Friedman (New York: Random House, 1972). As Greiner puts it in his excellent chapter on accountability for war crimes, "[T]he legal methods have to be described as self-release from law and statute." Greiner, *War without Fronts*, 334, and ch. 8 generally. Compare Joshua E. S. Phillips, "Inside the Detainee Abuse Task Force," *Nation*, May 30, 2011.

109. Barbara Keys, "The Forgotten Vietnamese Origins of U.S. Human Rights Legislation" (forthcoming); *Reclaiming American Virtue: The Human Rights Revolution of the 1970s* (Cambridge, MA: Harvard University Press, 2014). See earlier my *The Last Utopia: Human Rights in History* (Cambridge, MA: Harvard University Press, 2010), esp. ch. 4 on the post-Vietnam context of the turn in the United States to human rights.

110. The need to reform the laws of war in light of counterinsurgent realities was plain, but, unlike a few international actors, even eventual American human rights scholars were not yet arguing to supplement them with human rights. Compare Tom J. Farer, "The Laws of War 25 Years after Nuremberg," *International Conciliation* 583 (May 1971): 1–54 with UN Gen. Ass. Res. 2444 (XXIII) (December 19, 1968), 2674 (XXV) (December 9, 1970), 2852 (XXVI) and 2853 (XXVI) (both December 20, 1971), all on "Respect for Human Rights in Armed Conflicts." The American Society for International Law held a pioneering 1973 session on the subject (which Telford Taylor chaired): "Human Rights in Armed Conflicts," *Proceedings of the American Society of International Law* 67 (1973): 141–68. The most notable celebration of this attempted merger or infiltration remains Theodor Meron, "The Humanization of Humanitarian Law," *American Journal of International Law* 94, no. 2 (April 2000): 239–89. Falk himself never mentioned human rights in the relevant era, though from the mid-1970s on he did try to arrogate the language for the left. The most revealing early document is Falk, "La déclaration d'Alger et la lutte pour les droits de l'homme," in *Pour un droit des peuples: Essais sur la Déclaration d'Alger*, ed. Antonio Cassese and Edmund Jouvé (Paris: Berger Levrault, 1978); later see, e.g., Falk, *Achieving Human Rights* (New York: Routledge, 2008).

111.   18 U.S.C. 2340 and 18 U.S.C. 2441; Laura A. Dickinson, "Military Lawyers on the Battlefield: An Empirical Account of International Law Compliance," *American Journal of International Law* 104, no. 1 (January 2010): 1–28.

112.   Compare Nick Turse's brilliant *Kill Anything that Moves: The Real American War in Vietnam* (New York: Metropolitan, 2013)—which reveals the massive scope of atrocity in Vietnam, but without mentioning the deeper challenge that the mobilization of the era poses to the dominant contemporary moralization of American war today, which also focuses on atrocity.

113.   Compare Edward Keynes, *Undeclared War: Twilight Zone of Constitutional Power* (University Park: Penn State University Press, 1982); and John Hart Ely, *War and Responsibility: Constitutional Lessons of Vietnam and Its Aftermath* (Princeton: Princeton University Press, 1993).

114.   Compare Ryan Goodman, "Controlling the Recourse to Force by Modifying *Jus in Bello*," *Yearbook of International Humanitarian Law* 12 (2009): 53–84.

115.   Eric A. Posner and Adrian Vermeule, *The Executive Unbound: After the Madisonian Republic* (New York: Oxford University Press, 2011).

116.   Compare ibid., ch. 5; and Posner, *The Perils of Global Legalism* (Chicago: University of Chicago Press, 2009).

117.   Compare David Cole, "Obama and Terror: The Hovering Questions," *New York Review of Books*, July 12, 2012, which (over)emphasizes the policy shift President Obama carried out, under the influence (Cole argues) of just such a movement. Then see James Mann, *The Obamians: The Struggle Inside the White House to Redefine American Power* (New York: Viking, 2012) for an account emphasizing how Democratic foreign policy under Obama's presidency successfully transcended nagging worries about global intervention and violence first born in Vietnam and salient until recently.

War Crimes Trials during and after War

LARRY MAY

War and law sit in a tense relationship, often not well recognized by theorists writing in the just war tradition. Grotius says that wars "must be carried on with not less scrupulousness than judicial processes."[1] But the kind of scrupulousness needed for successful waging of war is quite different from the kind of scrupulousness needed for the successful pursuit of justice during trials. Achieving victory on the battlefield often requires having very high morale among troops, for instance, and yet achieving victory in a trial does not turn on such morale, and indeed can be achieved by playing off the low morale of troops who are convinced that they will be the next to be prosecuted if they do not cooperate and testify against their comrades.

It has seemed to some theorists over the centuries that war was either already criminal, or war involved suspending criminal rules. In both cases, the idea of guilt, traditionally the focal point of trials, was simply not appropriate during war. In addition, soldiers did not act on their own but on the command of others, and so their acts seemed to lack the intent necessary for criminal guilt. But the idea of war crimes is nearly as old as history itself. The oldest of codes place some limits on how war can legitimately be conducted, and the idea of prosecuting individuals who violate those rules of war can be seen at least as early as ancient Greece. In fact, arguably the first recorded criminal trial, the trial of Orestes for killing his mother, is tied up with the idea of whether Orestes' father, who was killed by his mother, acted appropriately during war in sacrificing his daughter to gain victory.[2]

Law is brought into tension with war in the very idea of war crimes trials. Most such trials occur after the war is ended, and here it is difficult to reproduce the sense of battle as well as even the issues that propelled the antagonists during war. It is as if law must wait until war is over to be able to achieve objectivity. But in this paper I ask not just about such trials but also about criminal trials for war crimes held while war still rages. In this respect, I will begin with Grotius, who forthrightly investigated these issues in the seventeenth century. For it is Grotius who not only discusses war but also war crimes in a way that aids in understanding how war and crimes are related.

In this paper I will consider the justifiability of retribution through war crimes trials, with special attention to the question of whether such trials should be held during wartime or after war ends. Contrary to most of the extensive literature on this topic, I will distinguish between trials conducted during war versus trials conducted in the aftermath of war. In the first section of this paper, I will begin by looking back to the just war tradition for guidance about how to view war crimes trials. In the second section, I defend the use of criminal trials for crimes committed during war, with special attention to the problems that result when principles of legality are mixed with the realities of war. In the third section, I will examine a U.S. case that was prosecuted during the Vietnam war, *Calley v. Calloway*, as well as several more recent cases from Iraq and Afghanistan. In the fourth section, I examine the arguments for holding war crimes trials *during* wartime, and I also examine arguments for holding war crimes trials *after* war ends. I look at how the principle of retribution should be seen in light of other *jus post bellum* principles. And in the final section I consider several objections to the views I have set out.

I. The Just War Tradition

States do not often seek legal permission before going to war. Yet law will often play a significant role at the end, and sometimes even during, a war, especially in the institution of war crimes trials. In this sense, war is often perceived through the lens of law, as was most notably true of the Nuremberg trial of the late 1940s that performed this function for World War II. Some have said that the My Lai trial, held in the late 1960s, played a similar role in respect to the Vietnam war. The relationship between law and war has been discussed for a very long time. I begin with the writings of Hugo Grotius early in the 1600s.

Hugo Grotius is the greatest of the secular just war theorists. In 1625, he wrote a treatise which to this day is still highly influential in international law. Grotius talks of a "great society of States" that is governed by the "law of nations."[3] The "common law among nations" is "valid alike for war and in war."[4] When the laws of nations, which include the laws of war, are broken, "a remedy must be found [so] that men may not believe that nothing is allowable, or that everything is."[5] Grotius also maintained that "in order that wars may be justified, they must be carried on with not less scrupulousness than judicial processes are wont to be."[6] In this respect, Grotius talks of the possibility that states, like individuals, would "league themselves together to establish tribunals."[7] And he follows this remark by pointing out that "law fails of its outward effect unless it has a sanction behind it," even as he also allows that law without sanction "is not entirely void of effect."[8] Thus Grotius anticipates international war crimes tribunals that would seek to punish individuals and perhaps also states that violate the rules of war, as established by the law of nations.

Grotius maintains that the law of *nations* is the source of the laws of war. But there are two crucial parts of the laws of war that are instead grounded in the law of *nature*, universal moral norms, not merely the law of nations. First, Grotius points out that the law of nations is largely based on agreements and pacts of states. And there is need of an obligation to obey pacts. The solution to this problem is that "it is a rule of nature to abide by pacts."[9] Second, for Grotius, some of the rules of war are grounded in "certain fundamental conceptions which are beyond question"[10]—namely, principles of natural justice, such as that one should not seize "that which belongs to another."[11]

In book I, chapter II of *De Jure Belli ac Pacis*, Grotius says that at certain times goodness is a narrow consideration. Think of it, he says, as "a point, so to speak, so that if you depart from it even the least possible distance, you turn aside in the direction of wrongdoing."[12] To perform an act without injustice is the key to living a good life. But what might otherwise be thought to be without injustice can change with only seemingly minor changes in certain circumstances. Because Grotius holds the general view that "the good of the innocent person should receive consideration before the good of the guilty,"[13] it will matter whether the one who is waging war is innocent or guilty, and in part this will be determined in light of whether the "legal formalities" of the rules of war have been followed. Grotius thus also anticipates the debate about whether a state's aggressor status taints all other acts that are taken during and after war.

For Grotius, what is crucial is whether or not a given act will "take away the rights of others."[14] Even the use of force that brings about the death of fellow humans can be "good" if that act does not take away the rights of those who are killed, since the "use of force which does not violate the rights of others is not unjust."[15] In particular, Grotius holds that "it is not unfair that each suffer the full extent of the evil he has committed."[16] Thus for Grotius it will matter whether one fights in a just or unjust war in terms of what can justifiably be done to that person during war, especially concerning which tactics during war are justifiable and which are not.

In an important, although somewhat elusive passage, Grotius sets the stage for the idea of war crimes trials when he says:

> Now then once it is proved that the inflicting of capital punishment could be lawfully retained after the coming of Christ, it is, I think, proved at the same time that in some cases war is lawfully waged, as, for example, against criminals gathered in a great number, and armed, who must be conquered in order that they may be brought to trial.[17]

The waging of war, and the killing of people that war necessarily involves, are sometimes justified because of the crimes of those against whom one fights this war, insofar as waging war is the only way to bring these criminals to trial.

While Grotius here seems concerned with crimes committed before the war started, it is an obvious extension of his doctrine to think also of crimes committed during early stages of a war. In war various legal "formalities must be observed."[18] And when they are not observed the individual in question has committed a war crime. In addition, Grotius argues that illegal orders to go to war, or to use illegal tactics in war, should not be obeyed. He says: "[If] the authorities issue any order that is contrary to the laws of nature or to the commandments of God, the order should not be carried out."[19] Indeed, it would be wrong to carry out the order, and in the case of the order to go to war, subsequent acts committed during war, which are based on the wrongful act of obeying the order to go to war, would also be wrong, despite the fact that they might otherwise be right. Grotius does not explicitly draw this inference, but it certainly seems consistent with the general line of argument of *De Jure Belli ac Pacis*.

When in book III Grotius sets out the "rules regarding what is permissible in war," he says that violating the rules of war can make one guilty and can change one's status concerning subsequent acts during war. Here is a crucial passage:

> [T]he fact must be recognized that our right to wage war is to be regarded as arising not merely from the origin of the war but also from the causes which subsequently develop. Just as in law suits a new right is often acquired by one party after suit has been brought. Thus those who associate themselves with him who assails me, either as allies or subjects, confer upon me the right to protect myself against them as well. In like manner those who join in a war that is unjust, especially if they can or ought to know that it is unjust, obligate themselves to make good the expenses and losses incurred, because through the guilt they cause the loss.[20]

Notice here that Grotius links both *jus ad bellum* and *jus in bello* considerations with those of *jus post bellum*. If a soldier participates in what is known, or should have been known, to be an unjust war, or engages in unjust tactics during war, that soldier incurs obligations after war ends to "make good expenses and losses incurred."

In the category of causes that arise subsequently to the onset of war are those having to do with the commission of war crimes, what Grotius calls violations of the rules of war. And yet Grotius is aware that such considerations as those described above can be abused. On the next page, he says:

> But, as we have admonished upon many occasions previously, what accords with a strict interpretation of right is not always, or in all respects, permitted. Often, in fact, love for our neighbor prevents us from pressing our right to the utmost limit.[21]

So Grotius urges that humanitarian concerns should motivate us not to punish severely those who have engaged in guilty acts. Rather, or so it seems, postwar reconciliation and reparations are more appropriate than is punishment.

Having established that it is unjust to wage war, or to participate in war, if that war is unjust, and that, as a matter of justice, people can then be punished for such injustices, Grotius also sometimes takes away "the privilege" of doing so. For, in some cases "a sense of honor may be said to forbid what the law permits."[22] He reminds us "that if the cause of a war should be unjust, even if the war should have been undertaken in a lawful way, all acts which arise therefrom are unjust from the point of view of moral injustice."[23] But just a few pages later, Grotius says that "from humanitarian instincts, or on other worthy grounds, he will either completely pardon, or free from the penalty of death, those who have deserved such punishment."[24]

And yet, as indicated above, Grotius does not rule out the prosecution of those who are guilty of crimes during war, as is also true in contemporary debates. He merely indicates that we should be motivated as much by humanitarian considerations as those of strict justice when dealing with those who have committed war crimes, especially "when anyone has done wrong not from hatred or cruelty, but moved by a sense of duty and righteous zeal."[25] This position in favor of humanitarian leniency for those who fight in unjust wars from good motives also anticipates what we will find in discussions of war crimes prosecutions in contemporary debates. But the general idea that war crimes trials, both for *jus in bello* as well as *jus ad bellum* violations, should occur early enough in war so that soldiers know what is expected of them is clearly something that Grotius provides support for.

II. A Defense of War Crimes Trials

A Grotian defense of war crimes trials would be drawn in terms of several factors. First, trials are generally justified so that wrongdoers do not have the sense that they can act with impunity. This obviously deals with both specific and general deterrence. But more important for a Grotian account, retribution must be had to set the scales of justice aright. War intersects with law so that a moral objective can be achieved. Of course, in a sense, law alone cannot achieve a moral objective. Here is one of the links between law and war.

Some kind of collective moral response is called for as a result of the injustice of initiating an aggressive as opposed to a defensive war, or the injustice of employing tactics or weapons during war that cause unnecessary suffering. In addition, as I shall argue later, a moral response is called for at the end of war that justifies the imposition of law upon war. In the Grotian account, war crimes trials are justified on moral grounds as a way to limit and ultimately provide a justificatory frame for how to think about the possibility of just war.

The reason that morality alone, through its sanction of blame, taint, and shame, cannot regulate war sufficiently without law is that war can never be effectively regulated and appropriately restrained except through institutions of collective liability. War is not a matter of individual isolated action. And war cannot be constrained by sanctions that are merely aimed at individual actors either. War involves the coordinated acts of many individuals, and properly to restrain war will require institutions that aim at collective liability.

A Grotian defense of war crime trials sees the institution of criminal trials as the legal institution that embodies the collective liability for wars wrongly initiated, wrongly conducted, or wrongly concluded. Contemporary debates in both philosophy and law have highlighted the importance of this Grotian insight. After providing several more layers of support for war crimes trials I will then turn to the question of whether such trials are better conducted during rather than at the end of war or armed conflict.

There are at least four goals of war crimes trials, two of which bear directly on *jus post bellum* principles. The first two goals are the traditional goals of retribution and deterrence for which all trials aim whether or not they concern war crimes. The second set of goals is nontraditional but important for securing a just and lasting peace: the goal during war of deterring soldiers from participating in atrocities or other acts of violence against civilians; and the goal, after war ends, of aiding in reconciliation by showing that even the victors will take responsibility for wrongs committed during even a just war. In this section I will say something relatively brief about each of these goals. Before doing so, let me say a bit about the problem of mixing principles of legality with the realities of war.

As indicated earlier, Grotius thought that war and law suits shared in common the idea that they should be pursued scrupulously. But war and law sit uneasily with each other when they are combined in the idea of a war crime. One of the problems is that during war many of the normal constraints that we all have during peacetime are cast off during war, most significantly the constraint against intentionally killing or harming. Yet, this statement is only partially true—soldiers can kill or wound each other, in certain circumstances, but the prohibition on killing or wounding civilians remains largely in place. Even so, it is often thought that holding soldiers responsible for killing civilians when such casualties are referred to as collateral damage by the politicians who send soldiers into battle presents conceptual and normative problems that are difficult to overcome.

The idea of committing crimes during war, when war already involves arguably the worst of crimes—intentionally killing human beings (who happen to be enemy soldiers)—strikes many people as at least odd. And given that soldiers are trained to inflict maximal damage on the enemy, to then say that the soldier has committed a crime, by doing just what the soldier was trained to do, seems unfair, especially if the soldier was following orders of a superior officer. Indeed, there is a very old tradition of saying that, where there is war, considerations of justice and law are out of place. Such an idea is still widely adhered to, especially by political leaders. Yet critics of the idea are now gaining ground, and international law is coming increasingly to embrace human rights theory instead of older notions of how to understand the relationship between war and law.

It seems to me that even on a traditional model soldiers should be held accountable for their crimes. The defense of the concept of war crimes is undergirded with the idea that soldiers should not see themselves as hired killers, but as professionals. And the best way to instill the sense of being a professional is that soldiers must conform to a code of honor. At least initially, one can understand the concept of war crimes as constituting a violation of a soldier's code of honor. This code of honor is a moral code, but over the years there has been an attempt legally to codify the moral code. With this legal codification has come a series of penalties for violating the code, including criminal sanctions for the most serious violations.[26]

There has been a difficulty in extending to soldiers the idea of committing a war crime, since most soldiers are only following superior orders. Various legal attempts have been made to try to indicate that certain orders are simply not legitimate and should not be obeyed by soldiers, lest they run afoul of the mandates of the soldier's code and bring upon themselves criminal liability. Soldiers are held liable for harms they cause in the case of orders that the soldiers should have known were illegitimate. But soldiers are not, as I indicated above, considered criminally liable for participating in unjust wars of aggression. Only those who planned or led the wars of aggression are currently held liable for the war crime of aggression. And soldiers are still not generally held liable for employing illegal tactics if they were ordered to do so, unless the orders were manifestly unjust.

With the shift to a human rights framework, where individuals are held accountable for violating the rights of others, the door has been opened to the idea of holding soldiers responsible for their actions, not just for murdering civilians but also for participating in unjust acts of aggression against states or peoples. Leaving aggression aside, the human rights framework allows for another, and perhaps stronger, basis for holding soldiers responsible for attacks on civilians. Here the idea is not just that soldiers are honor-bound to protect rather than attack civilians, but that soldiers have duties to civilians as fellow humans in just the same way that these soldiers, when out of uniform, would have duties to other people, simply because they are fellow humans.

And yet there is a serious problem that now arises—namely, why should enemy soldiers not also count as fellow humans who are deserving of protection rather than attack? In many ways the human rights rationale outruns even the most radical proposals for how to criminalize the acts of soldiers. For, at least in my view, the human rights rationale would potentially support the accusation of violations of the morality of war for what were previously viewed as normal acts of war, namely, the killing of one soldier by another soldier. If this position can be made plausible, then we would have to take seriously various forms of pacifism that have argued that normal acts of war are immoral, or at least so morally risky that soldiers should be counseled not to fight. And this would make pacifism a more serious challenger to the just war tradition than is normally recognized.[27]

But criminal liability needs more than the above-stated human rights rationale. There is the matter of intentions to deal with: soldiers do not typically attack enemy soldiers so as to take away their rights, but so as to achieve certain military objectives thought to be necessary to win what is perceived to be a just war. To be fair to soldiers who are often just trying to do their patriotic duty, only some of their acts should be prosecuted as criminal acts. As we next see, there may be some clear cases where soldiers have acted contrary to their duty and placed civilians into harm's way in attacking them as if they were enemy soldiers. When such cases occur, then both the traditional framework of honor and the contemporary framework of human rights come together to counsel that prosecutions of individual soldiers for war crimes should take place. Yet even in seemingly clear cases, problems arise nonetheless.

III. The My Lai Prosecution and More Recent Trials

There have been several high-profile domestic criminal trials for war crimes held during rather than after war, most significantly the trial of U.S. lieutenant William L. Calley, Jr., the main defendant charged in the My Lai massacre during the Vietnam war. Calley was charged on September 5, 1969, with premeditated murder for killing "not less than 102 Vietnamese civilians" in a hamlet in South Vietnam. Here is how the U.S. Court of Appeals described the facts:

> Lieutenant Calley was the 1st platoon leader of C Company, 1st Battalion, 20th Infantry, 11th Light Infantry Brigade, and had been stationed in Vietnam since December of 1967. Prior to March 16, 1968, his unit had received little combat experience. On March 15, members of the unit were briefed that they were to engage the enemy in an offensive action in the area of My Lai. The troops were informed that the area had long been controlled by the Viet Cong and that they could expect heavy resistance from a Viet Cong battalion which might outnumber them by more than two to one. The objective of the battalion was to seize the hamlet and destroy all that could be useful to the enemy.
>
> The attack began early in the morning of March 16. Calley's platoon was landed on the outskirts of My Lai after about five minutes of artillery and gunship fire. The assault met no resistance or hostile fire. After cautiously approaching My Lai, C Company discovered only unarmed, unresisting old men, women and children eating breakfast or beginning the day's chores although intelligence reports had indicated the villagers would be gone to market. Encountering only civilians and no enemy soldiers, Calley's platoon, which was to lead the sweep through the hamlet, quickly became disorganized. Some soldiers undertook the destruction of livestock, foodstuffs, and buildings as ordered. Others collected and evacuated the Vietnamese civilians and then proceeded systematically to slaughter the villagers. . . .
>
> After the killings at the southern edge of My Lai, Calley proceeded to the eastern portion of the hamlet. There along an irrigation ditch, another and larger group of villagers was being held by soldiers. . . . Calley ordered the start of firing into the people and he with Meadlo and others joined in the killing.[28]

Calley conceded that he had participated in these killings, and he was prosecuted for most of the killings.

The trial of Lieutenant Calley took place five years before the end of the Vietnam war. And while the trial was not properly a war crimes trial in the international sense, it did concern what were violations of the rules of war, as interpreted by the U.S. Uniform Code of Military Justice. Calley's defense was "that he was not legally responsible for the killings because there was an absence of malice on his part, [and] that he thought he was doing his duty in the operation, having been ordered by Captain Medina to kill everyone in the village."[29] I will just comment briefly on some aspects of this trial before going on to discuss more general issues about such trials that are conducted before the end of war.

First, the trial did have quite a significant effect on how the war was perceived by those who were serving in the military in Vietnam. The trial heightened awareness of the responsibility of soldiers to minimize civilian casualties as well as of the prohibition on targeting civilians. And especially since Calley was convicted by a court martial proceeding, there was a deterrent effect, at least judged by the reaction in the media to the trial and its outcome. No soldier wanted to be put on the cover of major news magazines back home because of alleged war crimes—indeed no one wanted to be known back home as a war criminal rather than a war hero. Even though arguably there were special circumstances in this incident, such as the lack of training by the U.S. personnel and the fact that civilians, even children, had been used as killers as well as human shields, it seems that there was a wide deterrent effect on misconduct by the U.S. military forces in Vietnam after Calley was tried and convicted.

Second, there were also strong effects on the ability of the United States to sustain troop morale as well as morale at home concerning the war effort. Many articles were written about how My Lai and other related incidents undermined support for the war and probably led to the strong decline in public support for that war. Of course this effect can be seen in two very different lights. One could say that this is a reason not to have wartime trials, since these trials make it very difficult for the war to be effectively fought to victory. Or one could say that this is a reason to have such wartime trials, since they make it hard for states effectively to wage wars contrary to the rules of war. The trial of Lieutenant Calley is often described as a watershed event for how the United States saw itself—not as a liberating force for good, but as a force for oppression and even atrocity.

While the trial court judge intimated that Calley could not get a fair trial because of the adverse publicity in the media prior to his trial, the appellate court disputed the idea that the publicity was all adverse. Indeed, the appellate court says:

> [A] survey conducted for and published by *Time* in the first week of January
> 1970 (when the publicity was at its peak) reached the conclusion that there was
> "considerable sympathy" for Lieutenant Calley among the people interviewed. "By

a margin of 55 percent to 23 percent, they believed Calley is being made a scapegoat by the Government."[30]

Of course this does not mean that soldiers were not deterred by Calley's prosecution, but only that the general public did not necessarily demonize Calley. And even if Calley was demonized, this fact would not necessarily mean that there was a deterrent effect, since most soldiers may simply see Calley as a rogue soldier, and not identify with him at all in a way that would affect their behavior.

The My Lai incident and the reaction to it are not uncommon among those cases where wartime trials have been held for violations of the rules of war. As I will indicate, there are competing advantages and disadvantages for such trials, but generally I believe that there is often much net good to be achieved by holding such trials. Even in the case where it is harder to wage war, or continue to wage war, after the disclosures of a war crimes trial, this is at least a mixed result since it is not clear that a state should want to pursue a war if the tactics it has to use are likely to be labeled war crimes. In rare cases this may not be true—namely, in cases in which a state is fending off invasion by a much stronger state. But even in this kind of exceptional case, war crimes trials would at least bring to soldiers' attention what the negative public reaction is likely to be regardless of the outcome of the war. Most important, states should look not only to the short-term consequences of wartime war crimes trials but also to the somewhat longer-term issue of what the society will be like at the end of war if that war has been conducted in a way that involves war crimes. This raises *jus post bellum* issues that I will address in subsequent sections.

In the Iraq and Afghanistan wars there have been war crimes trials conducted in the United States while those wars continue to rage. I will here set out some brief descriptions of those trials and some of the public reaction to them. In general, the public response to recent war crimes trials conducted during war is that both public and military morale has been adversely affected. As I said about the My Lai trial, this can be seen as both positive and negative. The declining morale has had an adverse impact on the support for these wars and for their continuation. And this is potentially negative if it is the case that these wars should have been fought. But it is also potentially positive in the sense that it has cast light on how even just wars (if they are) should be conducted, especially on the kind of restraints that should be placed on fighting.

The most widely watched trials were those that concerned the abuses at Abu Ghraib. In part, this was probably because of the sensational images that were leaked to the press. The trials concerned allegations of beatings, sexual assault, abuse, and torture of prisoners held in the Iraqi prison—a prison, Abu Ghraib, that had been infamous for torturing prisoners during Saddam Hussein's rule. The pictures that came to the attention of the public were often very gruesome, with dogs snapping at naked prisoners, or female soldiers performing simulated sex acts with prisoners, or hooded prisoners suspended by their arms from the ceiling.

The trials were court martial proceedings directed against lower-ranking soldiers and some officers. Staff Sergeant Ivan Frederick pleaded guilty and was given a sentence of eight years. Ten other lower-ranking soldiers were also convicted. The only officer to be convicted was Lieutenant Colonel Steven Jordan, who was convicted only of disobeying an order to keep silent about what happened at Abu Ghraib.[31] Unfortunately, the message was that commanders were not to be held responsible for the actions of their subordinates. But there was also a message sent to soldiers that they risked serious jail sentences for acting contrary to the laws of war.[32]

Another relatively recent war crimes trial conducted during war concerned the rape and killings of civilians by American soldiers at Haditha, Iraq, in 2006. Trials were conducted after a long debate in the media about how to regard such a blatant violation of human rights and the rules of war. President Obama described the acts as "cold blooded murder." Yet seven Marines had charges against them dismissed. One Marine involved in the Haditha killings still awaits trial as of the writing of this paper.

The most recent case to go to trial concerns U.S. Army soldiers forming themselves into a "secret self-described 'kill team' that repeatedly killed Afghan civilians for sport, posing for pictures with victims and taking body parts as trophies."[33] In a long interview with the *New York Times,* some of those who were involved said, "A lot of guys felt gypped . . . . All these other soldiers have these great stories about fire fights, then here we are, we're not getting anything. We had to just sit there and wait to be blown up."[34]

The more recent war crimes trials in the United States, while war was still raging, have had similar effects to that of My Lai. Popular support for the Iraq and Afghanistan wars reached their lowest levels right after these trials. One poll found that only one-third of Americans approved of these wars after President Obama described the Haditha killings as "cold blooded."[35] There has been a very healthy debate about whether to continue in these wars if it is likely that more war crimes will be committed by U.S. troops. Holding these trials during, as opposed to after, war certainly adds to the public consciousness about the pitfalls of sending teenagers into combat with images of a demonized enemy.

IV.　War Crimes Trials and *Jus Post Bellum* Principles

When war ends, the *jus post bellum* principle of reconciliation is often one of the hardest things to satisfy. Reconciliation is not merely about bringing two parties back together again, as if the relations between states or nonstate actors can be assimilated to the relations between a husband and wife who have had a spat and need to be reconciled. Reconciliation can involve merely a modus vivendi where both sides agree to leave each other alone and not act hostilely toward each other. Reconciliation sometimes also involves more than a modus vivendi, where the parties come to respect each other and can live side by side in mutual cooperation. In this latter kind of reconciliation, common respect for a rule of law is also required.[36]

The problem is that trials often involve adversarial proceedings that can intensify the ill-will that already existed among parties. There are ways to tone down the intensity of a trial on the part of the prosecutor, but it is very difficult to curtail tactics on the part of the defense.[37] Indeed, Martti Koskeniemi has suggested that there are often clashing world views that make it highly likely that war crimes defendants will try to make the fact of the trial the issue rather than their own guilt or innocence.[38] Reconciliation can be thwarted in a host of ways by the kind of postwar trial tactics displayed recently in the Milosevic and Saddam Hussein trials.

In an international (interstate) war, there are several types of reconciliation that must be effected. Most obviously, the two sides to a war, normally two states, must be able to go back to a state of peace and also a situation in which the parties are not acting unjustly. Since the previously warring parties most often maintain a common border, returning to a state of peace will mean that the peoples of the two states are able at least to maintain a modus vivendi with the peoples of the other state. Paradoxically, sometimes not prosecuting violations of the laws of war will make it easier to achieve this type of reconciliation.

In a nontraditional war, where a state faces a nonstate actor or where two nonstate actors vie with each other for control of an area, as in a civil war, there is even greater likelihood that the previously warring parties will have to achieve a modus vivendi reconciliation if any kind of peace can be obtained. Indeed, something stronger than a modus vivendi reconciliation is also normally needed in such cases, since the people will live among each other after the war is over. The parties will often have to accept respect for one another and perhaps also respect for the rule of law for lasting peace to be achieved after nontraditional armed conflict ends.

In general, there is also the reconciliation problem of how to reintegrate returning soldiers with the larger population, even if the soldiers are only returning from across the state's border, or from another part of the state. If the returning soldiers are tainted by the sorts of tactics they have employed, such a reintegration will be considerably harder than if they return as virtuous soldiers who have fought with honor.[39] Indeed, as I said, a Grotian defense of war crimes trials will help instill the idea of honorable fighting, the key to trying to make sure that soldiers do not merely regard themselves as hired killers and pillagers of the enemy forces. And this is crucial for how they regard those enemy forces and how they are regarded by their enemies after the war is over.

In a civil (intrastate) war, even more serious problems of reintegration are likely if soldiers were involved in war crimes that are unpunished. The parties to the war who often must now live alongside one another need to feel that the other side, whether victorious or vanquished, was respectful during the war even as its soldiers tried to kill the other side's soldiers. When war crimes are committed against your side, it is obviously considerably harder to convey that respect. If war crimes trials occur after war ends there will be no effect on how the war was waged. But if war crimes trials occur during war, especially early in a war, with corresponding deterrent effects, reconciliation after war's end is considerably easier.

The main positive advantage of war crimes trials during war is that wrongful tactics and practices can be stopped or deterred early enough in the current war to make a difference. And such a positive effect is quite considerable on a host of levels, both in international and civil wars. Reconciliation and the maintenance of a lasting and just peace are of central concern. In fact, the attainment of a just and lasting peace may be the only legitimate reason to have initiated war in the first place. It is important though that the resulting peace can be just, and this means that one should continue to worry about whether or not war crimes trials held during wartime will make it harder for a just defensive war or a war against an oppressor to be waged successfully.

After war has ended, mounting a war crimes trial poses serious difficulties for reconciliation. It is hard for the vanquished side not to see war crimes trials as "victor's justice." And it is harder yet for the victorious side to put their heroic soldiers on trial after war's end. Indeed, it is hard for the victorious side to think of their soldiers as anything but heroes. It is for this reason, among others, that there has been a recent trend toward holding post bellum war crimes trials in neutral states before international tribunals. The main disadvantage of these postwar trials, as I've been arguing, is that they create serious difficulties for reconciliation. In addition, postwar trials, at least of a traditional sort, greatly complicate efforts to repair as well as rebuild the rule of law and the infrastructures of a peaceful society.

War crimes trials during war can call attention to wrongful tactics that might not have been noticed in the afterglow of victory at the end of a war. And more important, the disclosure of wrongful tactics in the middle of a war will possibly make it harder for that war to be pursued to victory. This can be especially problematic during civil war, when it is a "cousins' war," to use the phrase employed during the U.S. Civil War in the nineteenth century. When "cousins" are committing war crimes against fellow "cousins," both sides may find themselves turning against the soldiers who have committed these wrongs. When war is disclosed with all of its horrors in the early stages of battle, few would think that its normal justifications hold much sway. Comparing the human slaughter of war with gains in territory or even gains in security is not easy for people back home when they see the enemy's soldiers as acting in disrespect of their own people.

The *jus post bellum* principle of reparation is also complicated by postwar trials, which often have quite different goals than those associated with repair. Reparations are very different from the kind of retribution that is the normal bailiwick of criminal trials. Reparations are backward looking, as is retribution, but they are very different in the way that the past is taken into account. Reparations are an attempt to repair a rift in the society with an eye toward better times in the future; whereas retribution looks back and seeks to make one pay for one's wrong without regard to what will then happen next.

A third post bellum principle, rebuilding the capacity to protect a state's population, requires a kind of consensus that is made harder to achieve by the presence of postwar trials that bring up more and more of the worst of the horrors of war. Of course, such events should not be swept under the carpet. The question is when is the best time to bring them to the public forum that trials normally represent. When these horrors are disclosed early enough for the tactics of a war to be changed, there is at least the possibility that something good can come from the disclosure of these horrors. After war ends, the disclosure can still achieve some good, but it is often at odds with the need for a society to move on.

Let us turn now to the case for war crimes trials *after* instead of during war. The major advantages of holding war crimes trials after war ends is that troop morale and hence also the ability to pursue victory are not affected; and in addition it is easier to secure the relevant evidence for a successful prosecution. In addition, there are some advantages for reconciliation as well—namely, that those who are vanquished will feel that they are able to achieve justice and closure in those cases where the acts of the victorious army wronged the vanquished, or vice versa. But once we get to the point where aggression trials are held, I believe that they are much better held at the beginning or during war rather than after the war ends. At least in part this is for the reason that troops then will be better able to decide whether or not to join or extricate themselves from an aggressive war.

The issue of morale, as I have indicated, can become a disadvantage as much as an advantage in some cases of postwar trials. But on the assumption that the war is just and its pursuit crucial for fending off aggression or stopping human rights atrocities, there are good reasons to support the war's success. And if holding war crimes trials during war hampers pursuit of victory in a just war, then on morale grounds perhaps the war crimes trials should not be conducted during but only after a war has ended. Morale is crucial to victory in most wars, both that of the soldiers and also of the populace. It is often thought that wars will be won when soldiers and civilians give their all for the war effort. Yet when the war becomes tainted by charges of abuse and atrocity committed by one's own soldiers, this morale is much harder to maintain.

Holding war crimes trials after war ends means that retribution will be the primary goal of such trials, or if deterrence enters in at all it will be long-term deterrence of acts of the sort that the trial concerns. It is for this reason that such trials are difficult to justify, since retribution is only one of the *jus post bellum* principles that need to be satisfied. And one of the problems is that since retribution is backward looking and most of the other *jus post bellum* principles are forward looking, pursuit of a just and lasting peace tends to favor the forward looking principles. And if instead emphasis is placed on retribution, it is hard for this not to look like simple revenge when it is allowed to trump other postwar principles that more surely lead to peace.

At least as important is that trials will be practically difficult to pursue during wartime. It is much easier to get needed evidence and witnesses when one does not have to worry about the dangers of traversing a battlefield to exhume bodies and obtain forensic evidence. It is also considerably easier to secure testimony after war ends than it is during wartime when such testimony is likely to be perceived as restricted because of its possibility of hurting the war effort. Indeed, if the evidence is currently available in the territory of the enemy, or where passage to the site of the evidence must proceed through enemy territory, it can be dangerous and often impossible to secure that evidence for trials conducted while the war is raging. The current attempts to get witnesses in the case of the president of the Sudan, Al Bashir, now at the International Criminal Court, have been almost as difficult as getting Bashir himself into the international courtroom. These practical problems mirror the conceptual and normative problems I have already addressed.

A final *jus post bellum* consideration is about a different sort of rebuilding, that which concerns the rule of law. It is not surprising that holding war crimes trials can often aid in the reintroduction of the rule of law in war-torn societies. This is best accomplished by trials that are held after war has ended, but it can sometimes be accomplished during a war as well. It may be surprising, though, that sometimes the rule of law is not best promoted by having high-profile, emotionally laden trials while a society is trying to heal from a devastating war. In such cases, the goal of establishing a lasting rule of law in a given society may require that war crimes trials be dispensed with.

Overall though, I continue to support post bellum war crimes trials. Both post bellum trials and those conducted during wartime have positive and negative consequences. In this paper I have expressed a weak preference for war crimes trials conducted during war, which is perhaps fueled by my distrust of the justifiability of most wars. And I have suggested reasons strongly to favor trials for aggression during wartime rather than waiting until a war is over. Holding war crimes trials is difficult in the best of circumstances. But war is just the kind of thing that should be restrained by the law.

V. Objections

I will finally consider a set of objections to what I have set out above. First, consider an objection based on the case concerning the indictment and arrest of President Al Bashir for genocide in the Darfur region of the Sudan. For there to be a trial held during the war in the Sudan, a war that seems to have no end in sight after many years of raging warfare, is not only difficult to stage but also of questionable consequences for the people who are the victims of the ongoing genocide. Tyrants who can temporarily evade international sanctions are also likely to be able to inflict very serious recriminations on the part of the population that has called for indictment or arrest.

While it is true that tyrants can exact serious penalties on their population, it is also true that letting tyrants get away with impunity is a serious problem, and one not just limited to the country in question. Serving notice on tyrants that their deeds will be overseen by the international community also acts as a deterrent to other tyrants and strong leaders across the world that their gross violations of human rights will be subject to similar oversight. So, in doing the calculation of what are the costs and benefits of indicting and arresting state leaders for gross violations of human rights, even while war rages, the deterrence value of such actions needs to be factored in along with the help for victims of tyrannical abuse worldwide. In my view, the right judgment was made in the case of Al Bashir.

A second objection is that the My Lai example betrays a potentially very costly consequence of holding trials in the midst of an ongoing war—namely, that the war will be very hard to pursue to victory, even if there is a just cause for fighting it. If Grotius is right to think that soldiers, and their leaders, would not fight wars whose tactics they believe to be unjust, and if it is hard to tell in the midst of a war whether tactics are indeed unjust, then war crimes trials will deter people from continuing those wars despite the fact that these might be just wars—that is, wars fought for just causes. Despite what I have argued above, it is often not for the best to stop a just war merely because it is being fought unjustly.

This is surely one of the most difficult issues raised by this paper. If we separate *jus ad bellum* from *jus in bello*, then we can see that wars can still satisfy the former even as they fail in some respects to satisfy the latter. But it is my view that these considerations are not separable in this way. When a war is fought in such a way that serious human rights violations have occurred, this will sometimes affect the justness of the war, both overall and even concerning the just cause aspect of the war. And in any event, soldiers as well as their leaders should be given the choice about whether to continue a war that is currently understood to be unjustly waged.

A third objection is that I have allowed considerations of reconciliation and other *jus post bellum* principles such as reparations to trump, or at least limit, retribution as important principles in *jus post bellum*. The victims of war or armed conflict often find it difficult to reach closure without a trial that prosecutes those who killed or harmed their relatives. While it is good to aim for reconciliation, so that a society can move on, it is a mistake to do so at the expense of victims and at the further cost of allowing perpetrators to think that they can act with impunity.

My response is to acknowledge that a delicate balance is called for in order to produce a peace that is also just in the sense that it does not run roughshod over the rights of victims and their families. In some of my other writings on these topics I have suggested that when victims are denied retribution so as to allow for a greater likelihood of peace they should nonetheless be given reparations, even if paying the bill must be had by enlisting those who did not cause the harms that are in need of being repaired.[40]

Finally, one could object that I have still not offered much help to those who are accused of victor's justice when trials are held against only one side either during or right after war ends. And because war crimes trials, either focused on *jus ad bellum* or *jus in bello* violations, are so likely to be simply skewed by victor's justice, it is a mistake to defend them at all. Indeed, recent history has shown that the tendency of war crimes trials for *jus in bello* violations to be show trials is getting higher. And there is no good reason to think that things will get better when *jus ad bellum* trials begin. Indeed, the determination that a state has engaged in aggressive war is so fraught with political considerations that it is very unlikely that anything like an objective judgment can be reached that does not favor the victor.

It is indeed incumbent on anyone who defends war crimes trials to take account of this serious objection. It is my view that war crimes trials can be conceived in such a way that they do not fall prey to the victor's justice objection. But I would be one of the first to admit that many war crimes trials, including the famous Nuremberg trial, have indeed looked more like victor's justice than proper trials. What is needed is for international oversight not to favor one side or the other, even when it appears that one side is clearly the aggressor. For even when a war is just, crimes concerning tactics can still be discovered and should be prosecuted, just as is true of war crimes committed by those who initiate aggressive war. War crimes trials conducted during or after war's end are defensible when they are supervised in such a way that impartial inquiry is made into the activities of both sides.

In this paper I have defended the use of trials for war crimes understood broadly to include violations of the rules of war, genocide, crimes against humanity, and the crime of aggression. I have indicated that trials conducted during war or mass atrocity have certain advantages over trials conducted when the conflict is over, including that it is hard to tell when mass conflicts have indeed finally ended. But I have also given reasons to think that trials conducted after the end of conflict are quite defensible. In terms of satisfying the jus post bellum normative principle of retribution, trials offer one of the best strategies, even if we must restrict such trials in light of other jus post bellum principles, such as reconciliation, reparations, and rebuilding.[41]

Notes

1. Hugo Grotius, *De Jure Belli ac Pacis* (On the Law of War and Peace) (1625), translated by Francis W. Kelsey (Oxford: Clarendon Press, 1925), 18.

2. See Aeschylus' play *Eumenides*, ed. and trans. Alan H. Sommerstein (Cambridge, MA: Harvard's Loeb Classical Library, 2008).

3. Grotius, *De Jure Belli ac Pacis*, 15.

4. Ibid., 20.

5. Ibid.

6. Ibid., 18.

7. Ibid., 16.

8. Ibid.

9. Ibid., 14.

10. Ibid., 23.

11. Ibid., 25.

12. Ibid., 52.

13. Ibid., 75.

14. Ibid., 53.

15. Ibid., 54.

16. Ibid., 58.

17. Ibid., 69.

18. Ibid., 97.

19. Ibid., 138.

20. Ibid., 600.

21. Ibid., 601.

22. Ibid., 716.

23. Ibid., 718–19.

24. Ibid., 733.

25. Ibid., 730.

26. See my book *War Crimes and Just War* (New York: Cambridge University Press, 2007).

27. See Larry May, "Contingent Pacifism and the Moral Risks of Participating in War," *Public Affairs Quarterly* 25, no. 2 (April 2011): 95–111.

28. *Calley v. Callaway,* 519 F.2d 184, 191–92 (1975).

29. Ibid., 193.

30. Ibid., 206.

31. See "Editorial: Abu Ghraib Swept under the Carpet," *New York Times,* August 30, 2007.

32. An interesting contrasting example is that most of the detainees held at Guantanamo Bay have not yet had any trial concerning their cases. It could be that the lack of such trials has contributed to the lack of public attention to the plight of these detainees in both Republican and Democratic presidential administrations. See the discussion of Guantanamo in Larry May, *Global Justice and Due Process* (Cambridge: Cambridge University Press, 2011).

33. Charlie Savage, "Case of Accused Soldiers May Be Worst of 2 Wars," *New York Times,* October 3, 2010, A1.

34. Luke Mogelson, "The Beast in the Heart," *New York Times Magazine*, May 1, 2011, 34–62, 37.

35. Rasmussen poll conducted in early April of 2011.

36. See the final chapter of Larry May, *Crimes against Humanity: A Normative Account* (New York: Cambridge University Press, 2005).

37. See the final chapter of Larry May, *Genocide: A Normative Account* (New York: Cambridge University Press, 2010).

38. Martti Koskeniemi, "Between Impunity and Show Trials," *Max Planck Yearbook of United Nations Law* 6 (2002): 1–35.

39. See Larry May, "Metaphysical Guilt and Moral Taint," in *Collective Responsibility,* ed. Larry May and Stacey Hoffman (Lanham, MD: Rowman and Littlefield, 1991).

40. See my paper "Reparations, Restitution, and Transitional Justice," presented at colloquia at Vanderbilt, Australian National, and Stanford universities, as well as at a conference at Sapporo, Japan.

41. For more on how the normative principles of *jus post bellum* relate to each other, see the first chapter of Larry May, *After War Ends: Normative Principles* (Cambridge: Cambridge University Press, 2012).

Index

Index

Abu Ghraib prison, 154, 210

Additional Protocol 1 (AP1), 30–31, 32, 34, 51, 56, 57

Additional Protocol 2, 51

Afghanistan War: civilians targeted by Taliban, 25, 43n4; compensation to civilians, 70; criminal acts of U.S. personnel, 47n52; war crimes trials during, 209, 210–11

Aggression: ambiguity, 178; crime of, 11, 62–63, 178, 181, 203, 205, 218; individual responsibility and, 62, 202; war crimes during wars of, 175, 200, 201

Air strikes: civilian casualties, 35–36; by drones, 1–3, 157; in Vietnam War, 165–66, 174, 175, 179–80, 190n52; in World War II, 179

Al-Awlaki, Anwar, 1–3

Al-Bashir, Omar, 215, 216

Alito, Samuel, 120

Allegiance school, 64, 65

Al Qaeda, 46n43, 72, 77, 85, 126–27n16

American Bar Association, 169

American Friends Service Committee, 176

American Revolution, 95–96

American Society of International Law, 172

Amnesty International, 39

Ancient Greece: rules of war, 7; war crimes trials, 198

Anthony, Henry B., 102

Anthrax, 84, 85, 126–27n16

Anticontagionists, 101

AP1, *see* Additional Protocol 1

Apocalypse Now, 166

Asymmetric tactics, 25

Atrocities: in colonial wars, 161; in Iraq War, 18, 40, 41, 157, 158, 182, 210–11; in Vietnam War, 159, 162–67, 168, 174–76. *See also* War crimes

AUMF, *see* Authorization for Use of Military Force

Aum Shinrikyo, 84

Australia, mousepox, 127n20

Authorization for Use of Military Force (AUMF), 2

Avian influenza, 85–86

Baez, Joan, 179, 195n99

Bales, Robert, 47n52

Bashir, Omar al-, *see* Al-Bashir, Omar

Baxter, Richard, 172, 191n63, 195–96n106

Belligerent reprisals, 52, 56

Benedict, Michael Les, 102

Bin Laden, Osama, 122

Biodefense: military role, 88–89, 90, 91; spending on, 121; state and federal roles, 90–91. *See also* Quarantine

Biological weapons: association with pandemic disease, 86–87, 89, 109; Cooperative Threat Reduction Program, 84; diseases in American Revolution, 95–96, 137n117; military research, 90; national security lens, 122; policy focus on, 121–22; preparedness efforts, 87; state use, 84; threat of, 84–85, 89, 122, 126–27n16; use

by nonstate actors, 84; U.S. laws and
policies, 84, 86–91

Bombing, *see* Air strikes

Boston Five, 177

Brierly, J. L., 9, 10

Brinkley, Alan, 158

British Empire, 164. *See also* Colonial
America

Bush (George W.) administration:
legal authorization of torture, 158;
unilateralism, 182. *See also* Afghanistan
War; Iraq War; War on terrorism

Bush, George W., 85, 107, 158, 159

CALCAV, *see* Clergy and Laymen
Concerned about Vietnam

Calley, William L., Jr., 40–41, 154, 206–9

Calley v. Calloway, 199, 206–9

Cambodia, U.S. bombing, 165–66, 175

Carter, Herbert, 164–65

Centers for Disease Control and
Prevention (CDC), 87, 88, 107, 108,
109

Central Intelligence Agency (CIA):
hunt for bin Laden in Pakistan,
122; Phoenix program, 163–64, 179;
targeted killings, 1

Chandler, Zachariah, 102

Chechnya, 70

Chemical weapons, 165. *See also* Weapons
of mass destruction

China: pandemic disease outbreaks,
85, 86; view of International
Humanitarian Law, 26

CIA, *see* Central Intelligence Agency

Citizens Commission of Inquiry into U.S.
War Crimes in Vietnam, 176

Civilian casualties: deliberate, 210;
Haditha killings (2005), Iraq, 18, 40,
41, 210–11; increase in, 60; of Taliban,
25, 43n4; in Vietnam, 164, 166, 178. *See
also* My Lai massacre

Civilian objects: classified as military
objectives, 33, 45–46n31; definition, 32,

34; dual use, 33, 45n30; war-sustaining
contributions, 34–35, 46n35

Civilian protection: customary practices,
27; efforts to promote, 23, 29, 30–31,
37–38, 43, 63; of enemy civilians,
48–49, 51–52, 54, 55, 63–64, 66–67;
enforcement, 24; harm limitation, 29,
35, 37, 38; human rights justification,
206; ignored by insurgents, 25; loss
of status, 44n12; measures by U.S.
military, 24; norms, 24, 29, 31, 37–38,
43, 179, 180, 204; precautions, 35–36, 53;
qualified, 28; risks taken by military,
59, 63–66; treaties on, 55. *See also*
Geneva Conventions; International
Humanitarian Law

Civilians, winning hearts and minds, 59,
76

Civil War, U.S., 9, 100, 101–2, 113, 213

Civil wars: International Humanitarian
Law and, 53; war crimes, 212, 213. *See
also* Insurgents

Clergy and Laymen Concerned about
Vietnam (CALCAV), 167, 174–75

Cold War, 3, 37, 161–62, 171–72

Collateral damage, 28, 63, 204. *See also*
Civilian casualties

Collective identities, 67, 78

Collectivism in International
Humanitarian Law: history, 50–52;
internal conflicts and, 53; issues,
74–75; meaning, 49; obligations, 53–54;
reparations, 54, 70–71; shift from,
48–49, 54–59, 75

Colonial America, quarantine laws, 91–95

Colonial warfare, 161, 164

Combatants: combat-related crimes,
47n52, 194n94; distinction from
noncombatants, 27, 29, 32, 164;
individual accountability for war
crimes, 67–69, 175, 176, 201, 205–6; as
individuals, 62; unlawful, 1. *See also*
Military

Commerce Clause, 91, 99, 101, 109, 116–19

Communalism, *see* Collectivism

Compagnie Francaise de Navigation a Vapeur v. Louisiana State Bd. of Health, 117–18

Compensation: for civilians, 70; for crime victims, 82n40, 83n44. *See also* Reparations

Confederate Army, 100, 101–2

Congress, *see* U.S. Congress

Connecticut,, quarantine laws, 97–98

Conscription, 62, 66, 79, 167, 170

Conservatives: criticism of Bush, 159; on law of war, 159–60, 182, 183; on war on terrorism, 159

Contagionists, 101

Cooley, Thomas, 117

Cooperative Threat Reduction Program, 84

Cordon sanitaire, 95, 102, 118, 123. *See also* Quarantine

Cornwallis, Lord, 95

Cosmopolitan individualism: implications, 74–79; issues, 74–75; meaning, 49–50; obstacles, 60–61; risk allocation and, 63–66; shift to, 48–49, 54–59, 75

Counterinsurgency: applicability of international law, 162; in Malaya, 164; in Philippines, 161, 162; rules of engagement, 164; U.S. doctrine, 38, 55, 59, 66; in Vietnam, 162, 164, 165, 179

Courts, *see* War crimes trials; *and specific courts*

Crime: combat-related, 47n52, 194n94; compensation for victims, 82n40, 83n44. *See also* War crimes

Crimes against peace, 10

Criminal law: application to suspected terrorists, 71, 72, 73, 74; punishment of individuals, 6, 72. *See also* International criminal law

Crown, Joseph, 168, 169, 170, 171, 173

Cumming, Hugh, 106

Cyber warfare, 26, 27

Darfur, *see* Sudan

DASR, *see* Draft Articles on State Responsibility

Defense Against Weapons of Mass Destruction Act, 84

Democracies, *see* Liberal democracies

Department of Defense, U. S., 59, 84, 109, 165

Department of Health and Human Services (HHS), 88, 107, 109

Department of Homeland Security (DHS), 86–87, 109, 115

Detention: of sexually dangerous prisoners, 119–21; of suspected terrorists, 71–74, 78, 154–55, 219n32. *See also* Prisoners of war

DHS, *see* Department of Homeland Security

Diplomatic protection, 52, 54, 56

Disease, *see* Pandemic disease

Dodd, Christopher, 89

Dolzer, Rudolf, 31–32

Domenici, Pete, 84

Dow Chemical, 165

Draft, *see* Conscription

Draft Articles on State Responsibility (DASR), 56

Drones, 1–3, 157

Dual use objects, 33, 45n30

Duffy, James, 179

Emancipation Proclamation, 113

Emergencies: federal responses, 108, 111, 115, 150n244; natural disasters, 88–89, 108, 111, 131–32n57. *See also* Biodefense; Pandemic disease

England: disease as weapon, 95–96, 137n117; Privy Council, 92–93; public health, 123; trade, 92–93. *See also* British Empire

Epidemics, *see* Pandemic disease

Equal application principle, 61–62

European Court of Human Rights, 70

Executive power, *see* Presidents

Failed states, 79

Falk, Richard, 155, 168, 169, 171–72, 173–75, 176, 177–78, 180

FBI (Federal Bureau of Investigation), 85

Federal Emergency Management Agency (FEMA), 108, 131–32n57, 150n244

Federalism, 90, 102, 109, 116, 118, 120

FEMA, *see* Federal Emergency Management Agency

Fenn, Elizabeth Anne, 95

Fifth Amendment, 1, 2, 110

Flu, *see* Influenza

Forman, James, Jr., 77

Frederick, Ivan, 210

Fried, John H. E., 169–70

Fulbright, J. William, 168–69

Geneva Conventions: of 1949, 9, 30, 44n12, 51, 52, 57, 161; of 1970, 9; Additional Protocol 1, 30–31, 32, 34, 51, 56, 57; Additional Protocol 2, 51; Common Article 3, 51, 162, 169; protected persons, 44n12, 52; U.S. accession, 161–62; U.S. violations, 158, 163

Genocide: in Darfur, 216; in Rwanda, 60. *See also* Nuremberg trials

Germany: national guilt, 68; Nazi regime, 5, 6; reparations, 54, 68. *See also* Nuremberg trials

Gibbons v. Ogden, 99, 117

Goldsmith, Jack, 158, 159–60, 163, 184n7

Gonzales v. Reich, 119

Greece, ancient: rules of war, 7; war crimes trials, 198

Grier, Robert, 113, 116

Grotius, Hugo: *De Jure Belli ac Pacis* (*On the Law of War and Peace*), 8–9, 200–203; on international law, 7–9; on just war theory, 9, 199–203; on law of war, 9, 11, 12, 19, 55, 198, 199–203; on war and law suits, 204; on war crimes, 8–9, 201–3

Guantanamo Bay prison, 71, 154–55, 219n32

Guerrillas, *see* Insurgents

Gulf War (1991), 54

Haditha killings (2005), Iraq, 18, 40, 41, 210–11

Haeberle, Ron, 154

Hagenbach, Peter von, 7

Hague Conventions (1899 and 1907), 9, 10, 30, 161, 165

Hamas, 73

Hamdi v. Rumsfeld, 1

Harris, Larry Wayne, 84

Health, *see* Pandemic disease; Public health

Health and Human Services, Department of, *see* Department of Health and Human Services

Herbert, Anthony, 163

Herodotus, 7

Hersh, Seymour M., 154, 155

HHS, *see* Department of Health and Human Services

Hitler, Adolf, 5

Hobbes, Thomas, *Leviathan*, 4–5, 19

Homeland Security Act of 2002, 86, 88

Homeland Security Department, *see* Department of Homeland Security

Hong Kong, pandemic disease outbreaks, 85

HRW, *see* Human Rights Watch

Humanitarian interventions, 77

Humanitarian law, *see* International Humanitarian Law

Humanity principle, 23, 28, 30, 31–32

Human rights: European Court of Human Rights, 70; individual responsibility, 205–6; law of war and, 181–82; norms, 56–57. *See also* International Humanitarian Law; International human rights law

Human rights movement, 181–82

Human Rights Watch (HRW), 33, 39, 43n2

Hurricane Katrina, 88, 89, 131–32n57

Hussein, Saddam, 25, 210, 211

ICC, *see* International Criminal Court

ICJ, *see* International Court of Justice

ICL, *see* International criminal law

ICRC, *see* International Committee of the Red Cross

ICTR, *see* International Criminal Tribunal for Rwanda

ICTY, *see* International Criminal Tribunal for the Former Yugoslavia

IHL, *see* International Humanitarian Law

IHRL, *see* International human rights law

IMT, *see* International Military Tribunal

Individual responsibility principle, 10, 67–69, 176, 201, 205–6

Individuals: accountability for war crimes, 10, 67–69, 175, 176, 201, 205–6; combatants as, 62; focus on, 48; relations with own government, 51–53; rights, 49–50, 55, 56–57, 79; tensions with states, 49, 59–61. *See also* Cosmopolitan individualism

Influenza, 85–86, 88, 107, 123, 128n27. *See also* Pandemic disease

Insurgents: as enemies, 53; international law and, 25; in Philippines, 161, 162; use of violence, 30; Vietnamese, 163–64, 174, 207; wars with, 26. *See also* Civil wars; Counterinsurgency; Nonstate actors

Insurrection Act, 114–15

International Committee of the Red Cross (ICRC), 33, 34, 43n2, 52, 59, 162

International Court of Justice (ICJ), 46n47, 53, 170

International Criminal Court (ICC): cases, 62–63, 215; establishment, 11, 58; goals, 39; indictments, 39; Rome Statute, 63; significance, 39, 42; U.S. view, 31, 36

International criminal law (ICL): cosmopolitan individualism, 67–68; evolution, 67; universality, 57–58. *See also* War crimes

International Criminal Tribunal for Rwanda (ICTR), 11, 57–58, 67

International Criminal Tribunal for the Former Yugoslavia (ICTY), 11, 36, 53, 57–58, 67, 211

International Humanitarian Law (IHL): balance and flexibility, 28, 38–39; challenges, 24, 25–27, 42–43; collectivism, 48–49, 50–52, 53–59, 70–71, 74–75; compliance with, 25–27, 36–37, 42, 56; distinction principle, 27, 29, 32; effects, 41–42; enforcement, 26–27, 38–41, 42; harm limitations, 53–54; humanity principle, 23, 28, 30, 31–32; humanization, 48–49, 60–61; international human rights law and, 53, 56–57; loss of relevance, 23; national policies, 23; necessity principle, 23, 28, 29, 41, 65; new technologies and, 26, 27; noncombatant immunity principle, 37; obligations, 53–54, 56, 57, 76; origins and development, 27–28; principles, 23, 27, 28, 29; progressive view, 23, 24, 27–33, 35–36, 39–40, 41–42; proportionality principle, 30–31; prosecutions of U.S. military, 24; specific provisions, 32–36; traditionalist view, 23, 24, 29–31, 32, 35–36; universal jurisdiction, 67. *See also* Civilian protection

International humanitarian law community, 43n2

International human rights law (IHRL), 52–53, 56–57

International law: American views, 29–30; Grotius on, 7–9; Hobbesian view, 5; tension between states and individuals, 49, 59–61. *See also* Law of war

International Law Commission, Draft Articles on State Responsibility, 56

International Military Tribunal (IMT), 9–11, 17–18. *See also* Nuremberg trials

International relations: idealist school, 3, 181; realist school, 3

Interrogation techniques, 163. *See also* Torture

Iraq: military, 25; reparations to Kuwait, 54

Iraqi Freedom, Operation, 33

Iraq War: Abu Ghraib abuses, 154, 210; atrocities, 157, 158, 182; compensation to civilians, 70; Haditha killings (2005), 18, 40, 41, 210–11; opposition, 156, 157; Vietnam War compared to, 156–57; war crimes trials during, 209–11

Islam, radical, 78

Isolation, 89–90, 97, 130n42. *See also* Quarantine

Israel: compensation to civilians, 70; detention policy, 73–74; military conflicts, 66–67, 76; Supreme Court, 73

Jackson, Robert, 10, 111

Jacobson v. Massachusetts, 105–6, 117

Jaffee, Jameel, 1–2

Japan, Aum Shinrikyo attack, 84

Jaspers, Karl, 68

Johnson, Lyndon B., 175, 180

Johnson administration, 169, 173. *See also* Vietnam War

Jordan, Steven, 210

Jus ad bellum: distinction from *jus in bello*, 9, 55, 61–63, 177; Grotius on, 9, 12; Vietnam War and, 156, 170; violations, 10; war crimes trials, 10–11, 178, 181, 203, 218. *See also* Aggression; Just war theory

Jus in bello: distinction from *jus ad bellum*, 9, 55, 61–63, 177; goals, 12; proportionality principle, 63–67, 180; violations, 10. *See also* War crimes

Jus post bellum: rebuilding rule of law, 215; rebuilding security, 214; reconciliation, 204, 211–13, 214, 217; reparations, 54, 68, 69–71, 202, 213–14; retribution, 204, 213–14, 215, 217, 218; war crimes trials, 198–99, 211–12, 213–16, 218

Just war theory: development, 50–51; Grotius on, 9, 199–203; Nuremberg trials and, 10–11; war crimes trials and, 199–203, 216–17, 218. *See also Jus ad bellum*

Kant, Immanuel, 55

Katzenbach, Nicholas, 169, 173

Kellogg-Briand Pact, 9

Kelsen, Hans, 5–6, 7, 10

Kennedy, Anthony, 119–20

Kennedy, David, 13

Keys, Barbara, 181

Kim Phúc, 165

Kissinger, Henry, 175, 179

Koh, Harold, 2–3

Kolko, Gabriel, 176

Korean War, 161

Koskeniemi, Martti, 211

Kosovo War, 34, 35–36, 112

Kuwait, Iraqi reparations, 54

Lang, Daniel, 164, 194n94

Laos, U.S. bombing, 165–66, 175

Law: criminal, 6, 72, 73, 74; Hobbes on, 4–5, 6, 19; natural, 4; relationship to war, 3–12, 19

Law of armed conflict (LOAC), *see* International Humanitarian Law

Law of nations, 200

Law of nature, 4, 8, 200

Law of war: conservative views, 159–60, 182, 183; development, 7, 9–12, 50–51, 161; Grotius on, 9, 12, 19, 55, 198, 199–203; liberal views, 182, 183; in United States, 3–4, 11. *See also Jus ad bellum*; *Jus in bello*

Lawyers Committee Concerning American Policy in Vietnam, 168–71, 172, 173, 190n52, 191n63

Leahy, Patrick, 89

Leftists, *see* Liberals

Legalism, 159–60, 168, 182

Leviathan (Hobbes), 4–5, 19

Liberal democracies: humanitarian aid, 59; norms, 55; popular sovereignty, 68–69; wars, 75, 76–77, 79

Liberals: criticism of Bush, 158; criticism of U.S. conduct in Vietnam War, 166–68, 177–78; on law of war, 182, 183; on war on terrorism, 158

Liberation Tigers of Tamil Eelam (LTTE), 26

Libya, NATO operations, 71, 75–76, 77, 112, 182

Lieber Code, 9, 51

Life magazine, 154, 163

Lifton, Robert Jay, 176

Lincoln, Abraham, 113

LOAC (law of armed conflict), *see* International Humanitarian Law

LTTE, *see* Liberation Tigers of Tamil Eelam

Lugar, Richard, 84

M23, 25

Malaya, 164

Marine Hospital Service, 99, 100, 103

Marshall, John, 99, 116

Maryland, quarantine laws, 96

Massachusetts: inoculating hospitals, 95–96; quarantine laws, 97

Massachusetts Bay colony, quarantine laws, 91, 92–93

Mayer, Jane, 158–59

McDougal, Myres, 169, 171–72

McWilliams, Carey, 168

Media, images of warfare, 60

Meeker, Leonard C., 169, 170

Mendlovitz, Saul, 171

Mercenaries, 58, 79

Meron, Theodore, 48

Michelman, Frank I., 29

Military: codes of honor, 205–6; conscription, 62, 66, 79, 167, 170; morale, 198, 208, 214–15; private contractors, 58, 79; reintegration of veterans, 212. *See also* Civilian protection; Combatants

Military, U.S.: Army Field Manual (1956), 66; biodefense role, 88–89, 90, 91; civilian protection measures, 24; counterinsurgency doctrine, 38, 59, 66; Counterinsurgency Manual, 55; culture, 165; domestic deployments, 114–16; draft, 66, 167, 170; International Humanitarian Law prosecutions, 24; Joint Publication 3-60, 34; justice system, 40; law enforcement role, 115; Military Manual (1956), 55; *Operational Law Handbook*, 33, 35; Posse Comitatus Act, 115–16; rules of engagement, 11, 37, 42, 47n54, 164, 179; training on law of war, 164–65; Uniform Code of Military Justice, 11, 36, 40, 207; Union Army, 9. *See also* Afghanistan War; Iraq War; Vietnam War

Military objectives, 32–35

Milosevic, Slobodan, 25, 34, 211

Minnesota Rate Cases, 106

Monterey Institute for International Studies, 85

Moore, John Norton, 172

Morgan's Steamship v. Louisiana Board of Health, 104, 105, 117–18

Morrill, Lot M., 102

Morse, Wayne, 168, 169, 170

Moyn, Samuel, 56

My Lai massacre: Calley trial, 40–41, 199, 206–9; description, 207; effects, 155, 168, 175–76; inquest, 180; investigations, 164–65; legal analysis, 171; photographs, 154; public reactions, 175–76

Myrdal, Gunnar, 171

Napalm, 165

Napoleon Bonaparte, 161

The Nation, 175

Nationalism, 49, 61, 65, 66

National Liberation Front (NLF; Viet Cong), 163–64, 174, 207

National security: biological weapons and, 122; pandemic disease and, 86–87, 90, 109, 110–12, 122; public health and, 87

NATO (North Atlantic Treaty Organization): Balkans operations, 34, 35–36, 70, 112; Libyan operations, 71, 75–76, 77, 112, 182

Natural disasters: federal assistance, 108; military role in response, 88–89, 111, 131–32n57

Natural law, 4

Nazi Germany, 5, 6, 68. *See also* Germany; Nuremberg trials

Necessary and Proper Clause, 91, 119–21

Necessity principle, 23, 28, 29, 41, 65

Neutral states, 51, 52, 213

New Yorker, 154, 158, 178–79

New York Times, 3, 89, 154, 165–66, 210

New York Times Book Review, 158, 176, 177–78

Nixon, Richard M., 179

Nixon administration, 170–71, 175–76. *See also* Vietnam War

NLF, *see* National Liberation Front

NMT, *see* Nuremberg Military Tribunal

Noncombatant immunity principle, 37

Noncombatants: definition, 44n12; distinguishing, 27, 29, 32, 164; in Vietnam, 164. *See also* Civilian protection

Nonstate actors: biological weapons use, 84; noncompliance with International Humanitarian Law, 25, 30, 42, 58; potential use of weapons of mass destruction, 27, 85; use of violence, 77–78; weapons available to, 58, 85. *See also* Insurgents; Terrorist groups

Norms: civilian protection, 24, 29, 31, 37–38, 43, 179, 180, 204; human rights, 56–57; of liberal democracies, 55; universal moral, 200

North Atlantic Treaty Organization, *see* NATO

North Vietnam: U.S. bombing, 165–66, 174, 175, 179–80, 190n52; visits by antiwar activists, 171, 173, 179, 195n99. *See also* Vietnam War

Nuclear weapons, *see* Weapons of mass destruction

Nunn, Samuel, 84

Nuremberg and Vietnam: An American Tragedy (Taylor), 177, 178–79, 180, 181, 194n91

Nuremberg Military Tribunal (NMT), 17, 177, 178, 179

Nuremberg trials: International Military Tribunal, 9–11, 17–18; precedent set, 175, 178, 181

Obama, Barack, 210, 211

Obama administration: *National Security Strategy*, 110; targeted killings, 1–3, 78, 79, 157; war on terror, 184n7. *See also* Afghanistan War

O'Connell, Mary Ellen, 1

Operational Law Handbook, 33, 35

Operation Iraqi Freedom, 33

Orestes, 198

Pacifism, 57, 60, 167, 206

Pakistan, CIA operations, 122

Palestinians, 66, 70, 73

Pandemic disease: causes of outbreaks, 113; mortality, 85–86; national security lens, 86–87, 90, 109, 110–12, 122; outbreaks, 85–86; preparedness efforts, 87; as weapon in wartime, 95–96, 100, 101–2, 137n117. *See also* Quarantine

Parity principle, 61–62

Paul, Ron, 1, 2

Peace: crimes against, 10; just and lasting, 213, 215, 217. *See also* Reconciliation

Philippines, 161, 162

Phoenix program, 163–64, 179

Plague, 84, 113. *See also* Pandemic disease

Police powers: public health laws and, 116–18; in U.S. Constitution, 91; of U.S. states, 98, 99, 102, 105–6, 110, 116–18

Policing: compared to warfare, 64–65; domestic, 77–78; positive assistance, 76; risking lives to protect citizens, 64; war as, 49, 75–77

Popular sovereignty, 68–69

Posse Comitatus Act, 115–16

POWs, *see* Prisoners of war

Precautions, for civilian protection, 35–36, 53

Presidents: legal constraints, 159–60, 183–84; war powers, 110–14. *See also individual presidents*

Prisoners of war (POWs): detention, 72; Geneva Conventions on, 161; obligations toward, 53; in Vietnam War, 162–63, 179

Prize Cases, 113

Progressive community: members, 43n2; view of International Humanitarian Law, 23, 24, 27–33, 35–36, 39–40, 41–42

Proportionality principle, 30–31, 63–67, 180

Prosecutions, *see* War crimes trials

Public health: adversarial framing, 122; federal role, 98–99, 100–105, 106–9, 120; national security lens, 87; in Pakistan, 122; policy issues, 121–24; reforms, 101; state laws, 97, 98–100, 101, 102, 103–4, 105–6, 116; surveillance system, 103; threats, 121; U.S. spending on, 121. *See also* Pandemic disease; Quarantine

Public Health Security and Bioterrorism Preparedness and Response Act of 2002, 87–88

Public Health Service, U.S., 106, 107, 118

Public Health Service Act of 1944, 106–7

Quarantine: constitutional concerns, 91, 109–21; definition, 130n42;

effectiveness, 89–90, 123–24; federal authority, 100–105, 106–9, 111–12, 113–15, 117–19; local authority, 91–100, 101; maritime, 92–94, 96, 100–101, 103, 105; military role in enforcement, 109, 112, 113–16; as response to biowarfare, 88, 89–90, 91, 109, 113–14; rights issues, 109–10; of travelers, 93, 94, 96, 101, 106–7, 113, 118; unintended consequences, 123; in wartime, 107

Quarantine laws: in colonial America, 91–95; federal, 87–88, 91, 98–99, 101, 102, 103, 104–5, 106–8, 109, 118; history, 91–100, 144n187; state, 92, 96–99, 103–4, 116–18, 130n42

Rajneesh cult, 84

Reagan, Ronald, 30

Rebels, *see* Insurgents

Reciprocity principle, 26–27, 56

Reconciliation, 204, 211–13, 214, 217

Rehnquist, William, 170–71

Reparations, 54, 68, 69–71, 202, 213–14

Retribution, 204, 213–14, 215, 217, 218. *See also* War crimes trials

Revolutionary War, 95–96

Rights: Grotius on, 200–201; of individuals, 49–50, 55, 56–57, 79, 109–10; quarantine and, 109–10; in wartime, 109. *See also* Cosmopolitan individualism; Human rights

Risk allocation, 63–66

Robert T. Stafford Disaster Relief and Emergency Assistance Act (Stafford Act), 108

Role school, 64, 65

Roosevelt, Franklin D., 160

Rostow, Eugene, 173

Rule of law, 40, 51, 211, 212, 213, 215

Rules of engagement (ROE): American, 11, 37, 42, 47n54; civilian protection measures, 37; factors in, 42; in Vietnam War, 164, 179

Rusk, Dean, 162, 169
Russell, Bertrand, 166–67
Russell tribunal, 166–67, 175, 176
Russia, war in Chechnya, 70
Rwandan genocide, 60. *See also*
    International Criminal Tribunal for
    Rwanda

Sacharoff, Mark, 171, 176
Salisbury, Harrison, 165–66
Sarin nerve gas, 84
SARS, *see* Severe acute respiratory
    syndrome
Sartre, Jean-Paul, 166, 176
Scalia, Antonin, 119, 120
Schell, Jonathan, 178–79, 193n83
Schmitt, Carl, 6–7, 55
Scott v. Harris, 3
Secret Service, 64
September 11 terrorist attacks, 46n43
Serbia: Kosovo War, 34, 35–36, 112;
    military, 25. *See also* Milosevic,
    Slobodan
Severe acute respiratory syndrome
    (SARS), 86, 88, 107. *See also* Pandemic
    disease
Sheehan, Neil, 176, 177–78
Smallpox, 93, 94, 95–96, 98, 101–2, 118,
    127n20, 137n117. *See also* Pandemic
    disease
Sohn, Louis, 172–73
Solatia payments, 69–70
South Vietnam: counterinsurgency, 162,
    164; political prisoners, 163. *See also*
    Vietnam War
Spanish Influenza, 86, 123
Spending Clause, 100, 109
Sri Lankan military, 26
Stafford Act, 108
Standard, William, 168, 169, 170
State: centralized, 5–6, 7; Hobbes on, 4–5;
    legal systems, 5–6, 7; loss of relevance,
    25; monopoly on use of force, 6, 51;
    relations with individuals, 78–79;

reparations, 54; responsibilities, 78–79;
    tensions with individuals, 49, 59–61
State Department, U.S., 2, 162, 169
State of nature, 4, 5
States, U.S.: biodefense role, 90–91; police
    powers, 98, 99, 102, 105–6, 110, 116–18;
    quarantine laws, 92, 96–99, 103–4,
    116–18, 130n42. *See also* Federalism
Sudan, 215, 216
Supreme Court, Israeli, 73
Supreme Court, U.S., confirmation
    hearings, 170–71
Supreme Court cases: *Compagnie
    Francaise de Navigation a Vapeur v.
    Louisiana State Bd. of Health*, 117–18;
    Gibbons v. Ogden, 99, 117; *Gonzales
    v. Reich*, 119; *Hamdi v. Rumsfeld*, 1;
    Jacobson v. Massachusetts, 105–6, 117;
    Minnesota Rate Cases, 106; *Morgan's
    Steamship v. Louisiana Board of
    Health*, 104, 105, 117–18; *Prize Cases*, 113;
    Scott v. Harris, 3; *Tennessee v. Garner*,
    3; *US v. Comstock*, 119–21; *Youngstown
    Sheet & Tube Co. v. Sawyer*, 111

Taliban, civilians targeted by, 25, 43n4. *See
    also* Afghanistan War
Targeted killings, 1–3, 58–59, 78, 79, 157
Taylor, Charles, 57
Taylor, Telford, 177, 178–81, 194n91,
    195n99
Technology: cyber warfare, 26, 27; drones,
    1–3, 157; International Humanitarian
    Law and, 26, 27; military, 58–59
Tennessee v. Garner, 3
Tenth Amendment, 91, 109, 116, 120
Terrorism: prevention efforts, 86–87;
    September 11 attacks, 46n43. *See also*
    War on terrorism
Terrorist groups: Al Qaeda, 46n43, 72, 77,
    85, 126–27n16; association with, 77;
    potential acquisition of weapons of
    mass destruction, 85. *See also* Nonstate
    actors

Terrorists: detention of suspected, 71–74, 78, 154–55, 219n32; identifying, 72

Thomas, Clarence, 120, 121

Tiedeman, Christopher G., 117

Torture: at Abu Ghraib, 154, 210; by colonial powers, 186n22; U.S. laws, 182; in Vietnam War, 163–64; as war crime, 186n22

Trade, quarantine and, 92–94, 96, 100–101, 105

Traditionalist view of International Humanitarian Law, 23, 24, 29–31, 32, 35–36

Treasury Department, U.S., 99, 100, 102, 103, 104, 105

Treaties: enforcement of, 5; impact, 60; laws of warfare, 51, 55; reparations, 54. *See also* Geneva Conventions

Trials, *see* War crimes trials

Tyrants, 216

Uniform Code of Military Justice (UCMJ), 11, 36, 40, 207

Union Army, 9

United Nations, 26, 169, 182

United States: biodefense, 88–89, 90–91, 121; biological weapons use and policies, 84, 86–91; Civil War, 9, 100, 101–2, 113, 213; detention of suspected terrorists, 71–74; foreign relations, 100–101; Guantanamo Bay prison, 71, 154–55, 219n32; human rights legislation, 181–82; IHL enforcement, 40–41; International Criminal Court and, 31, 36; law of war, 3–4, 11; payments to victims, 69–70; Revolutionary War, 95–96; September 11 attacks, 46n43; traditionalist view of International Humanitarian Law, 23, 24, 29–31, 32, 35–36. *See also* Military, U.S.; Presidents; Vietnam War

U.S. Congress: Authorization for Use of Military Force, 2; declarations of war, 111, 114, 182; House Armed Services Committee, 164–65; interstate commerce regulation, 119; quarantine laws, 98–99, 101, 102, 103, 104–5, 106–9, 111; Spending Clause, 100, 109; Tonkin Gulf resolution, 168; Vietnam War opponents, 168–69

U.S. Constitution: Article II, 91, 110–14; Commerce Clause, 91, 99, 101, 109, 116–19; Fifth Amendment, 1, 2, 110; Necessary and Proper Clause, 91, 119–21; police powers, 91; Spending Clause, 100, 109; Tenth Amendment, 91, 109, 116, 120

U.S. Marines, Haditha incident (2005), 18, 40, 41, 210–11

Unjust wars, *see* Aggression; Just war theory

US v. Comstock, 119–21

Vattel, Emer de, 8, 55

Versailles, Treaty of, 54

Veterans, 212. *See also* Military

Viet Cong (National Liberation Front), 163–64, 174, 207

Vietnam Veterans against the War, 176

Vietnam War: aerial bombing, 165–66, 174, 175, 179–80, 190n52; antiwar movement, 156, 163–64, 165, 167–68, 170, 177, 180; atrocities, 159, 162–67, 168, 174–76; chemical weapons use, 165; civilian casualties, 164, 166, 178; compared to Iraq War, 156–57; counterinsurgency, 162, 164, 165, 179; ideological rationales, 181; international criticism, 166–67, 170, 171, 173–74; international law and, 155, 156; Lawyers Committee, 168–71, 172, 173, 190n52, 191n63; legal claims of war crimes, 177, 178–81; legality debate, 155–56, 168–73, 175; moral aftermath, 181–84; morale issues, 208; moral objections, 167–68, 175; noncombatants, 164; post-9/11 debates and, 158, 160, 183; prisoners of war,

162–63, 179; public debates, 155–56; as quagmire, 158; rules of engagement, 164, 179; Tonkin Gulf resolution, 168; training on law of war, 164–65; U.S. withdrawal, 175; War Powers Resolution, 112–13, 171, 182. *See also* My Lai massacre

Vietnam War Crimes Working Group, 165

Walzer, Michael, 27

War: aversion to, 75–76; collective liability, 203–4; Grotius on, 8–9, 204; Hobbes on, 4–5, 7; as policing, 49, 75–77; relationship to law, 3–12, 19; rules of, 7, 9. *See also* Law of war

War crimes: accountability of commanders, 175, 180; collective responsibility, 68, 69; in colonial wars, 161; defining, 204–5; deterrence, 203, 204, 208, 212, 215, 216; effects on justness of war, 217; following orders defense, 10, 201, 205; Grotius on, 8–9, 201–3; humanitarian leniency, 202, 203; in illegal wars, 62, 175, 201, 202, 205; increased focus on, 156–57; individual accountability, 10, 67–69, 175, 176, 201, 205–6; punishments, 202, 203; Russell tribunal, 166–67, 175, 176; universal jurisdiction, 57–58, 60; U.S. laws, 182; in Vietnam War, 177, 178–81; violations of proportionality principle, 63, 180. *See also* International criminal law; My Lai massacre

War crimes trials: of Calley, 40–41, 199, 206–9; criticism of, 217–18; effects, 208, 209, 210–11, 212–13, 216–17; functions, 203; goals, 204, 213–14, 215; Grotian defense, 203–4, 212; Grotius on, 200, 201, 202–3, 216–17; historical, 7, 198; indictments, 57; international

tribunals, 11, 39, 57–58, 67, 211, 213; just war tradition and, 199–203, 216–17, 218; postwar, 198–99, 211–12, 213–16, 218; timing of, 198–99, 211–17, 218; as victor's justice, 217–18; in wartime, 198, 202–3, 207–11, 212–13, 214–17, 218. *See also* Nuremberg trials

War on terrorism: conservative views, 159; detention of suspected terrorists, 71–74, 154–55, 219n32; enemy combatants, 71–73; liberal criticism, 158; public debates, 154–55, 158–60, 183

War Powers Resolution (1973), 112–13, 171, 182

War-sustaining contributions, 34–35, 46n35

Weapons: of nonstate actors, 58, 85; precision, 58–59

Weapons of mass destruction: chemical weapons, 165; potential use by nonstate actors, 27, 85. *See also* Biological weapons

West Germany, reparations after World War II, 68

Westmoreland, William, 164–65, 179, 180

Wittes, Benjamin, 2

World Health Organization, 86, 118

World War I, German reparations, 54

World War II: German reparations, 68; strategic bombing, 179; *Yamashita case*, 180. *See also* Nuremberg trials

Wuterich, Frank, 41

Yellow fever, 92, 101–2, 103, 104, 107. *See also* Pandemic disease

Yemen, 1–2, 79

Youngstown Sheet & Tube Co. v. Sawyer, 111

Yugoslavia, *see* International Criminal Tribunal for the Former Yugoslavia; Serbia

The Amherst Series in Law, Jurisprudence, and Social Thought

EDITED BY

Austin Sarat, Lawrence Douglas, and Martha Merrill Umphrey

The Secrets of Law (2012)

Imagining New Legalities: Privacy and Its Possibilities in the 21st Century (2012)

Law as Punishment/Law as Regulation (2011)

Law without Nations (2011)

Law and the Stranger (2010)

Law and Catastrophe (2007)

Law and the Sacred (2007)

How Law Knows (2007)

The Limits of Law (2005)

Law on the Screen (2005)